Varga
1983

Pelican Books
Eurocommunism: Myth or Reality?

D1600223

Edited by
Paolo Filo della Torre,
Edward Mortimer
and Jonathan Story

Eurocommunism: Myth or Reality?

Penguin Books

Penguin Books Ltd, Harmondsworth,
Middlesex, England
Penguin Books, 625 Madison Avenue,
New York, New York 10022, U.S.A.
Penguin Books Australia Ltd, Ringwood,
Victoria, Australia
Penguin Books Canada Ltd, 2801 John Street,
Markham, Ontario, Canada L3R 1B4
Penguin Books (NZ) Ltd, 182–190 Wairau Road,
Auckland 10, New Zealand

First published 1979

Contents

Part One

1. Eurocommunism: Myth or Reality?
Arrigo Levi

1. 'Euro' or 'Neo'?

As far as is known, the word 'Eurocommunism' was invented by
the Yugoslav journalist Frane Barbieri, in an article in the
Giornale nuovo of 26 June 1975. He himself tells us[1] that the idea
came to him while reflecting on some writings of Manuel Azcárate
and Santiago Carrillo, leaders of the Western communist party
which has gone furthest in its polemic against Soviet communism.
He chose it to contrast with another term, 'neo-communism',
which had been used by other political observers including myself. He thought, rightly, that 'neo-communism' took for granted
a qualitative leap which in fact is still to be verified and defined.
It was wiser to speak of 'Eurocommunism', a simple abbreviation
for 'West European communism'. For once, wisdom had its
reward: the word caught on at once, and was eventually accepted
by the 'Eurocommunist' parties themselves.[2]

The problem remains whether this 'Eurocommunism' is also
a 'neo-communism', and if so to what extent: how far is it
tactical, and how far strategic? How far myth, and how far
reality? So much of the future, not only of the countries where
Eurocommunism is strong but of Europe as a whole, and therefore of the world, may depend on the answer which history will
give to this question.

For the time being, let us take 'Eurocommunism' to mean,
simply, 'the politics and ideologies of the principal communist
parties of Western Europe and of some others in the "capitalist"
world in the mid 1970s, together with the sense of mutual
recognition and affinity shown by those parties'. We can then
begin our search by reviewing the main answers currently given

to the questions we have posed: is Eurocommunism 'myth or reality'? There are essentially three answers: two of them simple and clear, the third difficult and obscure.

2. The simple answers

The simplest of all is to say that Eurocommunism is pure tactics, a snare and a delusion: a simple adaptation to the political conditions of the Western democracies. Such is the opinion of Jacques Chirac, as expressed in an interview with *Newsweek* (20 June 1977):

It is certain that there is a phenomenon which is essentially only window-dressing. The communist parties of southern Europe are trying to pursue a strategy which will allow them eventually to take power.

Eurocommunism is above all a wager which they would like us to accept on the capacity of communism to reform itself. The fact that the Eurocommunists are not denounced by Moscow is the real proof that they are not, in fact, sincere. It is a question of tactics. They are putting on a new varnish meant to create illusions about an ideological model more than a century old and unsuited to the demands of industrial societies. Eurocommunism is therefore a danger against which we must act.

Henry Kissinger and many others think much the same: they don't believe that 'communists . . . through some magic . . . have become democratic'.[3] This conviction is supported by communism's tragic history and by the evidence of so-called 'real socialism' as practised in all the countries calling themselves communist.

The other simple view is that the Eurocommunists are really nothing but social democrat turncoats, and only continue to call themselves communist in order to deceive the masses who still follow them, and whose hopes of revolution they intend to betray. This is the judgement untiringly repeated by the revolutionary 'New Left', in Italy and in France.

This accusation of 'social democracy' has also been levelled by

Moscow, at least as a warning, but not against all the Euro-communist parties together. So far only Santiago Carrillo has been accused (by authoritative Soviet journals) of revisionist heresy and, what is worse, of anti-sovietism. But the Spanish Communist Party as such has not been made the object of a real excommunication, like the Chinese and Albanian parties in the past. Relations between it and the Eastern Bloc parties have not been broken, and Carrillo himself is still received at the Kremlin, even though he was not allowed to speak at the sixtieth anniversary celebrations for the October Revolution.

Enrico Berlinguer, finally, has also been described more than once as a good social democrat and a moderate by non-Italian journalists, who lack the patience to track down the elusive reality of communism Italian-style and are anxious to provide their readers with clear and easy answers. Even some American academic experts on Eurocommunism have sometimes given the impression that they think much the same.

3. The third view: complexity and ambiguity

The third view is complex and it includes innumerable nuances. It is fair to warn the reader that this is where my own position (not necessarily shared by the authors of other chapters) is to be found: among those who believe that what is going on in the Eurocommunist parties is more than mere 'window-dressing', that Eurocommunism is really changing, by comparison with communism Soviet-style; but also that this change is not such as to turn the Eurocommunist parties into social democratic parties. Politicians who have spent their lives fighting communism – for a start, some of the leaders of the Christian democrats and other democratic parties in Italy – today believe that the Euro-communist leaders are 'sincere' in their statements.[4] But they are equally convinced that a profound ideological difference remains between their own parties (Christian democrat in Italy, socialist in France and Spain, and so on) and the communist parties of their respective countries. Equally firm are the Eurocommunist leaders themselves, in insisting on the substantial difference between their parties and other Western parties, and on the maintenance of their communist identity, different though it also is from that of ruling or 'traditional' communist parties.

Those of us who take this view are constantly obliged to try and make it more specific by drawing distinctions between one Eurocommunist party and another and, by updating our judgements, to keep pace with events. We also have to point to profound contradictions in the policies, behaviour and very identity of the Eurocommunist parties. Some of these contradictions fade away, while others remain or re-emerge. This, in turn, raises doubts about the Eurocommunists' future behaviour, about the substantiality of their new principles, and hence about their acceptability as allies.

Among believers in the *reality* of Eurocommunism there is thus constant debate about its precise nature. All of us see Eurocommunism as a transition not yet complete. But opinions differ on the point it has reached and even on the direction in which it is going – zig-zags and retreats being by no means ruled out. And hence there is also confusion and debate about the best way to deal with this 'explosive and magical' phenomenon, on how to prod it in the right direction: with reproofs or eulogies, by giving or refusing credit, with wagging finger or with open arms? Not only journalists and political scientists often seem unsure, but also politicians and statesmen – right up to the White House and the Kremlin, where those responsible for the peace and safety of the world show the same signs of confusion and uncertainty, leading one to suspect that in both superpowers there are discussions and differences of opinion about Eurocommunism at the very top.

4. Eurocommunism's birth certificate

These remarks are made without malice, simply to incite the reader to caution and scepticism, whenever he is offered any clear and final truth about Eurocommunism. It is as well to remember that here not only 'experts' but also Eurocommunist politicians themselves often appear uncertain – a point which will emerge clearly in the course of the book.

Before advancing further into a subject so complex and so ramified in space and time, the reader could do worse than refer to Eurocommunism's own statements of its principles, printed in the appendices (pages 330–38). The first, which is really the birth certificate of Eurocommunism – the first statement of political and ideological principles signed jointly by more than one party – is dated 11 July 1975. (It is to Barbieri's credit that he had found a name for the new-born movement a few days *earlier*.) The place of birth was Leghorn, one of the 'red cities' of Tuscany, where that day a meeting was held in the vast Piazza Repubblica. ('One of the biggest in Italy,' wrote *L'Unità* the next day, 'which no party but the PCI is capable of filling.') The speakers were the secretaries of the Italian and Spanish communist parties (PCI and PCE), Berlinguer and Carrillo. The two parties and their leaders had reached this rendezvous by a long journey through history, including revolutions, fascisms, persecutions, massacres and wars. What a generation earlier had been 'great powers' were now only middle-sized, if not actual satellites of the new superpowers. Between 1917 (from which both parties continue to date a new era of history) and 1975, the face of Europe and of the world had changed profoundly. Nearly sixty years after the October Revolution, and thirty years after the Second World War, which left the world divided into blocs, the communist parties of Spain and Italy found themselves locked in a Western camp which had proved unassailable by Soviet power. In this new world, the PCI and PCE declared their intention of acting on the basis of new principles.

5. Eurocommunism and the Soviet system

The second statement is the joint declaration of the PCI and PCF, dated 17 November of the same year. It is similar to the Italian-Spanish one, but is more detailed in its enunciation of the 'new freedoms' and in its identification of the historic values claimed by this new communism; more restrictive, it seems to me, in its description of the economic model – reflecting, clearly, the French party's more traditional approach to the question of nationalizations; but, as a whole, fuller and more solemn, closer to what the 'charter' of a new political doctrine should be like; involving therefore a deeper commitment, less related to local or ephemeral issues, more ambitious and 'universal' in its scope.

Like the first, this document proposes a policy of accommodation with other 'popular' forces, of broad alliances. Like it, too, it avoids referring to Leninism by name, whereas it does mention the January 1974 Brussels Conference of West European Communist Parties. It denounces 'monopoly capitalism' as 'chief enemy of the working class', but, while criticizing the 'interference of US imperialism', it also denounces 'all foreign interference'. In short, there is little 'Soviet' about this text, which virtually ignores what was later to be called 'real socialism' and puts forward a new doctrine in its place.

These themes have been repeated, with variations, in innumerable declarations, articles and writings. As the reader will find out, only the Spanish communists – Carrillo and Azcárate – have gone so far as to say explicitly that the society they imagine (pluralist, democratic and so forth) is socialist, whereas Soviet society no longer is. The Italian and French communist parties have been careful not to deny that Soviet socialism *is* socialism; indeed, Berlinguer (for instance, in his Milan speech of 30 January 1977) explicitly restricts his criticism to 'certain illiberal features of the political régimes in some East European countries'.

More critical statements by both Italian and French communist leaders can be found, but so can vigorous defences of Soviet socialism and reaffirmations of Leninist faith. Only once, but in an undeniably important and binding context, has Berlinguer fully affirmed the 'universal' value of Eurocommunist ideology: in his speech in Moscow on 2 November 1977, at the solemn celebration of the sixtieth anniversary of the October Revolution. Speaking after Brezhnev, Berlinguer said:

Experience has led us – as it has led other communist parties in capitalist Europe – to the conclusion that democracy today is not only the ground on which the class enemy is obliged to yield, but also the historically universal value on which an original socialist society must be founded ... That is why our united struggle ... is geared to realizing a new, socialist society, which will guarantee all freedoms – personal and collective, civil and religious – the non-ideological character of the state,[5] the possibility for different parties to exist side by side, and pluralism in society, culture and ideals.

Here the challenge to the 'Soviet model' is quite explicit. But it must not be forgotten that this challenge comes from inside, not outside, the Soviet system and the communist movement.

6. A common heritage

Whether or not you believe in the sincerity of these statements, you cannot deny that the Italian, French and Spanish communist parties – and others which more or less follow their line, even outside Europe (Japan, India) – have solemnly stated a new doctrine, and have striven to be believed when they affirm that this is not merely tactical, but represents a fundamental ideological change. Before considering the reasons which lead many observers to think that this is not enough to make those parties *democratic* (in the ordinary sense of that word), we should draw the reader's attention to the complexity of the different national experiences which have led the Italian, French and Spanish to reach common conclusions.

There are, in fact, two questions that need answering. First, how does it happen that *in all three countries the majority or at least an important part of the left has chosen to be communist rather than socialist or social democrat*? Secondly, what is it that pushed these communist parties, after decades of working in different national conditions but with equally rigid fidelity to Soviet ideology, to evolve now in a 'Eurocommunist' direction?

On the first point, it is impossible not to be struck by the fact that, in the West, communism is strongest in the three Latin countries bordering the Mediterranean. The words 'Latin' or 'Mediterranean' can be used as a label implying a whole series of social and economic characteristics, connected in various ways with relatively late industrialization, with a particular class structure and a particular tradition of the state. There is also a strong temptation to inquire in another direction: is it significant that all three are Catholic countries? These points are put forward more as suggestions for future historical research than as keys to the solution of current problems.

Or again: two of the three countries, Italy and Spain, have been through a period of fascist rule. The former, indeed, is the motherland of fascism – an ideology which, defined as 'the nationalism of underdevelopment', is still enjoying a world-wide success. Fascism lasted twenty years in Italy, from 1922 to 1943; and twice that, but later, in Spain – from 1936 to 1976. Certainly a comparative study of the roots of fascism in the small and medium 'Latin' bourgeoisie, and of the roots of communism in the proletariat of the same countries, would be anything but irrelevant to an understanding of our present theme. And finally, it is remarkable that in all three countries the 'Left' has almost never been in power. Effect . . . or cause?

Turning to the reasons why these parties have moved from Leninist-Stalinist communism to Eurocommunism, it is easy to point to other shared experiences. All three parties operate in a 'Western' historical and geographical context: they are subjected to the cultural influences, and have to work within the rules, of Western democratic society. Their declared hostility to this 'capitalist' society and their adoption of revolutionary goals are deeply rooted, strongly held and durable attitudes. The Soviet link and the identification with the ideals of the October Revolution are the symbol of this determination to *break*, which sets them apart from other Western parties. Yet all three have been forced over a long period to face up to Soviet reality, and more than once have found the experience traumatic. The contact with the world of Stalin has, however, been much closer for the two parties driven into exile by fascism than for the French party. This leads one to wonder whether the personal experience of Italian and Spanish leaders in Moscow might explain their greater propensity to seek different and more independent roads, their readiness to reject the Soviet myth, whereas the French party remained Stalinist for much longer. Thus the first stirrings of Eurocommunism are already apparent in the behaviour of Togliatti immediately after his return to Italy from Moscow in 1944. In his case there is a clear affinity with the determination (in part surely genuine) to find 'different roads to socialism', expressed by some communist leaders in Eastern Europe who later met a tragic end.[6]

All three of the Eurocommunist parties long shared the dream of revolution and believed passionately in the 'communist ideal'; but for equally long they were tormented by the bitter contrast between this ideal and the 'real socialism' of the Soviet Union. They shared in a great myth and a great disappointment. Yet the myth has not been completely abandoned, and the disappointment has not driven any of these parties to a total breach with its own past. Continuity is the hallmark of their development: none of them has yet had its 'Twentieth Congress'.

7. Continuity, change and contradiction

Visibly, their development is conditioned by events outside themselves: they follow history more than they direct it. The stages of development are marked for all of them by certain dates relating to events on which they had little or no influence, but from which resulted sudden and drastic changes in their policies or their ideological positions.

The October Revolution itself, and later the Soviet world, were sufficiently distant and unfamiliar to lend themselves to mythification by the masses. The unshakeable faith of these parties in Lenin's successors, the heirs of the October Revolution, was proof for an incredibly long time against all kinds of disclosures, until the moment – late indeed – when the most shattering revelations were made by the heirs of the heirs themselves. Yet not even then did one of these parties engage in a corresponding denunciation of *its own* past. Nothing was repudiated. None of the parties broke up or lost its faith. Instead there began, by fits and starts, a development which revealed a growing capacity for independent judgement, but which was often diverted, slowed down or accelerated by sudden, unforeseen events outside.

In 1956, the very year of the Twentieth Congress and the year in which Togliatti invented 'polycentrism', the Soviet invasion of Hungary was still approved by all these parties, without reservation and almost without hesitation. Then a series of events, culminating in the invasion of Czechoslovakia in 1968, revealed the gradual crumbling of the Soviet myth, which stood up less well to each succeeding blow: in 1960–62 the Sino-Soviet rift; in 1964 the fall of Khrushchev. By 1968, the destruction of Dubček's communism in Czechoslovakia could no longer be defended, but was harshly and irrevocably condemned. In a sense, Eurocommunism was born then, at dawn on 21 August 1968, when Soviet tanks entered Czechoslovakia and Dubček was arrested. This was the Soviet response to Togliatti's 'polycentrism': the two doctrines can coexist, but remain fundamentally irreconcilable.

During the same period, more gradually but equally unmistakably, the myth of the Soviet Union's economic and social superiority also withered. Little by little the Soviet model was revealed as actually inferior in technical and material terms to its 'neo-capitalist' counterpart, while Soviet society emerged as culturally sterile and unattractive. The only lively element, dissent, continued to be brutally repressed. To all this the Western communist parties clearly felt themselves ever more alien and hostile. Conversely, their sense of belonging to the West grew stronger, and from this resulted a series of political choices tending to 'integrate' them into a Western society which they no longer categorically rejected. In 1969, PCI deputies first entered the European Parliament; but in that year the Twelfth Congress of their party was still condemning NATO outright. Not until 1974, during the preparations for the Fourteenth Congress, did Berlinguer clearly and unequivocally accept the Atlantic Alliance as an element in the strategic balance on which détente was founded, and one moreover which does not allow for the unilateral departure of a country like Italy from the alliance to which it belongs; and not until 1976 did he say, first in an interview, then on television in front of millions of viewers, that he felt 'safer on this side than on that'.[7] Marchais has never said as much.

Two impressions emerge from this necessarily condensed synthesis of an extremely complex history: that of a close dependence on external conditioning factors, and that of an evolution which, though gradual – at times even accidental, and certainly fraught with contradictions – is none the less a 'one-way' process. Put simply, it goes from East to West, from Leninism to democratic socialism. It is hard to resist the optimistic feeling that this process must culminate, sooner or later, in the complete 'Westernization' of the parties concerned and the end of the Leninist heresy.

At this point, however, it is wise to remind ourselves of what we said at the beginning: that many people who live in contact with Eurocommunists, and not a few scholars and politicians outside the countries concerned, see the whole of this development as ambiguous and full of illusions. The ranks of the unconvinced are still well-manned, and many even of those who do believe the change to be real and sincere are constantly troubled by doubts and anxieties because of the incomplete and contradictory nature of the process. And the more one believes that there must be a definite finishing-post in the form of complete 'Westernization', the more one is exposed to constant disappointments and surprises.

The Eurocommunist parties have changed greatly from what they were, and are very different from the parties of the Soviet

Bloc; but they also remain different, in too many ways, from traditional Western parties. Here we are on shifting ground, where any situation report is likely to be out of date within a few months. Yet, strange as it may seem, some contradictions not only persist but appear more acute as the process of change progresses.

Writing at the beginning of 1978, I shall try to point out some of the most glaring contradictions; some of the logically incompatible attitudes which coexist in the ideology and behaviour of the Eurocommunist parties; some of the peculiarities which make these parties so 'different', whether one sets them in a Western or an Eastern context; some of the characteristics which give them an identity so uncertain and difficult to define. (Togliatti once said that those who didn't believe the PCI was a democratic party were like those fools who, seeing a giraffe for the first time, declared: 'It doesn't exist, it's too different.' Which shows that even Togliatti found it almost unnatural that a communist party could be democratic.)

8. Motives for doubt

The most important element in the uniqueness of the Eurocommunist parties, which sets them apart from all other parties in the West, is their own clear consciousness of being different. They themselves are the first to say that they are different, to reiterate their rejection of 'capitalist' society, and to reaffirm their pretension to represent an alternative system – even if they then find it more difficult to say just what this alternative consists of.

Their sense of being different is expressed, first and foremost, by continuing to proclaim, proudly and firmly, that they are *communist*. 'The PCI has remained, does remain and will remain a communist party,' repeats Berlinguer, in the sincerest tones, to anyone who doubts it.[8]

One expert on Eurocommunism, Aldo Rizzo, wrote of the

P C I in mid 1977 (though the remark is equally applicable to the other Eurocommunist parties):

The PCI had changed greatly from its historic and ideological origins; its political proposal – for a socialism to be built in freedom, with a multi-party system and an alternation of parties in power – had by now little to do with its remote Leninist roots or with the Soviet model which for half a century the Italian Communists themselves had exalted. And yet, even thus changed, the PCI still identified with the whole of its history, not disowning even the murkiest episodes through an explicit and 'cathartic' self-criticism. Whereas the CPSU had had its moment of trauma, admittedly short-lived, with the Twentieth Congress and the Khrushchev speech, the PCI, after passing through the whole long tunnel of Stalinism, had avoided any embarrassing confession, any rigorous self-analysis, and claimed to have been broadly in the right in all the most varied and contradictory moments of its history. Everything was presented as evolution, nothing as a break or a qualitative leap. Besides, the apostles of pluralism were in many cases the very same who had been the instruments of Stalin's campaign against Tito or had applauded the repressions in East Berlin, in Poznan and in Budapest.[9]

The most eloquent symbol of this unrepudiated identity remains, in the late 1970s, the Moscow connection – never denounced or denied, sometimes summed up in the formula 'autonomous but present'. Present, that is, in the capital city of communism for congresses, for celebrations, for high- and medium-level meetings; sometimes in heated polemic, but still present; respected, but also (except for Carrillo) respectful of the 'socialist' character of Soviet society – the only socialism yet put into practice. Those in the West who criticize Berlinguer on his visits to Moscow for 'embracing Brezhnev and not Medvedev' (Moscow's 'Eurocommunist' dissident, whose writings are published by the PCI's Rome publishing house) are always firmly slapped down in the communist press. The Eurocommunist parties protect some dissidents but not others; and they tenaciously refuse to be pushed, as they put it, 'into the area of anti-Sovietism'.

These protestations of an enduring *communist* identity

inevitably keep alive a ferment of doubts and anxieties, since so much of the new doctrine is, on the face of it, irreconcilable with what is meant by 'communist' in any language. Once the new Eurocommunist values are proclaimed as 'universal', how can the maintenance of the special relationship with countries of the Soviet Bloc, where these values are constantly and systematically denied, be justified? If the Eurocommunist parties are really 'giraffes', why do they continue to keep such dissimilar and dubious company?

Other reservations about the credibility or completeness of the change relate to further incongruities or discords in the new doctrine. To start with, the internal organization of the parties remains tightly bound up with the practice of 'democratic centralism', which, of course, means that minorities may not be formed, nor dissent organized, within the party. The result is an impression of compactness which, curiously enough, sometimes helps to attract votes, as a symbol of 'solidity' and seriousness. It should be said, though, that this compactness is much less than it used to be. The internal debate is more visible, the disagreements much less disguised. In 1976–7 there were many cases of arguments between PCI leaders being carried on in the non-party press – something which would have been unthinkable not long ago.

There are also doubts about the independence of the Eurocommunist parties, arising from their choices in foreign policy. They often seem instinctively to align themselves with Soviet positions; for instance, in condemning the neutron bomb or in supporting pro-Soviet forces in the Middle East and Africa.

Other questions concern problems of doctrine. The new 'identity' has been shaped in part by ideological debates; for instance, on the concept of 'dictatorship of the proletariat', which the French and Spanish communists have explicitly dropped; on Marxism-Leninism (still referred to in the statutes of the PCI); or on the key Gramscian concept of 'hegemony'. The Eurocommunist parties have built up Gramsci as forerunner of Eurocommunism, probably much exaggerating his originality. In particular, they have tended to contrast Gramsci's 'hegemony' with Lenin's 'dictatorship of the proletariat'. But socialist and democratic thinkers (notably Norberto Bobbio) have pointed out that Gramsci's hegemony in fact has little to do with the pluralism and multi-party system proclaimed by the Eurocommunists. If pluralism were simply the tool of a Gramscian hegemonic strategy, the democratic spirit of the Eurocommunists would have little credibility.

These issues have provoked fierce debate during 1976–7, especially in Italy, forcing the PCI leaders, in evident discomfort, to carry their ideological reflections further: the results so far are hardly conclusive. The fact that the party did not impose any strict taboos in the discussion is itself important. But the resulting image of Eurocommunism's 'ideal society' is none the less somewhat confused, owing to the wide variety of raw materials that have gone into it – and the mix varies considerably from one party to another. There are obvious chunks of Marxist, Leninist and Gramscian tradition; there are populist attitudes, and a great undifferentiated mass of concepts, ideas and sociological hypotheses drawn from the most varied Western sources. In short, the Eurocommunists are not at present capable of presenting a clear picture of their model of society. But one can frequently glimpse, even in the most up-to-date and 'civilized' of their ideologists and politicians, absolutist attitudes which betray the survival of traditional communist influences. Even Berlinguer's 'historic compromise' strategy, although derived from a critical reflection on the maximalism of the Chilean Left under Allende, contains within itself the underlying ambition to bring Italian society to a point of no return. That ambition, still genuinely revolutionary, is what gives Eurocommunist parties their strength. But it is also one of the basic reasons for the mistrust which they continue to arouse.

9. Reactions, East and West

Eurocommunism seems at present to be at a middle point between different ideologies. It is not capable of clearly presenting a social model, or utopia, of its own; yet it rejects, more or less clearly, all the other models both of East and West. It reflects, and is moulded by, the whole of contemporary history.

Yet it would be unfair to lay too much stress on its derivative, externally determined character, for it, too, has in its turn become an important factor of change and is felt as a destabilizing element far outside its own countries, far outside Europe itself.

Here it is enough to draw the reader's attention to the chapters dealing with Eurocommunism's effects in Eastern Europe and in the United States. It has been much debated whether, in the context of détente, the disruptive effects of Eurocommunism may be greater in the East or in the West. Is it Moscow's Trojan horse in the West, or the cutting edge of a Western 'forward policy'?

That Eurocommunism is an element of destabilization in the Soviet power system has been repeatedly argued by many dissidents and exiles, including Medvedev, Mlynar and Sakharov. Others, like Solzhenitsyn and Amalryk, are less or not at all inclined to believe in this possibility, and much more inclined to fear the negative effects in the West, where Eurocommunism may help to reduce 'vigilance' and weaken resistance to the Soviet threat.

Similar uncertainties are reflected in the behaviour of the two superpowers. But, in general, the Americans have stuck to their policy of firm opposition and scepticism, while the Russians, for all their polemics, threats and warnings, continue to recognize these parties as 'communist', not heretical. Rightly or wrongly, then, the superpowers are agreed in proceeding with caution and in not yet recognizing any irreversible transformation or change of camp. Some American and European advisers find Washington's position too rigid. They fear that America's clear negative, helpful though it is to anti-communist political forces in countries like Italy and France, may become counter-productive when

Eurocommunist parties increase their share of power (and even enter government): at that point the effect could be to 'throw the Eurocommunists back into the arms of Moscow' and thus render the most catastrophic prophecies self-fulfilling.[10]

But the governments of Moscow and Washington seem to be incited to caution, suspicion and incredulity, either by realism or by their imperial responsibilities. Brezhnev (like Suslov) and Carter and Brzezinski (like Nixon and Kissinger) seem concerned above all to maintain balance and stability in Europe and the world. Indeed, the destabilization of the Soviet imperial system would arouse as many fears as hopes in Washington.

10. The challenge to the East: from within

During 1977 there were some signs that the process of change, inherent in Eurocommunism, was halting or even turning back. While the Spanish party alone made the leap to denouncing Soviet society as 'non-socialist', the Kremlin's harsh response induced the Italian and French communists to stress the difference between their positions and that of Carrillo. Some senior figures in the PCI, including Amendola, went so far as to say that 'Eurocommunism doesn't exist', since 'each party works out its own independent strategy' and there is no question of setting up a new International.[11]

On the other hand, Berlinguer did make his Moscow speech, quoted above (page 15), asserting the 'universality' of Eurocommunist doctrines. And on 26 January 1978, in a speech to his party's central committee, he took one more step forward. While he, too, denied any intention of setting up a new organizational centre, he repeated that Eurocommunism arose from the convergence of certain 'essential' features common to the Western parties: pluralism, the 'indissoluble' link between democracy and socialism; the quest for 'unity – not only at trade-union level – of the European labour movement' together with socialists and Catholics; and finally the task, to which the Eurocommunists are called, of 'making a contribution, perhaps a decisive one, to the qualitative renewal of the existing socialist societies, in the direction of a full democratic development'.

The challenge which Berlinguer thus issued to the 'existing socialist societies' will certainly not have passed unnoticed in Moscow. The words have a flavour of irreversibility, of personal commitment, for which the price could be high. Dubček paid very dearly for saying much less. There is courage and intellectual integrity in this position.

Yet we must be careful not to miss the more profound significance of such statements and messages to the East. After Berlinguer's Moscow speech, Ugo La Malfa, the veteran and respected leader of the Italian Republican Party, said it was now clear that the PCI 'had taken up a new international position'. I am not convinced of that, and the Italian communists themselves do not agree with the interpretation. They are always keen to prove that, notwithstanding the serious tensions and differences, and the exchanges of challenges and warnings, the special relationship with the 'existing socialist societies', and thus with Soviet Russia, is still there and remains for them fundamental.

In my view the error of interpretation arises from an incomplete understanding of the pride which Berlinguer – and no doubt Marchais – takes in himself and his party. He issued his challenge from within the Kremlin – as it were, from inside the family circle. He was not and did not wish to be outside, but inside the great international system composed of what he himself called, in the same speech, 'the revolutionary and progressive forces – parties, movements, peoples and states'.

In the summer of 1977, Berlinguer told me himself that he thought that Soviet Russia had not excommunicated the Eurocommunist parties 'so as not to be left in isolation'; and he added that he believed Soviet Russia would change, as Spain had changed. Yet, for this very reason, Berlinguer and the whole group of Eurocommunist parties intend not to shut themselves off in the West, but to maintain a special relationship with the Soviet world, in order to maintain their influence on it from within, as communists, being convinced that, despite its 'illiberal features', Soviet society is still 'socialism'. About the same time, another major figure in the PCI, Bufalini, said that 'the imbalances' visible in Soviet society 'are due to mistakes, not to natural necessity', and that 'not even these [Stalin's purges] could wipe out the socialist ideals and socialist bases' of Soviet society.[12]

It may even be that the stronger the PCI's Eurocommunist vocation becomes, the more it will want to reaffirm its position as an 'insider' in dealing with the problems of the Soviet Bloc. On the day after his challenging speech on the 'universality' of democratic principles, Berlinguer paid a visit of 'cordiality and friendship' to Brezhnev, at the end of which they solemnly affirmed, while respecting each other's independence, their 'voluntary internationalist cooperation, as comrades, and the solidarity between communist and workers' parties'.

What, then, are we to think of the 'credibility' of the Eurocommunist parties? Amendola once answered, 'No one can guarantee our honesty. The tricksters will always believe that we are tricksters. Honest people will try to judge us by what we do, and I myself cannot claim that everyone should take us at the value of our promises.'[13] That seems fair enough.

So we must judge by deeds (remembering that, in politics, words too *are* deeds). Sticking to the facts, we can say that this generation of Eurocommunist leaders – the children of Togliatti, of Thorez and of La Pasionaria – are sincerely expressing their own complex personalities and world views, essential parts of which are: (a) the affirmation of typically Western and democratic values (the 'Euro' component); (b) the reaffirmation of the ineradicable and never-repudiated communist tradition, which derives both from Lenin's totalitarian and from Gramsci's hegemonic vision; and (c) the maintenance, so far as is in their power, of the close and ambitious link with 'real socialism'. East is East and West is West: but in Eurocommunism the twain meet and live side by side. One can, after all, be contradictory and even ambiguous without being insincere.[14]

11. The challenge to the West: also from within

In the past, the Soviet Union has never hesitated to pronounce excommunications, even against the Communist Party of China, when it saw heresy threaten the solidity of its own camp and the monolithic nature of the parties directly under its control. In the long run, the existence of a polycentric, diversified camp is incompatible with the 'monolithism' on which the Soviet power system is based; but up to now the military power of the Soviet Union has been sufficient to contain this threat, resolving by force a very intricate system of political equations. Moscow has therefore not found it necessary to go beyond a 'semi-excommunication' of Carrillo – more a warning than anything else, and as such not without effect. Evidently Moscow does not find the Eurocommunist challenge to its power system too dangerous, or at least it considers that the damage caused so far is less than the advantage which can be derived, today or tomorrow, from the growing influence of some of the Eurocommunist parties in their respective countries. But what has happened up till now is not a basis for hard predictions about what may happen in the future. What has been tolerable until today may no longer be tomorrow. And a rigidly authoritarian, closed, pyramidal and gerontocratic political system like the Soviet one does not change by degrees: changes are, by definition, never predictable, but sudden and surprising. The Soviet Union *may* change 'like Franco's Spain'. Indeed, it surely will change; but the changes, when they come, may be very surprising ones.

This digression on the Soviet factor is necessary, since too often explosive events in the 'socialist societies' have provoked sudden accelerations and veritable qualitative leaps in the development of Eurocommunism. But we should not forget that while the effect of events in the East has in most cases been to drive the Western communist parties away from their 'spiritual mother', there was also a moment (the 'Prague spring') when the liberal development of an Eastern communist régime seemed capable of resolving all the Eurocommunist parties' contradictions and solving the problem of their identity by enabling them to identify with a 'real socialist' country, which was certainly much more liberal than the USSR but could hardly be called 'democratic' in the Western sense of the word. There could therefore be changes in the East which would bring the Euro-communist parties closer to the existing communist governments instead of driving them away.

But it is not on such as yet unknown factors that a strategy for dealing with Eurocommunism should be based. My own view, as should by now be clear, is that Eurocommunism is indeed a reality, not a myth, but a reality that is complex, contradictory, ambiguous, rich in obscure and unpredictable potential. (How much simpler if it were indeed simply a delusion!) The evolution and transition which are its essential characteristics do not appear to be irreversible one-way developments. The Eurocommunist leaders have not yet been able to tell us enough about their model of society (perhaps they themselves do not know enough) to overcome the fears of those who can see only one fixed point in the process: namely, the point of departure, communism old-style.

But what Eurocommunism has achieved is to preserve intact, and almost certainly to strengthen, the vitality of parties which, had they stayed put in their pro-Soviet dogmas, would have been deserted by a large part of their electorate. The ability to adapt shown by the leaderships of these parties has been considerable: the renewal has been carried through without splits and with significant electoral gains in the case of the PCI; without splits and with limited electoral losses to the socialists in the case of the PCF. The result of ten years' change has been to preserve for these parties a position of importance, even if they remain an essentially regional force. In the new European Parliament, the communist group should represent between 10 and 15 per cent of the electorate – smaller, therefore, than the socialist, moderate and conservative groups.

In today's Europe, in short, the line put forward by the communists, however uncertainly and ambiguously, has its place, and that place may even expand as the continent moves towards unity. The Eurocommunists accurately reflect the political views of a mass of voters, no longer only from the working class, who share the aspirations for 'revolutionary' change which for a hundred years have been associated with Marxist and socialist ideologies. *The Eurocommunists have not been 'parachuted' into Western Europe: they have here their deep and vital roots.* The development of advanced industrial society has not emptied of meaning the political message which the Eurocommunists – now closer than ever to the socialists and social democrats – continue to transmit.

History will say whether the evolution of the Western communist parties constitutes 'a victory for democracy' or foreshadows a defeat. But if it is true, as I have argued above, that the growth of Eurocommunism has been largely conditioned from outside, then there is still plenty of room for further conditioning by other political forces. We have the chance to influence both the future development of the Eurocommunists and, more generally, the growth of democracy – civil, social and political – in the industrialized countries. My own vision of the future is in terms of 'more democracy' rather than 'more socialism': I believe the spectre that will haunt Europe, East and West, is not that of communism but of democracy. To give it flesh and bones, it is indispensable that different forces play their part, in accordance with the rules of pluralist societies – that is, through advances and defeats, through bouts of renewal and pauses for careful consolidation.

Within this framework, the Eurocommunists have their place and their function. It depends on the strength and vitality of the rest of us whether they go back to being a totalitarian and authoritarian challenge to democratic values. In other words, the premise (and perhaps also the conclusion) of any analysis of the Eurocommunist phenomenon could be this: that the problem in Italy is not the PCI but Christian democracy; that in France or Spain it is not the PCF or PCE but the socialist parties, and so on. The problem is not so much the threat, nor even the hope, of Eurocommunism, but the greater or lesser capacity of the West as a whole to establish itself as a stable and living democratic society, as a balanced and self-sufficient group of nations, and as an essential part of a well-ordered and developing world economy. To reach these goals we may find, if the 'cunning of Reason' so wills it, that the challenge of Eurocommunism, too – complex and enigmatic, disturbing and fascinating – will in the end prove useful, important, even indispensable.

January 1978

Notes and references

1. See M. Steinkühler, *Euro-Kommunismus in widerspruch – Analysis und Dokumentation,* Cologne 1977, p. 389. Steinkühler's interview with Frane Barbieri, reproduced here, appeared in *Deutschland Archiv*, 4, 1977, pp. 347–50. Barbieri has had an illustrious career in Yugoslavia, both as a journalist and as a political figure. Among other things, he has been deputy editor of *Politika*, and editor of the weekly *Nin*. He then wrote for *Giornale nuovo*, and is now with *La Stampa*. In fact the journal *Nin* (issue of 26 December 1976) wrongly attributed to me the paternity of the term 'Eurocommunism', and this term was at once taken up by Jean-François Revel of *L'Express*, and used in his book *La Tentation totalitaire* (Paris, 1976, p. 361). Enzo Bettiza also wrote of 'neo-communism' in *Encounter*, January 1978, p. 20.

2. Used for the first time officially by a communist leader, Enrico Berlinguer, on the evening of 3 January 1976, in a meeting held at the Porte de Pantin in Paris, along with Georges Marchais (Aldo Rizzo, *La Frontiera dell'Eurocommunismo*, Bari, 1977, p. 3). Among other things, Berlinguer said: 'It was neither us, nor you, French comrades, who coined the term "Eurocommunism" in reference to the issues on which our parties converge. However, the very fact that this term has such a wide currency in the international press, and raises in different fields so many questions and hopes, is a clear sign of the interest with which our two parties are regarded . . .' Note the restricted and defensive use of the expression made by Berlinguer.

3. From the NBC documentary on Eurocommunism, transmitted in January 1978 (*Newsweek*, international edition, 23 January 1978).

4. 'There are fundamental differences between the communist positions of yesterday and today. Now they see NATO as a guarantee of equili-

brium. They are all in favour of European development. They recognize the need for firms to make profits. But these new elements, which are genuine, have to find their place within a general judgement about the possibility of such a policy being put into practice. All this could be of extraordinary interest for the development of Italian politics, but to judge it correctly you need a dose of prudence and scepticism.' (Giulio Andreotti, interviewed in *Le Monde*, 2 March 1977).

'It's difficult to lump together men like Cunhal, Berlinguer, Marchais, Carrillo. So far Carrillo is the only one who has tried to lay the foundations for a systematic doctrinal revision. Of course Eurocommunism has aroused a lot of interest but, like all great hopes that fail to bear fruit, it runs the risk of provoking great disappointment. Of course you must give it time, but I feel some impatience.' (Bettino Craxi, Secretary of the Italian Socialist Party, interviewed in *Le Monde*, 4 September 1977).

'I attach the greatest importance to Berlinguer's Moscow speech [on the 60th anniversary of the October Revolution]. For me it's the clearest possible turning-point. After that speech it is no longer possible – without grave intellectual dishonesty – to dispute the PCI's new international alignment.' (Ugo La Malfa, President of the Italian Republican Party, interviewed in *La Repubblica*, 6 November 1977).

5. In the documents quoted above, the phrase had been 'secular character of the state' (*laicità dello Stato*).

6. One of the arguments most frequently put forward against the credibility of the Eurocommunist parties' new 'democratic pluralism' has to do with the experience of the 'people's democracies', the East European countries enclosed in the Stalinist sphere of influence. There too the communist parties, immediately after the war, preached a more or less 'pluralist' doctrine and proclaimed their determination to follow 'national roads to socialism', different from the Soviet, revolutionary road. Henry Kissinger has more than once reminded us of these embarrassing precedents, notably in his Washington speech of 9 June 1977 at the international conference on 'Italy and Eurocommunism'.

It is not difficult to find passages in the speeches of Georgi Dimitrov, Ernö Gerö, Władisław Gomułka, Klement Gottwald and other communist leaders of 1946–7 showing a not superficial similarity with the Eurocommunist texts quoted above. Togliatti, in fact, said analogous things upon his return to Italy in 1944, speaking of the 'New Party'. 'We do assuredly not propose a régime which is based on the existence, and the domination, of one sole party' (speech in Naples, April 1944, quoted in Rizzo, *La Frontiera dell'Eurocommunismo*, p. 25).

The argument of Kissinger is sufficient to insinuate a precise and persistent doubt: but I do not think it is in itself enough to prove the present declarations of the Eurocommunist parties false. During a seminar discussion held by a private organization which I attended in October 1977, the West German academic Richard Löwenthal answered Kissinger, who was advancing this argument, with a series of historical arguments which were also valid. Among other things, he noted that the 1946-7 declarations of Dimitrov and others were made in countries rigidly closed in the sphere of Soviet power, occupied by Russian troops, and with Stalin's consent. He pointed out that the present Eurocommunist declarations are made in totally different historico-geographical conditions.

One could add that the history of the people's democracies shows that at least some of the communist leaders of this period genuinely desired to follow a different road from the Leninist-Stalinist line, and wanted to build a road different from the Soviet variety. Several of them paid dearly for their heretical ambitions, even with their lives. Having said that, the speeches in question do remain disquieting, and cannot simply be put to one side, as did one of the top PCI leaders in a *Newsweek* interview of 30 January 1978. He said: 'It is absurd to think that after thirty years, history can repeat itself, in another part of Europe and in different conditions. It is absurd, stupid to say that what happened in Czechoslovakia and Poland after the Second World War can happen again, and that communists in France and Italy will do the same thing.'

This assurance is important, but hardly enough to efface the deep impression left in the Western memory of the tragic events in Eastern Europe after the Second World War – at least, not so long as there remains a substantial link between the Western communist parties and the Eastern heirs of Stalin.

7. Rizzo, *La Frontiera dell'Eurocommunismo*, p. 61. In the televised press conference of 15 June 1976, closing his electoral campaign and speaking to twenty million viewers, Berlinguer said: 'We believe ... that to construct the socialism we desire, the true socialism that is Western Europe's best hope of saving itself from decay – the great hope of the mass of workers, of women, and young people – it is more fitting that we stay in this area. This guarantees us the socialism we want, a free socialism, a plural socialism ...' This text was reproduced in full

in the next day's edition of the communist daily, *L'Unità* (16 June 1976). In *L'Unità*'s account of the Berlinguer interview with the *Corriere della Sera*, the passage containing the same concept had been omitted.

8. Speech at the Festival of Naples, 20 September 1976.

9. Rizzo, *La Frontiera dell'Eurocommunismo*, p. 96.

10. R. Christopher, 'Italy, the Upside Tickle and the Downside Risk', *Newsweek* international edition, 12 January 1976.

11. Speech of Giorgio Amendola, at the Festival of Modena (*Corriere della Sera*, 6 September 1977).

12. From the official interview of Paolo Bufalini (*L'Unità*, 6 November 1977) on the occasion of the 60th anniversary of the October Revolution.

13. Interview with Enzo Biagi, *Corriere della Sera*, 6 November 1977.

14. In an article published in February 1977 in the official Christian democrat weekly, *La Discussione*, Andreotti described as '. . . wise, the behaviour of the Italian communist leaders in not facing at this stage the problem of ideological revision, but to have concentrated on the renewal of their praxis'. In so doing, said Andreotti, the PCI leaders have been able to 'avoid the consequences of what in the eyes of many other communists, Italian or not, would have seemed like heresy'. The ideological revision would come later, 'motivated by the need for coherence, and compatibility with effective pluralism' (cf. editorial in *La Stampa*, 15 February 1977).

2. From Comintern to Polycentrism: the First Fifty Years of West European Communism
Neil McInnes

Political parties with an elaborate, explicit ideology always rationalize changes of policy, even (or especially) if these are sudden and merely tactical, by arguing that they are derived from an unchanging theory. What the party does now, it is said, is what it always did, or grew gradually and reasonably out of it. Any sudden change would mean that the party had previously fallen under the leadership of traitors who had betrayed its ideology and had therefore just been purged. In either case, the party's history must be constantly rewritten to prove this continuity or that rare act of treachery among the leadership. When the party in question is the communist party, which in its long history has advocated everything and its opposite, the rewriting of its past is a labour of Penelope, forever recommenced, never finished. It is facilitated by the fact that the communist party has no memory: its members are mostly young people, honestly ignorant of the past; few of them stay in the party for long; and the records are party secrets.

The major West European communist parties, which reluctantly adopted the label 'Eurocommunist' to denote their latest strategy, are busy rewriting their past to justify it. A remark of Maurice Thorez in an interview given to *The Times* in 1946 is discovered to be the very programme of Eurocommunism; the Spanish party recalls that it began its present course during the Civil War; while the Italian party asserts that it is all to be found in Gramsci, one of the very founders of the party.

A more disinterested study of the parties' history throws doubt on these discoveries, but it does not support the assertion of the communists' enemies, that Eurocommunism is a sudden, and therefore probably tactical, manoeuvre, aimed merely at winning

electoral advantage. The differences of opinion between the
Soviet Union and the major Western parties are deep and long-
standing, so that what is now called Eurocommunism has been
developing for at least twenty years. Premonitions of it can be
found, but not always where the communists say. And when they
do accurately recall some such anticipation, they forget to add
that soon afterwards their party changed tack and said the exact
opposite. This is the familiar difficulty of evaluating the policies
of a Leninist party, one that practises rigid discipline to enforce
a 'party line' which is in reality a zig-zag, a succession of con-
trasting tactical swings.

The foundation of these parties in 1920–21 was meant to
acclimatize that sort of organization, a peculiarly Russian invention, in Western soil. A Leninist party had successfully carried
out a revolution in Russia and, simply in order to defend it and
give it its full significance, it was now necessary to export the
revolution to the more advanced capitalist countries of West
Europe. Parties calling themselves communist, and insurrections
styled 'Soviet republics', had already sprung up across Europe,
more or less spontaneously, for the whole continent was in a
revolutionary ferment. The central empires had collapsed after
their military defeat, while the victorious Western governments
had broken the promises they had made to their working classes
during the long war. Few westerners knew what a Leninist party
was, let alone a soviet, but the more embittered and adventurous
were ready to join one. The Russian leaders sought to systematize
these revolutionary movements in a new Communist (or Third)
International. This Comintern would be one, single globe-girdling
party, of which the national agencies would be the local sections.

At a first congress in March 1919, the Comintern (which was
almost entirely Russian despite its international label) called for
communist parties to be formed everywhere, and at a second
congress in July–August 1920 it required them to agree to a precise constitution or set of statutes, the so-called '21 Conditions'.
Because the European situation at the moment was revolutionary
– the Red Army was advancing on Warsaw as the second congress convened – the conditions were severe, demanding the

maximum of aggressiveness and discipline from the new Western recruits. Some of the conditions duplicate others, but the principal ones called for the following: a party structure labelled 'democratic centralism', defined as a quasi-military discipline under the command of a highly centralized leadership; submission to a supranational authority, the Comintern; defence of the Soviet Union; periodic purges to maintain each party's purity; a strictly controlled party press, which would advocate the dictatorship of the proletariat and mercilessly criticize the bourgeoisie and its reformist accomplices, the socialists; the expulsion and vilification of those reformists as traitors to the revolution; communist infiltration of the trade unions; vigorous support of colonial revolts; and the establishment of a parallel organization that could, when necessary, operate underground.

Most Western socialists found these conditions unacceptable, but in their parties there was usually a section – here a minority, there a majority, but almost everywhere the youngest members – ready to accede to them. Yet few of those who agreed with them took them altogether seriously. They did not realize (for the fact had no precedent) that the Russians intended to interfere directly and ruthlessly in Western communist parties, as well as to set up regular schools to train their members in running the 'party of a new type' and in engineering violent revolution.

All the same, the new parties came out fighting: their first actions were violent, such as the German party's desperate bid to seize power in March 1921, and their mood was uncompromising when it came to dealing with their former comrades, the socialists. These latter and their trade unions were, as Lenin and his colleagues told a meeting of trade unionists in 1920, 'the last support of dying capitalism ... the watchdogs of capitalism that bark furiously at anyone who approaches their master's lair ... the last bourgeois barricade that the working class in revolt must storm in order to triumph ... more despicable even than the kings of the stock market and the sharks of capital'.[1] Gramsci was no more tender towards the socialists who were fighting to stop the rise of fascism in Italy, and he scornfully accused them of 'trying to hold Italian society together and even to avert that collapse that issued naturally from the ferment of corrosive acids inoculated into Italian society fifty years ago'.[2]

This phase of violent sectarianism soon ended, for it was everywhere drowned in blood. The Red Army was decisively stopped before Warsaw, and the westward march of the revolution ceased. The German revolutions collapsed, the Hungarian and Bavarian 'Soviet republics' were suppressed, and the great strikes and factory occupations in Italy, France and Czechoslovakia were defeated. A third congress of the Comintern met in Moscow in June–July 1921 to draw the lessons of these setbacks and particularly of the failure of the revolution in Germany, upon which the Bolsheviks had been counting to strengthen their own. As Borkenau said, 'At the time it seemed a tremendous lesson, of universal application, which would never now be forgotten. Everybody in the Comintern believed that never again would a similar experiment be attempted, and that the communist parties would now settle down and try to win over the majority of the workers.'[3]

Indeed, in mid 1921 the communist parties did change tack, but they did not abandon the Leninist strategy; they simply turned to another of its resources, the united front. This meant, as the Comintern explained in December 1921, offering an alliance to the social democrats, whom they had deserted in 1920 and had abused ever since. Zinoviev, Lenin's faithful spokesman, explained the reversal in tactics from ultra-revolutionism to a united front by saying in 1922:

> The workers want unity. Not to take account of that state of mind would be to make sectarians of communists and to help the social democrats . . . But we could not always respect that sentiment because the social democrats were using it to the profit of the bourgeoisie. We had to make the split. Now let's change roles: the splitters will be the socialists and not us . . . We are on the eve of a new surge of the working class.[4]

Actually, far from a new surge of the working class, there soon after ensued the fascist march on Rome and the dictatorship of Primo de Rivera in Spain. The communists had left it too late to change tactics, and besides, as Zinoviev's words abundantly show, the change was not sincere. The proffered unity was understood as collaboration between communists and socialists *against* the leaders of the socialist parties. That tactic was known as 'the united front from below'; it would have been 'from above' if cooperation with the socialist leaders were intended. The communist party in Germany was gravely weakened, and the continued though disguised hostility to the socialists had disastrous consequences in Italy and Spain, and yet the communists were not distressed for they were working on the theory, 'After the deluge, us!' They were convinced that their hour would strike only after the social democrats had been discredited in the eyes of the workers, if needful by defeat at the hands of the fascists, whereupon the workers would turn to their good shepherds, the communists.

As Gramsci put it later:

In 1921–2 the party had this official conception: the coming of a fascist or military dictatorship was impossible – a conception very similar to the other one about the inevitable replacement of a fascist régime by a socialist one, similar because it too was based on the idea of a mechanical and automatic resistance of the working class to dictatorship without the need of political direction. At that time we undervalued the sullen and latent resistance of the industrial bourgeoisie to fascism and we did not consider that a social-democratic government was possible . . . this conception hamstrung our political action and led us into many mistakes.[5]

Gramsci said that in a letter to Togliatti, but not in a public document. The lessons of Germany and Italy were not drawn and the Comintern was to go on making the same mistakes.

Limited and hypocritical as the united front was, it none the less marked a sudden switch from the ultra-revolutionary tactics of the period 1919–21. The turn was too sharp for many Western communists to take, and within the French, Italian and Spanish parties there was resistance and dissent. The Comintern drew the conclusion that the Western parties needed to be Bolshevized, that is, purged and disciplined to the point where they would make such turns without question. The aim was not to exclude the supporters of one strategy and approve the advocates of another, but to expel both if they could not accept the need for absolute discipline and tactical suppleness. At a given moment, a communist might be 'too far left' or 'too far right' or even 'too centre', but one thing he could not be was too obedient to the line dictated from Moscow. There was no way of knowing what that line might be, because in Moscow at that time there was taking place a struggle for power among Lenin's survivors, a struggle in which Stalin was now left, now right, now centre, whichever seemed to bring him nearer absolute power. By the time Stalin's victory was complete, in 1927, the Spanish party was outlawed, the Italian party was being hounded under Mussolini's laws of exception, and the German and French parties were seriously weakened; in the leadership of the latter, the police seem to have been as well represented as the proletariat.

Incredibly, however, these bedraggled troops were then ordered from Moscow into a new phase of left sectarianism, under the slogan 'class against class', which was to last until 1934. West Europe then got its first taste of disciplined communist aggressiveness on a massive scale. The experience left an indelible impression and it is responsible for much of the hostility towards communists that became inseparable from democratic sentiment. Later phases of communist sectarianism, as during the Cold War, only served to revive these painful memories. The communists' behaviour at this time exemplified a paroxysm of political folly and bad faith which justified the frequent comparison with their bosom enemies, the Nazis.

Stalin launched his first Five-Year Plan of industrialization in 1928, and he affected to fear that the West would attack the Soviet Union before it could 'build socialism'. He decided that the Western communists could help defend the Soviet Union by subverting, or at least disorganizing, Western nations. For that, they must first get rid of the obstacle constituted by the social democrats, who were preaching democratic collaboration against Nazism and fascism and thereby spoiling a promising revolutionary situation. Once the socialists were out of the way – and there would be nothing wrong with accepting fascist help to get rid of them – the workers would flock to the revolutionary banner.

Perhaps there would first be an interlude of fascist rule, but it would be short.

The Amsterdam-Pleyel Movement (a forerunner of the post-war Peace Movement) was set up to propagandize against 'imperialist warmongers', and the Western communist parties set to the task of annihilating the 'social-fascists', the 'social-patriots' or 'social-chauvinists', that is, the social democrats. In Germany and Austria, menaced by the rise of Nazism and the deepening economic crisis, the Comintern predicted imminent revolution; communist gains at elections were impressive. The communists attacked socialists – both verbally and physically – more than they did Nazis, and they even cooperated with Nazis in agitation against the socialist administration of Prussia. This campaign was kept up even *after* Hitler's victory in January 1933. In the Nazi jails, where both sides soon disappeared, the socialists remained 'social-fascists' for the communists.

In France from 1928, the communist party suspended the electoral arrangements whereby communists, socialists and radicals desisted at the second round of an election in favour of the leftist best placed in the first round, in order to ensure the defeat of the Right. The communists thereby lost many representatives in the Chamber of Deputies, but they had the satisfaction of seeing the socialists lose many more of theirs. The French party's membership slumped from 65,000 in 1926 to 28,000 in 1932, since fewer and fewer Frenchmen were ready to participate in this suicidal enterprise. Undaunted, the communists went to the lengths of joining in a demonstration with French fascists against the Daladier government in February 1934. There, too, the advent of Hitler had not opened communist eyes. As late as June 1934, Thorez, the secretary-general, was proclaiming, 'The party is organizing the break-up of the bourgeois army. It is practising the anti-militarism of Lenin and the Bolsheviks.'[6]

The moment the Spanish party regained its liberty with the inauguration of the Spanish Republic in 1931, it hastened to follow identical Comintern instructions with a virulence that today, in retrospect, shocks Santiago Carrillo, the present secretary-general:

On the proclamation of the Republic, the then small communist party, as narrow and sectarian as it was combative, rushed out into the streets to proclaim the necessity to install soviets and to smash the bourgeois state. That was the period of the tactic 'class against class', which in many ways resembles the ultra-leftist positions of today [1977], although in Spain none of today's ultra-leftists, with the exception of tiny and dubious groups, are as extremist as our party was then.[7]

Marvelling at the foolishness of these policies, Carrillo says elsewhere:

Today when I ask old comrades, 'How could you organize a general strike in Seville in favour of soviets?' they explain, 'The delegate of the Comintern came to Seville with one of the party leaders named Adame and said to us: There has to be a general strike for soviets. If they had asked us what a soviet was, we could not have answered. But we had influence inside the trade unions and we had courage, and so we started a general strike for soviets.' That policy led the party to be, at the time of the Republic, nothing but a little group on the margin of events.[8]

Carrillo insists that all this was done on Comintern instructions, and this was true of all the communist parties' actions at this time.

The Comintern in fact simply ran the Western parties in the period after Stalin came to power. Previously, the Comintern always had its man in each party, who was not necessarily a Russian but always a foreigner.[9] He managed the clandestine apparatus that the party was required to set up, and he advised the secretary-general and the politburo. He could, in turn, be influenced by their advice, but they could not dismiss him. However, from 1931–2 Moscow's interference in the Western parties became more massive than that. The Comintern sent a whole team of militants with foreign experience to run the French party, for example. One of them, Ceretti, was 'elected' to the central committee in quite irregular conditions, but the others stayed in the shadows and directed the party, unknown, needless to say, to the majority of members.[10] The Spanish party was similarly taken over by Comintern agents then and, more visibly, during the Spanish Civil War.

The secret apparatus of the Comintern which these delegates represented had been set up in the 1920s to carry on, or prepare, revolutionary activities which would be blatantly inconsistent with the Soviet government's diplomatic relations with other governments. The Comintern, Moscow told the British government when it protested, was an independent organization over which the Soviet government had no control! The headquarters of the secret apparatus, none the less, were within the Kremlin. Called at first ORG (Organization Bureau) and later OMS (International Communications Bureau), it maintained radio links with the illegal communist parties and with the clandestine organizations of the lawful parties. It ran for them training schools for professional revolutionaries.

In 1928, when the 'class against class' line was adopted, it was decided to intensify this work in Western Europe. A Vestsekretariat headed by the Bulgarian Georgi Dimitrov was set up in Berlin, for the prime target was Germany. When Hitler came to power, the office was transferred to Copenhagen and later, in 1937, to Paris. In 1928, moreover, there was established the International Seamen's and Harbourworkers' Federation to work in collaboration with the Vestsekretariat. It was based in Hamburg, and later in Copenhagen and Oslo. Known as the International Seamen's Club, it was an espionage and sabotage organization. It employed communist stewards and sailors as couriers for the Comintern, it arranged clandestine passages for agents, and it supplied propaganda material to communists the world over. It laid elaborate plans to sabotage the commerce of Western nations, notably Germany and Sweden, in the event of war with the Soviet Union. It perpetrated acts of sabotage against ships carrying arms to Franco's forces when the Spanish Civil War began, and against a Polish passenger ship apparently as retaliation for a border incident between the Soviet Union and Poland. Not only were there fires and explosions in ships in port, but several were wrecked at sea with loss of life. By that time, the Comintern's secret apparatus was locked in an 'unseen war' with the Gestapo.[11]

How close were relations between the communist parties and this secret organization? In theory they were separate, but in fact there was overlapping membership, and the leaders of the parties must have guessed what was happening. A member designated for secret work would resign from the party, and thereafter the party would want to know nothing about him; some thereupon became members of the Soviet party. Of course, when a party was outlawed in its own country, as many were in the 1930s, this pretence was dropped and the small number of militants ready to take the risk of working for the clandestine party became conscious collaborators of the secret organization. In other times, card-carrying members of the party might act as couriers or 'letter boxes', or they might put up an incognito comrade, but without directly participating in espionage or sabotage. Apart from one dubious case in 1929, the French Communist Party, for example, has never been implicated in any espionage affair. Even in the ultra-revolutionary period of 1928–34, the role and purpose of the communist parties in countries where they were legal was quite distinct from sabotage and espionage on behalf of Soviet Russia. Abundant right-wing accusations to the contrary have never been substantiated.

Their role then was, as it continued to be after the war, to influence public opinion in the democracies in favour of Soviet foreign policy and to intimidate Western governments which might oppose that policy. For that purpose, legitimate political activity usually sufficed, especially in countries like Italy and France where the parties came to have extensive electorates and numerous representation in parliament. Street demonstrations, the use of cover organizations or fronts, infiltration of trade unions and even resort to mob violence were regarded as legitimate in cases where it was desirable to make communist support seem greater than it actually was, but the intent was always to intimidate rather than to subvert, i.e. literally to overthrow a government and seize power. As Richard Pipes has said:

In this connection a few words must be said about the function of foreign communist parties which is often misunderstood. Communist parties are not used for purposes of subversion except in the most backward areas of the world because, being vulnerable to penetration by police agents, they cannot provide the necessary security. KGB agents who have been uncovered in the West not only had no connection with local communists but made every effort to appear conventional. Nor are these parties thought of as alternative governments to take over after the existing governments have been overthrown. When, after World War II, the Soviet Union occupied Eastern Europe it did not put in positions of power local communists but communists trained in Moscow. Once the East European client states had been solidified, the local communists were purged as thoroughly and with even greater vindictiveness than adherents of the so-called 'bourgeois' parties . . . Useful as they are, one must not overestimate the importance which the Soviet leadership attaches to foreign communist parties. It much prefers to establish working relations with the foreign elites; and there is enough evidence on hand to indicate that when the interests of the Soviet Union require it, foreign communist parties are readily sacrificed. They are only one element in the calculation of forces, and not the most weighty one at that.[12]

Maybe the West European communists began to sense that in 1934, to feel that Moscow was willing to put them in an impossible situation by prolonging the sectarian line beyond all reason. There are signs that they began to realize the error of that policy before Stalin did. Santiago Carrillo claims that it was the French and Spanish parties that first saw the urgency of uniting with the socialists and other democrats, in opposition to fascism,[13] because the communists in the field realized before the Moscow high command that 'the dogmatic line was restraining the development of the party and in a sense alienating it from the masses'.[14] French communists argue that their party defied Stalin, to force the new line on a reluctant Comintern. It is quite likely that there was discussion within the Comintern, and the French may well have taken the initiative,[15] but it would have made no progress had it not been for Stalin deciding, on grounds of Soviet foreign policy, that a change of tactics was needful. He had at last perceived the fact that a fascist alliance of Germany, Italy and eventually France would be more dangerous to the Soviet Union than to the Western democracies. He determined to seek an alliance with France against Germany, and he instructed the communists to join with French democrats (in fact with the traditionally anti-German Right) in supporting French rearmament. The coincidence of the switch to Popular Front tactics in France and Spain with other developments in Soviet foreign policy (entry into the League of Nations in 1934, the Mutual Assistance Pact with France in 1935) is too obvious for us to accept the idea that the veritable puppets who then headed the communist parties forced the change on Moscow. Besides, as we shall see, the new tactics had limited application, in that they never implied anything like the 'union of the Left' or the 'historic compromise' proposed today by the communists, and they were abandoned overnight when Soviet foreign policy suffered its next metamorphosis, in 1939.

At all events, the French party (the PCF) signed an agreement with the socialists in July 1934 for joint action in defence of democracy, an agreement that was extended to the Radicals soon after. This led in July 1935 to the Popular Front electoral alliance, which was approved as an example of the new communist line at a Comintern world conference in August 1935 (its seventh and last). That Popular Front alliance went on to win a majority in the Chamber of Deputies in April 1936. Léon Blum formed a government of socialists and radicals, which the PCF refused to join though it promised its support in the Chamber. Thorez, it is said, wanted the communists to accept portfolios in Blum's ministry, but the Comintern vetoed direct participation. Similarly in Spain, a Frente Popular was formed headed by the socialist Largo Caballero, but the PCE, on instructions from Moscow, refused to join the ministry. (It entered the Republican government only in September 1936, after the Civil War had begun.) Carrillo today wonders whether that refusal was not a fatal mistake which actually led to the Civil War and the subsequent Francoist dictatorship.[16] He likewise believes that if the PCF had joined Blum's ministry, this would have strengthened resistance to fascism throughout Europe.[17] On the contrary, I have argued elsewhere that open communist participation might have exasperated the fascists, because 'fascism fed on the Bolshevik danger and would have prospered faster if the communists had joined the socialists [in governments]'.[18] There were no other Popular Fronts. The British Labour Party stolidly continued to expel members who proposed one.

The French communists dissolved their parallel 'red' trade unions when the Popular Front was formed, but they kept up their sniping on the socialist leaders, and they worked hard at infiltrating socialist organizations while they kept their own organization aloof and ready to switch to radically different tactics at short notice. Democracy, it seemed, remained the enemy of the communists as much as if not more than capitalism, and their avowed objective was, by way of whatever compromises might be necessary, to install a Soviet society in the West. This was just when the Soviet original was beginning to assume its most diabolical features, in the mass deportations and the fake trials.[19] Thorez was still explaining in 1936 that a 'true popular front' would mean the establishment of soviets and the dictatorship of the proletariat and not a 'vulgar policy of ministerial collaboration', i.e. what the communists were offering in 1977.

The Popular Front, which was arguably one of the most disastrous governments France has ever had, has become a legend on the Left. It is credited with having wrested from the capitalists the wage increases, the forty-hour week and the paid annual holidays that were consecrated in the Matignon Agreement of June 1936. One could as well credit the Pompidou government with having wrested the massive wage increases conceded in the Grenelle Agreement of May 1968. In reality, in both cases, the concessions were made after totally unexpected mass strikes and factory sit-ins, which the communists, in both cases, anxiously tried to control once these had begun spontaneously. The electoral victory of the Popular Front sparked a brushfire of direct action, even before Blum could form his cabinet. It was brought under control only at the cost of concessions which ran directly counter to Stalin's original foreign-policy aims: the French economy was weakened, and French social tensions exacerbated, to the point where France was no longer a useful ally against fascism, as was to become clear in 1940.

Whatever the Popular Front did for Stalin, the Spanish and French parties soon found that it did them a power of good. In the previous, sectarian phase, the parties had lost up to three quarters of their members, showing once again that the violent

Leninist conspiracy would never flourish in Western soil. In contrast, during the phase of collaboration with democrats, however calculated and insincere, the membership prospered. When the Spanish Republic was inaugurated in April 1931, the Spanish Communist Party (PCE) counted barely 800 militants, but by February 1936 it had 30,000 members. These had risen to 84,000 in June of that year, and to 100,000 in July, and it went on to enrol 300,000 members during the Civil War (not counting the half-million members of the Youth Organization run by Santiago Carrillo). The French party's membership swelled from 28,000 in 1932 to 280,000 in 1936, and then to 320,000 in 1938.

These latter gains were to be wiped out by the Hitler–Stalin Pact of 1939. (By then, of course, the PCE had followed the Italian, German and Portuguese communist parties into the jails of fascism.) The French communist leaders were ready to see their troops melt away and to lose the confidence of 'a whole disgusted generation', because they had been trained to believe that the defence of the Soviet Union's foreign policy (which they saw as the defence of the one bastion of communist collectivism in the world) was their prime obligation. A popular, tolerant mass party might be the best instrument for that at one moment, but immediately afterwards a small, patient, hardened Leninist machine might be better suited to Moscow's purpose. That was the case in 1939–41, when the rump of Western communism defended the German-Soviet Non-aggression Pact, denounced the 'imperialist sham-democracies', forebore to breathe a word against Hitler and, when the war that Stalin had helped to unleash broke out, deserted in the face of the enemy rather than participate in a war which, for communists, merely betrayed the 'contradictions' of predatory capitalism.

Harry Pollitt, the secretary-general of the British party, was alone among Western leaders in arguing that the war became an anti-fascist one, and ceased to be imperialist, the day Hitler attacked Poland. For that, he was obliged to abandon his functions – until the German attack on the Soviet Union proved he had been right too soon. The other Western communist leaders and their few remaining followers faithfully applied Comintern

instructions, even though this entailed acts of treason in time of
war, and thereafter collaboration with the Nazi occupying power.
As recently as 1977, the parties were still trying to scrub this blot
from their scutcheon, using forged documents and falsified testimony to hide the fact that, on Comintern orders, they preferred
the good graces of the Soviet Union's Nazi ally to the service of
their own governments and resistance movements. They sought
permission to bring out communist newspapers in occupied
France, Belgium and Scandinavia (they secured it in Belgium,
Denmark and Norway, and some such editions were actually
printed in Germany); they were ready to cooperate with local
Quislings; they refused to take part in the Resistance; and they
kept up propaganda against Germany's lone opponent, Britain,
on a scale that well served Berlin's designs.

Their attitude changed when Hitler launched his attack on the
Soviet Union. However, it did not change quickly in Norway,
where the party was slow to join the Resistance,[20] and it never
changed decisively in Holland, where the wartime record of Paul
de Groot, the secretary-general, led to a party inquiry at the
Liberation.[21] Most other secretaries-general passed the war in
Moscow, in accord with the Leninist doctrine that the party boss
is a sacred vessel more valuable for the future than the rest of
the party put together.[22] Their lieutenants at home led the parties
into energetic and often heroic resistance work, which forced the
admiration of their partners. Indeed, after rallying belatedly to
the Resistance, the communists practised it with a terrorist im-
placability that some of their partners (for instance de Gaulle)
sometimes found impossible and counter-productive. The influence they thereby won in the occupied countries disturbed
Western governments (particularly governments in exile), and it
was to allay such anxiety that in May 1943 Stalin dissolved the
Comintern. The parties were thus 'dispensed from the obligations
resulting from the statutes and the congresses of the Comintern',
to quote that organization's final declaration. This did not mean
that they were absolved from obedience to Moscow, but the
orders that Moscow transmitted to them at the Liberation were
of a quite different sort from the generally aggressive instructions

the Comintern had put out. In brief, Stalin told the West European parties to curb the revolutionary enthusiasm engendered by the Resistance and to collaborate with the democratic régimes set up under American and British auspices. Communists who could not be curbed were ruthlessly purged by leaders who had spent the war in Moscow.

Paul de Groot and Earl Browder were so conciliatory towards the end of the war that they proposed to liquidate the Dutch and US communist parties, respectively, in broader socialist parties; they were condemned by Jacques Duclos of the PCF, speaking for Moscow. The non-revolutionary line adopted by the Italian Communist Party (the PCI) and by the PCF at the Liberation caused great disappointment within their ranks (and corresponding relief outside them), and it has been deplored ever since by leftist critics who claim that a revolutionary situation existed in Italy and France. Yet the only time an official communist voice has reproached them with it was when Tito was delegated to throw it in their face in 1947 – shortly before being expelled from the movement himself.

In accord with Stalin's directives, the communist parties entered post-war governments across Western Europe: in France, Italy, Belgium, Luxemburg, Austria, Denmark, Norway, Finland and Iceland. The Greek party, operating in a country whose fate had not been settled to Stalin's satisfaction, was alone in practising violent revolution; and the Spanish party kept up a desperate and costly guerrilla war against Franco.

No communist party made so complete an adaptation to the post-war parliamentary line as the PCI. It has never since departed from it, at least at the level of municipal and regional politics. Returning from eighteen years of exile, Palmiro Togliatti, the secretary-general, proposed in a speech at Salerno in March 1944 that representatives of all the anti-fascist parties serve in a government under King Victor Emmanuel III. A national government was formed a month later under Marshal Badoglio, and Togliatti (like Benedetto Croce) was part of it. He remained in successive governments under the monarchy and then in the newly founded republic, latterly with the rank of vice-president of the council of ministers. The PCI collaborated in the writing and adoption of the republican Constitution, and ever since it has identified itself as a party 'within the constitutional arc', claiming that the Italian Constitution needed no more than updating and thorough application to accommodate every communist demand. If that is true, it is because the communists saw to it that certain wide-ranging provisions were written into it from the start.

In contrast to the PCF, the Italian party, in its second, postwar incarnation, has always considered itself (whatever opponents might think) an integral component of Italian parliamentary democracy; indeed, as a founding father of the republic. It never felt isolated, even when the 'opening to the Left', the admission of the socialists to the government in 1963, was undertaken precisely in order to isolate it. It never retreated into a political ghetto, nor aimed to constitute a 'counter-culture' on the fringe of Italian society. On the contrary, it participated in post-war reconstruction, collaborated in parliamentary deliberations (especially the off-the-floor horse-trading in parliamentary commissions) and gladly accepted whatever particle of power it could win at every level of the administration from the municipalities upwards. It sought to avoid confrontation, except for one impressive display of power when an attempt was made on Togliatti's life in July 1948. In fact, by a slow movement of encirclement, it *absorbed* Italian socialism.

The PCI was aided in this characteristically Italian manoeuvre by its peculiar history and character. It had been defeated by fascism before it could be effectively Bolshevized, and throughout its long eclipse it remained the affair of a small number of intellectuals with a gift for organization, until they could recreate it, virtually *ex nihilo*, as a mass party at the end of the war. None of its leaders, from Bordiga by way of Gramsci and Togliatti to Berlinguer and Amendola, was a worker. None of them was inclined to follow what Gramsci called the Byzantine-Napoleonic example of Stalin, or to accept such Soviet fads as Zhdanovism, the dictation of 'socialist culture' from above. This is not to imply that they were independent of Moscow from the beginning, but their broad domestic backing, which brought great economic power and numerous footholds in the Italian power structure, enabled them gradually to win a measure of autonomy. Being communists, they used it to choose the Soviet side in the most important issues of the day. Their democratic version of democratic centralism (that is, the party remained heavily centralized but the fixers and arbitrators who set the party line seldom applied Stalinist methods, as Thorez loved to do) proved politically advantageous. From 5,000 or so in 1943, the PCI membership grew to 2·6 million (including the youth federation) in 1951. Fascism had made Italians a nation of 'joiners', so big parties were the rule, but it had not made them docile, and the PCI was never an effective Leninist machine.

The PCF likewise rallied to the new (Fourth) French Republic. Amnestied of the crime of desertion, Thorez returned to Paris in 1944, under the terms of a deal between Stalin and de Gaulle. He endorsed the national-front line, disarmed the communist militia and made it plain that revolution was not on the agenda. True, the communists pushed the purge of wartime collaborators with a characteristic intolerance, not to say savagery, but they renounced any intention of seizing power. They proposed re-unification to the socialists. Spurned, as they no doubt expected to be, they delegated five ministers to de Gaulle's government, where they enthusiastically supported post-war reconstruction. Thorez served as vice-president of the council of ministers and earned grudging respect as an administrator. He showed he could stop strikes, and incidentally signed the Act that unleashed the first Indo-Chinese War. This policy agreed with the PCF, too, for by the time the communists were expelled from the Ramadier government in May 1947, they claimed over 900,000 members. That was no doubt an exaggeration (which did not stop them claiming a million members soon after), but the party was obviously several times the size of the organization that had committed political suicide by approving the Hitler–Stalin Pact.

The PCF during its passage in government managed to 'colonize' several ministries and to infiltrate all the public services, to an extent that required years to undo. Yet, compared with the PCI, their penetration of French society was less thorough, and the break – when it came – more complete, because the PCF had retained the stigmata of an aggressively proletarian party. In that, it was true to an old French tradition of 'social racism' or working-class tribalism. This enabled it to provide an intermittently successful imitation of a Leninist machine. Thoroughly Bolshevized and long accustomed to accepting Moscow's dictation, the leaders of the PCF were distrustful of parliamentary work, inept at compromise and suspicious of intellectuals. They were ready to swallow any Stalinist propaganda and to follow any directive from Moscow, no matter how impolitic.

This was to matter when the break in the national front in France came in 1947. Contemporary historians are re-examining the origins of the Cold War and reappraising the responsibilities, as between Moscow and Washington, for the sudden change in the international climate that occurred then. None of that will change the facts as concerns the communist parties. Whether thrown out by their coalition partners or called out by Moscow, they went quietly and thereafter threw themselves whole-heartedly into the defence of Soviet foreign policy, which was soon openly aggressive. Moscow sought to coordinate their work by founding, in September 1947, the Cominform, a shadowy reincarnation of the Comintern which included the governing parties of East Europe and the PCF and PCI.

The Spanish party resented the formation of the Cominform, not just because it was excluded from it and not advised about it, but also because it had already become touchy about surrendering any of its freedom of movement to a new world organization.[23] Its recollection of Soviet interference during the Civil War was still smarting. The French and Italian parties, on the other hand, submitted meekly. The Cominform's first act was to attack them for their submissiveness to the Anglo-Americans at the time of the Liberation, but the attack came from the Yugoslavs, in accord with the communist practice of assigning dirty work to a candidate for imminent disgrace. Thorez and Togliatti, scenting what was coming, stayed away from that first meeting, and Togliatti

managed to evade the responsibilities Stalin had in mind for him
in the new organization.

The Yugoslavs' criticism helps to explain some of the venom
of the Latin parties when Tito was expelled from the movement
the next year, but the animosity of the French communists was
remarkable. It is one aspect of their reckless behaviour throughout the Cold War – behaviour that some of them now confess
bordered on political hysteria. They not only believed the absurd
allegations brought against East European 'Titoists' in the fake
trials of 1949–52, but they staged imitations of those trials in
their own ranks.[24] They not only carried adulation of Stalin to
the utmost limits of baseness and bad taste, but they practised
an identical cult of the 'personality' of Maurice Thorez.[25] They
adopted the worst excesses of Zhdanovism in cultural affairs;
they defended Lysenko's spurious 'proletarian science' of
genetics;[26] and they propagated palpable untruths about France's
economic situation, such as the theory of 'absolute pauperi-
zation'.[27] No lie about the United States was too grotesque, no
flattery of the Soviet Union too sickening for the infinite credulity
of a French communist. Anyone who disagreed, or demurred,
with the party line was pursued with scurrilous abuse.

Naturally they also joined vigorously, as did all the communist
parties, in uncompromising attacks on US foreign policy, on the
defence preparations of Western governments and on France's
colonial wars. Their espousal of the cause of Soviet foreign
policy extended from epic scenes of denunciation in parliaments
to violent street riots, from the manipulation of numerous front
organizations [28] to the massive imposture of the World Peace
Movement founded in April 1948. The Italian communists, who
were excommunicated by the Catholic Church in July 1948, were
scarcely less ferocious in their street demonstrations against the
NATO commanders Eisenhower and Ridgway in 1951 and 1952
than the French were in riots between 1949 and 1952.

The two parties lost members during this era of systematic
fanaticism, but the PCF lost few votes (it even gained some in
1956), while the PCI's electoral audience grew at each successive
consultation. Indeed, the imperturbable progress of the Italian

communist vote since the war, through all sorts of domestic and international crises, has been decisive for the Italian republic and for the appearance of Eurocommunism:

June 1946	4,356,686 votes	19%
June 1953	6,120,809 votes	22·6%
May 1958	6,704,454 votes	22·7%
April 1963	7,763,854 votes	25·3%
May 1968	8,557,404 votes	26·9%
May 1972	9,085,927 votes	27·2%
June 1976	12,620,509 votes	34·4%

These electoral advances brought with them (and in turn are explained by) increasing communist penetration of local government, of the press and broadcasting (radio and television), of the universities and the cooperative movement, and even of the police and army. In other words, Italian communism ceased to be merely a Soviet agency and became a national party which, however far from power, represented one possible future for Italy. The party continued to be dependent for its basic ideology and for its distinctive political appeal on the *example* of the Soviet Union, the land where the possessors had been dispossessed and where exploitation had therefore supposedly ended. But in most other ways it became less dependent on the Soviet Union as it won, within Italy, its own sources of votes, power, money and respectability. Naturally, it paid for this national status by exposing itself to all the influences of Italian political life. Thus it became more open and tolerant, less monolithic, more democratic at the base (where the cell disappeared in favour of constituency-sized units) and more *interclassista*. That is, it ceased to pretend to be a proletarian party and even abandoned claims to be more of a 'people's party' than its main opponent, the Italian Christian Democrat Party. By recognizing in its adversary a movement of the same sort as itself, however different their respective moralities, the PCI opened the way to the 'historic compromise'.

What mattered more to other communist parties was that the PCI made these advances while – and presumably because – it took its distances from its avowed model, the Soviet Union. Thanks to Gramsci and Togliatti, the Italian communists had not been Stalinist sycophants even when they maintained that the Soviet way was the right one for Italy. They were eager to seize upon signs of de-Stalinization, after the tyrant's death in 1953, as justification for further inflection of their domestic policies. The extent of the PCI's integration into Italian political life is shown by the fact that its deputies voted for three quarters of the laws enacted between 1948 and 1968, usually for the good reason that some at least of their amendments had been accepted.

The Spanish party, obviously, could not seek integration into Francoist society for it was illegal and in exile – and even in its most convenient place of exile, France, it was declared illegal in 1950. Nevertheless it managed to achieve a certain autonomy by maintaining several foreign bases other than Moscow. (Dolores Ibarruri, the party president, lived in the Soviet capital, but Santiago Carrillo was unique among prominent exiled communists in having spent no more than six months there.) Those bases were in Czechoslovakia, Romania and France, where, despite the law, Carrillo lived for over twenty-five years. Many party members returned clandestinely to Spain at the end of the Second World War. Their networks were regularly dismantled by the police, but their press attained a certain circulation and communists were active in the illegal strikes that began in 1947. Communist guerrillas tried to invade Spain from France in 1945, and the party kept up sporadic raids until officially abandoning that line in October 1948; it claims that later raids, which continued till 1952, were the work of isolated groups.

The party was convinced throughout this period that Franco was about to fall at any moment, and it turned to less violent methods only with the conviction that they would hasten that eventuality. It sought to get its members elected to the vertical trade unions of the fascist régime, as Stalin had advised it to do in 1948; and it managed to take over the Comisiones Obreras after 1962 when these were set up as parallel trade unions by other leftists, against initial communist opposition.[29] The Francoist governments, for whom communism served as a bogeyman, probably exaggerated the extent of the PCE's influence, but the party was happy to accept the reputation of being the régime's best-organized adversary. By 1953, the leadership, still in the hands of an old guard composed of Uribe, Mijé and Lister, was being challenged by younger men led by Carrillo, Fernando Claudín and Ignacio Gallego. These latter were more keenly aware of the changes taking place in Spain, not least in the party's own support there as intellectuals and some middle-class people joined its ranks. They pressed for new policies, notably as to alliances, that would reflect that change.

The Italian and Spanish parties, then, were poised ready to greet the liberalization heralded by Khrushchev's secret report to the Twentieth Congress of the Soviet party in 1956. Not so the French party. It had accepted uncritically Stalin's last hallucination, the 'doctors' conspiracy' to murder him, and, after his disappearance in 1953, it clung to a rigid Stalinist orthodoxy. It had its own Stalin, in the person of Maurice Thorez, and even its own Zhdanov in Laurent Casanova. Its only contributions to French politics were to join in any motley coalition of opponents seeking to bring down the ephemeral governments of the Fourth Republic, while opposing the Indo-Chinese War and using its trade-union affiliate, the CGT, to disrupt French industry and administration.

Khrushchev's report in 1956, which denounced some of Stalin's crimes and consolidated the end of the terror, was plainly expected by several Western communist leaders. It could have contained few revelations for any of them who had lived for years in Moscow under Stalin. Yet they denied all knowledge not only of its contents but of its very existence. It is now established that Togliatti, Thorez, Ibarruri and others saw it while it was being read by Khrushchev or even slightly before,[30] but they decided to keep quiet about it, at Soviet request. They were all the more inclined to do so because it put them in an invidious position. They were free citizens living (even if in exile) in free countries, but they had volunteered acquiescence in a monstrous system of oppression and falsehood, acquiescence which within the Soviet Union could only be obtained by terror.

The Spaniards were the first to draw political conclusions from the new Khrushchev line. The 'Young Turks' led by Carrillo and Claudín had been attacking the 'authoritarianism' of Uribe with increasing insolence, till they faced expulsion from the party in 1956. Once Dolores Ibárruri read the Khrushchev report, she realized they had anticipated the future. From that moment Carrillo was the *de facto* party boss, although he was not officially designated secretary-general until 1960. Significantly, Carrillo merely wanted to accept the Khrushchev policy of de-Staliniization, because it suited him politically, but not to discuss the question further. Claudín, on the other hand, realized that the party would have to analyse its Stalinist past and not fob critics off with the label 'personality cult'. This was the beginning of the rift between two men who had been 'like brothers' through years of exile, which was to culminate in the expulsion of Claudín (and of Jorge Semprun) in 1964. Only in 1977 did Carrillo publish the analysis of the Stalinist state that all the communists' critics had awaited since 1956. Right from that year, however, the PCE launched its new policy of National Reconciliation, the first of a series of offers to collaborate with Spanish democratic forces. None of them, down to the Pact for Liberty, had much echo inside Spain.

The PCI seized, similarly, upon Khrushchev's statement that in some 'highly developed capitalist countries' a coalition of 'all patriotic forces' led by the working class could win a parliamentary majority and effect 'radical social transformations'. This revisionist farewell to revolution in favour of the peaceful way to power was written into the PCI programme from 1956. Togliatti went further by rejecting the 'personality cult' as an adequate explanation of the Stalinist system and by calling for 'polycentrism', a notion which, however vague, implied a reduction of Soviet influence over Western parties and a devaluation of the Soviet model as a pattern for Western communism.

The PCF in contrast refused to adhere to the Khrushchev line or to acknowledge de-Stalinization. Thorez conspired with Khrushchev's Russian opponents, who wanted to disown his report, and when they were defeated and it became necessary to kotow to the new master of the Kremlin, Thorez flirted with Mao

Tse-tung, whose rejection of de-Stalinization was to lead to the Sino-Soviet split. Thorez was not serious in this flirtation, but he won a bargaining position that he could exploit to the full in 1961: he agreed to rally to Khrushchev's support against China if Moscow would accept a purge of Khrushchev's liberal supporters inside the PCF. Two leading members were tried, convicted and demoted, thus leaving Thorez free to pursue his total opposition to the 'semi-fascist régime' of de Gaulle, and, of course, to continue to run the party as his private property. In the long run he was obliged, by the contrast of the PCI's electoral successes and his electoral failures, to incline the PCF's policies towards the Khrushchev line and even to follow the Italian communists in adopting a more independent stance. But the main point is that by 1960 Moscow was reduced to bargaining and negotiating with men like Thorez, its own creatures whom once it had ordered to obey *perinde ac cadaver*.

The Sino-Soviet split was by then weakening Moscow's position in the movement, but so too was the discredit Khrushchev had thrown on all forms of communism by his admission of Stalin's terror. This confession stimulated on the Left, both within the communist parties and without, a reconsideration of the whole history of communism since 1917 and a rereading of Marxism itself. Once the Bolshevik Revolution was admitted to have ended in tyranny and mass murder, historical materialists were bound to ask how that was possible, and, the personality of one man being no sufficient explanation, to ask whether the deviation had not occurred earlier in the movement's history, perhaps in Lenin's day or even earlier. Official answers from Moscow were no longer accepted, for it had lost its pre-eminence, and from 1956 was hard put to maintain by brute force even a semblance of respect in its own camp. It could not lay down the law on theoretical questions for Westerners. This awakening of the critical spirit on the Left led to the heretical reinterpretations of Marxism that became public in the disorders of 1968 and to the rebirth of an ultra-Left as a permanent feature of the European political landscape. It led also to the deviation now known as Eurocommunism.

Moscow could not foresee all that, but it was swiftly evident that communism was in crisis (a condition the communists had always reserved for capitalism). The Hungarian uprising in 1956 did not trouble Western communist parties unduly, though it alienated members who saw that, however sincerely Khrushchev might condemn Stalin's methods, he was obliged to make use of them to maintain communist rule in the satellites. In 1957, Moscow called the first world conference of communist parties since the days of the Comintern. (The Cominform, discredited by its anti-Tito campaign, had been wound up the previous year in April, when Khrushchev was preparing a reconciliation with Tito.) The conference was meant to overcome the movement's crisis and to reassert Moscow's pre-eminence. All the participants, including Mao, paid lip-service to that pre-eminence, but this was a papering over of differences. Underneath, the splits continued to widen. The same act of communist decorum was repeated at another conference in 1960, although by then the Russians and the Chinese, by interposed Albanians, were at loggerheads over Khrushchev's revisionism. That conference ended with a piece of triumphant hypocrisy that needs to be recalled when later communist differences are being discussed: 'The speculations of the imperialists, the renegades and the revisionists about the possibility of a split in the socialist camp are built upon sand and doomed to collapse. All the socialist countries treasure the unity of the socialist camp like the apple of their eye.' Within months, two members of that camp were on the verge of war.

The substance of the Sino-Soviet dispute was of little interest to the Western communists. They have never, in twenty years, let themselves be manoeuvred by the Russians into a unanimous condemnation of Peking. Yet that is not from any sympathy with the Chinese, who have made no effort to understand the gravamen of the Western parties' quarrel with Moscow and have evinced no understanding of the conditions in which the Western parties must operate. For all this mutual indifference, the Chinese challenge hastened the Westerners' challenge to Moscow, because the Sino-Soviet split damaged Russian prestige, abolished Moscow's monopoly over the notion of revolution and obliged the Kremlin to seek political support from erstwhile subordinates. Above all, it demonstrated communism's failure to conquer nationalism. The very vice in socialist internationalism that brought Lenin to denounce it and found a new International was discovered to have eaten the heart out of communist internationalism too. Neither movement had been able to withstand the trial of governmental responsibility without succumbing to nationalism. What the Western communists had obediently denounced in Titoism from 1948 to 1956 was now seen to be the general case for all communist régimes. They were national régimes first, and their pretended internationalism was not even a secondary interest but merely the foreign-policy cover for their fundamental nationalism.

That was probably enough to suggest to Western communists that they, too, would have to put national concerns higher in their programmes and to reconcile themselves to domestic, national political traditions – even if as a first stage towards *their* variety of national communism they had to use a pseudo-internationalist figleaf like 'Eurocommunism'.[31] If it was not enough to suggest that to them, then they were soon convinced by the Soviet Union's new foreign policy of 'peaceful coexistence'. This plainly put the Soviet interest in good relations with Western governments ahead of the political ambitions of the relevant parties. The PCI has not objected to peaceful coexistence, for it saw that it was essential to its gradual approach to the 'area of government' in the peculiar conditions of Italian politics. But the PCF has bitterly resented Moscow's cooperation with de Gaulle and his successors, just as the PCE was incensed by Moscow's courting of the dying Franco. The French and Spanish communists protested that internationalism was a two-way affair, and if Moscow expected their loyalty, it would have to show a care for their domestic political problems. But that, as we have seen, is something Moscow has never done. The communist parties are expendable; or at least (since only the Polish and Egyptian parties have literally been expended), they must be ready to suffer crippling losses of prestige, membership and electoral support whenever Moscow requires. But that is something that the Western communist leaders, with their new-found political appetites and their solid domestic base, are no longer as ready to accept as they were in 1939.

By the mid 1960s, Western communists had come to see that if political power was what they wanted, then the Russians were unreliable allies in seeking it. Thorez had already called them 'unpredictable', and Togliatti said they could be incomprehensible. Two new developments strengthened that distrust. First, Khrushchev had persuaded them to accept peaceful coexistence by arguing that it would provide the conditions that would enable the Soviet Union to outclass the United States. If the Soviet Union were, as Khrushchev promised, soon to 'bury the USA', the Western communists need do little but sit still and wait for communism to demonstrate its overwhelming superiority in every field. Thereupon they would be received in public office by unanimous acclamation, or at most after just a little *putsch*. Instead, the Soviet Union encountered a series of humiliating agricultural disasters and economic failures that made it dependent upon the West. That threw doubt upon the whole collectivist project. Inevitably, Western communists began to say they were no longer collectivists (least of all in agriculture), and to seek political allies who assuredly were not.

Secondly, and in direct connection with some of those failures, the Russians showed that they had not solved the succession problem. Most Western communists, with greater or less good grace, had rallied to Khrushchev. Even the PCF came to accept his policies, to de-Stalinize, and to liberalize its views on culture. Just when they had managed this difficult emotional 'transfer' from Stalin to Khrushchev,[32] he was unceremoniously unseated in the palace revolution of 1964. Khrushchev's fall embittered Western party leaders [33] more than non-communists have perceived. It shook their bureaucratic sense of security and made them ridiculous as converts to democratic procedures in their own countries. Until the Soviet Union resolves its succession problem (which will be difficult in the absence of democracy), it will recurrently embarrass Western party bureaucrats in the same way.

Thus, by the time the Czechs began their experiment in communism 'with a human face' in 1968, the Soviet party on the one hand and the major West European parties on the other hand had accumulated a whole catalogue of contentious issues and divergent interests. None of that allowed one to forecast that the breach over the Czech affair would go as far as it did, but it was plain that the Western parties had come a long way from the days when they were small, fanatical and occasionally violent sects, ready for any sacrifice in defence of Soviet foreign policy but powerless in the face of the Kremlin's displeasure. To be sure, everything in their history testified to their tactical resilience and disinclined observers from placing trust in the solidity of any one position the communists might take up. But the story of those same communist zig-zags and reversals also showed that when the communist parties have changed position from democratic collaboration to pro-Soviet violence, they have done so at the cost of reducing themselves to rump parties of negligible influence in Western political life.

Notes and references

1. Arnold Toynbee *et al.*, *The Impact of the Russian Revolution*, London, 1967, p. 118.

2. Franco Catalano, *Storia dei partiti politici italiani*, Turin, 1965, p. 293.

3. Franz Borkenau, *World Communism*, new edition, Ann Arbor, 1962, p. 218.

4. Jules Humbert-Droz, *L'Oeil de Moscou à Paris*, Paris, 1964, p. 13.

5. Catalano, *Storia dei partiti politici italiani*, p. 294.

6. Maurice Thorez, *Oeuvres*, livre II, tome 6, pp. 169–70.

7. Santiago Carrillo, '*Eurocomunismo*' *y Estado*, Barcelona, 1977, p. 147. (English translation: '*Eurocommumism*' *and the State*, London, 1977.)

8. J. A. Vidal Sales, *Santiago Carrillo: Biografia*, Barcelona, 1977, p. 58.

9. Examples were Gerhard Eisler (in the US party), M. N. Roy and Sen Katayama (in South America), D. Petrovski (in Britain), Matthias Rakosi (in Italy), Heinz Neumann (in China and Spain), and so on.

10. Roland Gaucher, *Histoire Secrète du Parti Communiste français*, Paris, 1974, pp. 238–41.

11. Erik Norgaard, *Revolutionen de udeblev*, Copenhagen, 1975; and *Den usynlige Krig*, Copenhagen, 1975.

12. Richard Pipes, 'Operational Principles of Soviet Foreign Policy', *Survey*, vol. 19, No. 2, pp. 52–3.

13. Carrillo, *'Eurocomunismo' y Estado*, pp. 144–6.

14. S. Carrillo and S. Sanchez Montero, *P.C.E.*, Bilbao, 1977, p. 12.

15. Annie Kriegel, *Un autre communisme?*, Paris, 1977, pp. 133, 156–7.

16. Carrillo, *'Eurocomunismo' y Estado*, pp. 153–4.

17. ibid., pp. 145–6.

18. Toynbee, *The Impact of the Russian Revolution*, p. 125.

19. Fernando Claudín, *Eurocomunismo y Socialismo*, Madrid, 1977, p. 98–9.

20. Haakon Lie, *Hvem kan vi stole på? En dokumentasjon om Norges Kommunistiske Parti under den tysk-russiske alliansen 1939–41*, Oslo, 1974, p. 118.

21. Wouter Gortzak, *Kluiven op een Buitenbeen. Kanttekeningen bij enige naoorlogse ontwikkelinge nvan het Nederlandse communisme*, Amsterdam, 1966, pp. 22–3.

22. A doctrine that explains the otherwise curious (Marchais said 'lamentable') exchange of Vladimir Bukovsky for the secretary-general of the Chilean Communist Party, Luis Corvalan, in 1976. Such Soviet investments in party bosses can pay off handsomely, as the case of Alvaro Cunhal showed after fourteen years in Moscow; see Francisco Ferreira, *Alvaro Cunhal, Herói Soviético: Subsídios para uma biografia*, Lisbon, 1976.

23. Carrillo, *'Eurocomunismo' y Estado*, p. 165; Claudín, *Eurocomunismo y Socialismo*, p. 34.

24. Charles Tillon, *Un Procès de Moscou à Paris*, Paris, 1971.

25. Philippe Robrieux, *Maurice Thorez: Vie secrète et vie publique*, Paris, 1975, pp. 290–91, 375–80 and 604; Jacqueline Mer, *La Parti de Maurice Thorez, ou le bonheur communiste français*, Paris, 1977.

26. D. Lecourt, *Lyssenko: Histoire d'une 'science prolétarienne'*, Paris, 1976.

27. Dominique Desanti, *Les Staliniens*, Paris, 1975.

28. Neil McInnes, *The Communist Parties of Western Europe*, London, 1975, pp. 11–17.

29. Julio Sanz Oller, *Entre el fraude y la esperanza: las Comisiones obreras de Barcelona*, Paris, 1972.

30. After twenty-one years of prevarication, the PCF politburo admitted as much on 13 January 1977.

31. For the theory that Eurocommunism (before the word) was a 'polycentrist legitimation' to hide the return to national communism, see McInnes, *The Communist Parties of Western Europe*, pp. 153–6.

32. Not the Dutch party, however. Rather than make the transfer to Khrushchev, Paul de Groot took the party out of the world movement. He returned to it in 1977, apparently to mark his disapproval of Eurocommunism.

33. Åke Sparring *et al.*, *Röd opposition: Europas kommunistiska partier och Chrusjtjovs fall*, Stockholm, 1965.

Part Two

3. Il compromesso storico:
the Italian Communist Party from 1968 to 1978
Giovanni Russo

The Breach with the Soviet Union

No one can say that the internal policy of the Italian communists has not been decisively affected by their ties with Moscow. But, from the party's foundation at Leghorn in 1921 onwards, fidelity to the Soviet Union was constantly intertwined with the struggle to implant communism in Italy, the one alternately taking priority over the other. Here are a few famous examples:

1926: Antonio Gramsci writes to Palmiro Togliatti in Moscow, expressing the PCI's disagreement with Stalin's treatment of the internal opposition in the CPSU. Gramsci asks him to show the letter to Stalin. Togliatti is careful to do nothing of the sort.

1939: Umberto Terracini, co-founder of the party and one of those closest to Gramsci (who was now dead), condemns the alliance between the Soviet Union and Hitler's Germany. For this he is expelled from the party by the comrades interned with him, to be readmitted only after 1945.[1] (Both Gramsci and Terracini were out of line with the Stalinist positions adopted by the party's clandestine *centro dirigente* and by Togliatti as one of the secretaries of the Comintern.)

1956: Expulsions and resignations of party leaders and intellectuals who opposed the Soviet intervention in Hungary.

All these upheavals in the PCI were directly connected with the problem of its relations with the Soviet Union, as also were the successive shifts between alliance and polemic in relations with the socialists – and, indeed, Berlinguer's proposal for the historic compromise itself. These two elements (fidelity to the Soviet

Union and the autonomy of the PCI) coexisted and struggled with each other, but before 1968 it was always the former which prevailed.

Only in 1968, with the condemnation of the Soviet invasion of Czechoslovakia which smashed Dubček's 'socialism with a human face', did the contradictions between external and internal policy decline, though even then they did not disappear. This condemnation, which prepared the ground for the change of direction into which Enrico Berlinguer was to lead the party, reflected the will of Luigi Longo, who represented and still represents 'continuity' with the past. Communist historians like Paolo Spriano or influential leaders like Giorgio Amendola and Giancarlo Pajetta argue that there has always been a 'continuity' in the policy of the PCI since the so-called 'Svolta di Salerno'. (On his return to Italy from the Soviet Union in 1944 after the liberation of southern Italy by the allies, Togliatti obliged the reluctant communists, who believed that revolution was imminent, to collaborate with the monarchy and with the government of Marshal Badoglio – then based in Salerno – in the name of the unity of all anti-fascist forces in the war against the Germans. But it has also been said that he did so on orders from Stalin, who had been the first to recognize the Badoglio government.)

The PCI remained Stalinist, or at least wore Stalinist clothing, for a long time, even though Togliatti conceived and presented the party as a force for the construction of Italian democracy.

Yet the invasion of Czechoslovakia found the party mature enough to express judgement on it in terms different from the Hungarian revolt, which by contrast was unconditionally approved. Togliatti had died in 1964 and his post of secretary had been taken by Longo, a man of the old guard who was regarded as even more closely linked to Moscow. In reality, Longo knew that the major obstacle to the PCI's advance in the eyes of Italians was its dependence on the Soviet Union. For this reason in 1964 he did not hesitate to publish, without consulting the Soviet leaders, the 'Testament of Yalta' – the document written by Togliatti just before his death.

The Yalta testament is a very explicit criticism of the 'achievements of socialism', of Khrushchevism, and of the CPSU's international policy. In it Togliatti explained the dramatic nature of the crisis in the international communist movement (the breach with China), and said that it was necessary to find more flexible mechanisms of unity.

Already in 1956 Togliatti had developed the theory of 'polycentrism', which is the origin of Eurocommunism, since it denies the totally predominant role of the CPSU.

The decision to condemn the Soviet intervention in Czechoslovakia was not an easy one,[2] but the expression of 'profound dissent' was clear. It was taken both to give credibility to what Togliatti had called 'the peaceful road to socialism' and as a way of maintaining an equidistant position on the China question. The PCI had consistently criticized the positions of Mao Tsetung, but had also made every effort to avoid an international conference which would excommunicate the Chinese party. 'In Czechoslovakia an independent road of autonomous development was struck down,' says Luca Pavolini, 'and if the PCI had not come out against this it would have been contradicting its own thesis of a different model and a national road to socialism.'

Besides, in 1968 events were happening in Italy which obliged the PCI to emphasize its autonomy. There was the student agitation which had started in late 1967, before that in France. As Giorgio Napolitano admits,[3] the PCI did not at first understand 'the significance and implications of the explosive growth of the student population'. The student agitation was the forerunner of the awakening of the workers which brought about the great strikes of autumn 1969, after the series of spontaneous struggles in the factories from 1968 onwards.

On another side was the working-class agitation caused by the discontent of hundreds of thousands of young southerners who had emigrated to the big towns and factories of the north – the only true and great social revolution to occur in post-war Italy – and their consequent politicization. The uncontrolled growth of cities provoked social imbalances which are at the root of the crisis that the country is at present living through. Also in 1968 began the decline of the centre-left formula of government (based on an agreement between Christian democrats, socialists, social democrats and republicans), whose object had been to head off the communist advance by introducing economic and social reforms. In the elections of May 1968, the PCI in fact improved its position, winning 26·9 per cent of the votes, but the Christian democrats were still four million votes ahead, with 39·1 per cent. The United Socialist Party (formed by the merger of socialists and social democrats in 1966) withdrew from the government after the elections and the prime minister, Aldo Moro, was obliged to resign. Thereafter the centre-left lived through a series of convulsions but had finally expired by the time of the elections of June 1976.

Berlinguer's rise to the party leadership

Enrico Berlinguer, who became for the first time a member of parliament in 1968, emerged as the dauphin of Longo after the PCI's Twelfth Congress, held at Bologna in February 1969. His election by the central committee as deputy secretary of the party made it clear to all that he was to be the new leader. This confirmed the reduction to the status of 'notables' (as it were, a council of elders) of the leaders of the intermediate generation – Giorgio Amendola, Pietro Ingrao and Giancarlo Pajetta – though they remained very powerful in the party and influential with public opinion.

Amendola, son of an illustrious liberal victim of fascism, had been the symbol of the choice of communism as sole alternative to fascism made by the children of the traditionally liberal intellectual bourgeoisie. He had believed in the myth of Stalinism,[4] like every other communist, but was now considered the spokesman of the pragmatist wing of the party which was ready to make an agreement with the Christian democrats in order to get into power. In some respects, Amendola can be considered a forerunner of Eurocommunism – as is shown by his speech at the

Eleventh Party Congress on the Communist Workers' Movement in the West, which provoked a polemic with Togliatti, and by his proposal after Togliatti's death for a united party with the socialists. Pietro Ingrao, who had always been the leader of the left wing of the PCI and favoured a strategy of alliance with the Catholic Left to win power by the parliamentary road together with the socialists, counted among his followers the Manifesto group later forced to leave the party. He came from the group of anti-fascist students in Rome who joined the party during the war. He is now the Speaker of the Chamber of Deputies.

Giancarlo Pajetta, today 'foreign minister' of the PCI, is one of the eight members of the political secretariat. He has always represented within the party the tradition of the barricades, and is also famous for his cutting asides, the most famous of which is, 'As a very young man Berlinguer joined the party . . . leadership.' Between Amendola's pragmatism and Ingrao's maximalism, Longo (and other senior figures in the party) chose Berlinguer as the man best qualified to overcome these divisions, because he had always been an orthodox follower of Togliatti and had never shown a preference for either of the two wings. Berlinguer's only rival was Giorgio Napolitano, who was supported by Amendola.

Berlinguer had made his whole career in the apparatus, showing great talents as an organizer. His Marxist training also included the influence of leaders of the movement of 'Catholic communists' which had an ephemeral existence immediately after the war. The main representative of this movement was Franco Rodano, who is believed to have inspired the 'historic compromise'.[5] Berlinguer was not at that time a conspicuous personality in the party. But that was the result of his taciturn character, his meticulousness and his tenacity – all the fruits of his Sardinian origin. He come of an old but minor noble family. His father was a well-known socialist lawyer related to the most important Sardinian families. Berlinguer soon became very popular, not only because the PCI is an enormous public-relations machine, but mainly because he aroused the sympathy of the Italian public by his simple life-style and modest character. He has a normal family, a Catholic wife whom he takes to church on Sundays even if – like the old-style liberals – he doesn't himself attend the service.

The first big problem he had to confront as deputy secretary of the PCI was the conference of seventy-five communist and worker parties held in Moscow in June 1969, in spite of the PCI's reservations. Faced with the main leaders of the pro-Soviet communist world, Berlinguer quietly but decisively stated: 'We reject the idea that there can be a single model of socialist society valid for all situations.' He repeated his party's refusal to condemn China, even though describing the Maoist line as erroneous, and affirmed that 'not every difference of opinion can be explained in terms of "deviation" from a doctrinal purity whose guardianship could always be disputed'. He confirmed the disagreement over Czechoslovakia, deplored the Soviet intervention and re-affirmed the 'pluralist' road to socialism in Italy, proclaiming that 'the model of socialism for which we call on the Italian working class to struggle is different from any other existing model'. The PCI approved only one part of one of the four clauses of the final resolution and abstained from voting on all the rest.

In 1969, too, a series of internal events were to have a great influence on the PCI. There was the split in the United Socialist Party, which once again divided the socialists from the social democrats. In the autumn of 1969, known as 'the hot autumn', the trade unions took the lead in major strikes while both the objective of the struggles and the structure of the trade unions themselves were transformed, the officials being for the first time elected directly from below, by the workers. The workers no longer demanded only wage increases, but also sought to win 'power' in the factories.

There was in the PCI a group of communists who wanted the party to put itself at the head of the 'movement' to overthrow the power of the Christian democrats through united mass action. The leaders of this group published a monthly review, *Il Manifesto*. This was an infringement of the principle of democratic centralism, and after the congress they were 'struck off' (*radiati*) by the PCI at a meeting of the central committee in

November 1969 for indiscipline: another sign of the change in the times since the 1950s when they would have been expelled with a ritual condemnation for 'political and moral indignity'. 'Striking off' (*radiazione*) was a comparatively light punishment. The Manifesto group was the first organized movement on the left of the PCI and was to become for a few years, especially among young people and intellectuals, a theoretical and political reference point: the review was transformed into a daily newspaper which also marked a technical and professional breakthrough in Italian journalism.

With the strike wave of 1969 came the beginning of what was to be known as the 'strategy of tension', with a series of bomb attacks, including the dramatic fascist attempt in December 1969, causing many deaths and becoming sinisterly known as 'Strage di Piazza Fontana'. In all these unhappy events the state secret services seem increasingly to have been involved.

This strategy of tension, aggravated by the social crisis and by the appearance of the extreme left terrorism of the Red Brigades, was one of the main reasons why the PCI sharpened its attacks on the ideology and the methods of the extra-parliamentary groups which sprang up on its left. The PCI was anxious on the one hand to confront the dangers of the strategy of terror and to maintain the democratic framework, and on the other to combat the danger that the economic crisis might push to the right a part of the middle classes – the small- and medium-sized employers, the shopkeepers and the small farmers. At the same time it was anxious to reabsorb the student agitation, as Longo had succeeded in doing in 1968. In 1970–72 there was a major reshuffle of PCI cadres, bringing in many young people from the student movement. During these years the economic and social gap between North and South and the contrast between the great wealth of some and the despair in the ghettos and slums of Rome and the outlying districts of Turin and Milan became more and more glaring.

Twenty-two years late, in June 1970, the elections for the regional institutions prescribed by the constitution of 1948 were finally held. In Emilia-Romagna, Umbria and Tuscany, the communists and socialists won a majority and formed left-wing governments. As a result of these same elections the revolt of Reggio-Calabria occurred in the South in protest against the fact that it had not been chosen as the regional capital. The revolt was stage-managed by the neo-fascist MSI, but its roots lay in the discontent, not only economic and social but also moral, of the southern population. For similar reasons there were revolts in the Abruzzi. These were eloquent proofs of the political failure in the South not only of the Christian democrats but also of the PCI itself. Here, again, the PCI was taken by surprise and recognized only belatedly the real causes of these upheavals. While ever weaker centre-left governments followed one after the other, at the end of 1971 the most intransigent representative of Christian democracy, the President of the Senate, Amintore Fanfani, was defeated in his attempt to become President of the Republic; the Left, too, was unable to impose either of its own candidates, and in the end Giovanni Leone was elected with the support of fascist votes.

After Leone's election, a single-party Christian democrat government was formed under Andreotti, but, on 26 February 1972, it was defeated in the Senate on a vote of confidence. Elections were fixed for 7 and 8 May.

This situation made it necessary to give greater responsibility to Berlinguer, especially as Longo was ill at the time. In fact, at the Thirteenth Party Congress he took over the post of party secretary, while Longo became party president. With Berlinguer as secretary, a number of men emerged alongside the old and already well-known leaders to form the new ruling group in the party: Gerardo Chiaromonte, Armando Cossutta, Fernando di Giulio, Carlo Galluzzi, Ugo Pecchioli, Alfredo Reichlin, Aldo Tortorella and Achille Occhetto. Among the most influential between 1972 and 1975 would be Paolo Bufalini, Emanuele Macaluso and, above all, Armando Cossutta who was to deal in particular with the party's internal relations but would also be charged with delicate missions to the Soviet Union and other Eastern Bloc countries.

The 'historic compromise'

The general election was marked by a confrontation between the PCI and the Christian democrats. The communists made some small gains, but the Christian democrats, led by one of Fanfani's closest associates, Arnaldo Forlani, still won 38 per cent of the votes – an undeniable success for them. There was, however, a notable advance of the monarchist and fascist Right. There was clearly a swing back to the Right. For the forces on the Left of the PCI, the 1972 election was by contrast a real disaster. Between them they managed to waste more than a million left-wing votes. The most striking débâcle was that of the left socialist party, PSIUP, which lost all its seats and virtually disappeared. Most of its members joined either the PCI or the socialists, while a minority joined the Manifesto, only to split from it later on. Also defeated were the Manifesto group itself, and the Movimento Popolare dei Lavoratori, led by the former president of the Catholic Trade Unions, Livio Labor, and supported by the left-wing Catholics. It appeared that the so-called 'New Left' had been defeated for good.

In June, Andreotti formed a new government returning to the 'centre' formula of the 1950s (that is, including liberals and excluding socialists). This was the government which took Italy out of the European currency 'snake', thereby inaugurating the era of hyper-inflation, and which also introduced on-the-spot detention as a method of dealing with the problems of public order.

On 24 July 1972, the united trade-union federation was formed by the three trade-union movements: CGIL (communist and socialist), CISL (Christian democrat) and UIL (republican, socialist and social democrat). This was an attempt to save trade-union unity. The federation was to prove in the following years one of the main instruments of the 'historic compromise' tactics to control the discontent of the masses. In the meantime, Berlinguer and the PCI vigorously opposed the Andreotti government. In 1973 there were repeated general strikes in support of trade-union demands. There were also new acts of violence. Within the Christian democrat party itself there was a growing conviction that a new centre-left government should be formed, and after the party's Twelfth Congress, which reinstated Fanfani as secretary, such a government was formed by Mariano Rumor (8 July 1973).

This was the Italian situation, marked by growing inflation, working-class struggles, threats of a shift to the right, and fears of a *coup d'état*,[6] in which Enrico Berlinguer, after the military *coup* in Chile, launched his proposal for a 'historic compromise'. Between 28 September and 9 October 1973, there appeared in *Rinascita* three articles by Berlinguer which brought about what the communist historian Paolo Spriano considers 'more than a turning-point, a leap in the dark' in the history of communist politics. In these articles, Berlinguer asserted that the Left would not be able to govern the country even if it obtained 51 per cent of the votes. He thus swept aside the hypothesis of an alternative to Christian democracy and argued that it was necessary to strive patiently for an agreement with the Christian democrats, who could not be regarded simply as a conservative party. The words 'historic compromise' appear only once, at the end of the last article. Yet these words were to change not only the internal but also the external policies of the PCI and were to be the origins of Eurocommunism.

In the articles, Berlinguer says that

> the events in Chile make it clearer, against all illusions, that the character of imperialism and especially of North American imperialism is still economic and political suffocation, the spirit of aggression and conquest, the tendency to oppress peoples and to deprive them of their independence, freedom and unity whenever the concrete circumstances and the balance of forces allow it.

After asserting that US intervention was of decisive importance in Chile, and that this tendency of imperialism can be checked only by a change in the balance of forces within the peoples aspiring to liberation, but that international imperialism is capable of inflicting severe defeats on the forces animating the struggle, and after coming out against the division of the world into blocs, Berlinguer observes that there is a

need to continue struggling tenaciously on the international level to advance the process of détente and coexistence and to develop all its positive potential and, at the same time, to pursue in each country the battles for national independence and for the transformation in a democratic and socialist direction of the economic, social and political structures.

Our party has always taken into account the unbreakable connection between these two levels. On the one hand we have always tried, as Togliatti taught us, to evaluate coolly the general context of international relations and Italy's position in it. On the other we have sought to judge exactly the balance of internal forces in our country. In particular, we have always given due weight to the fundamental fact that Italy belongs to the politico-military bloc dominated by the USA and the inevitable implications of this fact. But our consciousness of this objective fact has certainly not condemned us to inertia or paralysis.

In a meeting with workers at a factory in Ravenna on 8 November, Berlinguer repeated:

It's not by obtaining 51 per cent of the votes that the left-wing parties can be sure of governing and achieving their work of renewal because a vertical split down the middle of our country would not be in the interests of the country and would ruin the experiment of renewing our society. That is what has happened in Chile.

The themes developed by Berlinguer in the articles were, then, the decisive weight of US intervention in Chile; the influence of imperialism in preventing progress; the policy of détente; the appeal to Togliatti's thesis of 'Italy's advance towards socialism in democracy and in peace', with a reference to Gramsci's thought; the line of unity from the war of liberation against fascism to the 'Svolta di Salerno'; the assertion that the dilemma between peaceful road and non-peaceful road of struggle for the advance of socialism is abstract and schematic; the necessity of consensus for a transformation of society by democratic means; the problem of alliances, since the PCI does not want a collapse of the economy but to guarantee the efficiency of the economic process even in the critical phase of transition to a new social order. Berlinguer argued that the PCI was seeking a democratic alternative, not a left-wing alternative, and that relations with the Catholic world had to be defined on three levels: one with the Church, one with the Catholic movements and groups which had taken an anti-capitalist and anti-imperialist position, and one with the Christian democrats, considered as a party representing a variety of social and political groups, not all of them necessarily conservative. To the final question, 'What is to be done?', Berlinguer replied that a new great historic compromise was needed between the forces representing the vast majority of the people, namely communists, socialists and Christian democrats.

During the following years, Italian politics were to be profoundly changed by these 'reflections' of Berlinguer, of which at first neither their opponents, nor the socialists, nor the communists themselves from the grass roots to the middle cadres, understood the enormous implications.

The Referendum on Divorce

In 1974, the PCI's approach to the 'area of government' (or eligibility to form part of the governing majority, if not of the government itself) was speeded up. The party activists made an enormous propaganda effort to prepare the reluctant rank and file for possible collaboration with the Christian democrats, which up to then had seemed to party members an absurd hypothesis. The economic situation was deteriorating constantly, inflation was accelerating and there was the prospect of galloping unemployment. The oil crisis seemed to throw Italy back into the pre-industrial era. Obscure forces were at work in the shadows. There were more fascist acts of violence, but left-wing terrorism was also becoming more aggressive. The Red Brigades were organizing more efficiently. Some of their members were young students, often from Catholic schools, for whom Marxism meant armed struggle against the capitalist system; others were workers recruited at Fiat in Turin or at factories in Milan and Genoa. Their ideology mingled quasi-Christian mysticism, social conscience and Marxism with Guevarist and 'Third World' theories. A typical example is their leader Renato Curcio, an outstanding graduate of the Institute of Sociology in Trento – an academy set up by a Christian democrat regional government, but which became a hotbed of the Red Brigades. The brigades have continued to carry out attacks on Christian democrat leaders, on journalists, magistrates and industrial managers.

On the political level, the central issue of 1974 was the referendum on divorce, demanded by a committee of traditional Catholics and at once supported by many Christian democrats, including Fanfani. The secretary of the Christian democrat party himself, Arnaldo Forlani, who was also the most influential representative of Fanfani's wing of the party, was one of the first to sign the demand for the referendum. It was 1972 all over again. The PCI feared a radicalization of politics – that division into two opposing blocs which Berlinguer has always called 'the greatest disaster', and which the referendum was bound to provoke. Paolo Bufalini, who had daily contacts with the Christian democrats, with the other non-Catholic parties and with the Vatican establishment, tried till the last moment to reach a compromise on an amendment of the law which would have avoided the referendum. The PCI was accused by the radical party of wanting to 'sell out' a great social achievement. But Fanfani, now secretary of the Christian democrat party, was determined to have the battle. He was sure that he could win the referendum and then reconstitute the anti-communist alliance on which Christian democrat power had been built since 1948. And, in the end, Fanfani got his way, despite many doubts within the Christian democrat party itself.

As soon as the PCI realized that the referendum was unavoidable, it mobilized its formidable and tentacular party machine. On the other side, the Church mobilized its parish priests – at least in the South, for the impression in the North was that it did not commit itself one hundred per cent. Fanfani stomped the country, holding meetings in which he urged the repeal of divorce as the only civilized choice, raising the bogey of the collapse of the family. In the South, and Sicily especially, he tried to make use of the most backward customs. Against him were ranged all the non-Catholic parties: socialists, radicals, liberals, social democrats and republicans. The communist party adopted a quieter tone, respecting Catholic beliefs and presenting divorce as a remedy for secret ills and sorrows which were the real cause of the crisis of the family. For the first time since the war, Christian democrats had to fight a campaign with only the fascist extreme Right on their side, while, on the other side, the pro-divorce alignment included not only the PCI, which was its central axis and decisive in ensuring its success, but also non-Catholic parties like the Liberals, who had always been anti-communist, and the 'Catholics of dissent'.

The referendum was held on 12 May. The result was far better for the pro-divorce camp than even the most optimistic radicals had dared to hope: 59·3 per cent voted 'no' (against the repeal of the divorce law), and 40·7 per cent 'yes'. Up to the last minute, Berlinguer and many of the other PCI leaders had feared a defeat. The result at once took on great political importance because it showed that the Christian democrats could be isolated and beaten. Even so, the PCI, instead of stepping up its opposition to the government, continued to pursue the historic compromise. To understand this attitude we must remember that 1974 also saw new acts of violence by the extreme Right, including the 'Strage di Brescia', where eight people were killed and dozens injured by an explosion during an anti-fascist rally. A few days later, two members of the neo-fascist MSI were assassinated at their party's Padua office by the Red Brigades. On 4 August, the international express train, the 'Italicus', was derailed just outside Bologna, causing six deaths and many injuries. Like the Brescia bombing, this was attributed to the secret fascist organizations, Ordine Nero and Ordine Nuovo.

A new ministerial crisis was provoked by the social democrats, and there was talk, as so often since Leone became president, of an early general election. The crisis lasted fifty-one days, at the end of which Moro formed a government. The republicans returned to office with La Malfa as deputy prime minister, while the socialists and social democrats supported the government from outside. The centre-left was now in its death-throes.

In 1975, the economic crisis worsened and political violence spread. The Christian democrats took law and order as the theme of their campaign for the local and regional elections, while the PCI tried to present itself more and more as the opposition party seeking to rescue the country's institutions and restore order without sacrificing freedom. (It was in this year that parliament approved the 'Legge Reale' giving the police wider powers for the use of weapons. The PCI voted against Communist influence increased among intellectuals, in schools and universities, and began to affect small and medium-sized businessmen, as well as farmers – classes traditionally regarded as opponents and hitherto impenetrable to communist propaganda. The PCI began to distinguish between 'productive' and 'parasitical' classes, adopting a strategy of 'dialogue' with leaders of enlightened, 'Agnelli-style' big business which it contrasted with the parasitic rentier class. The PCI's economists began to revise their theory of profit, regarding it as a positive factor in so far as it is directed towards production. The historic compromise was thus extended to the economic sphere. The party surprised many people by coming out in favour of private enterprise and against the extension of the public sector, thus breaking with the generally accepted notion that the communists want to nationalize all firms. The party's Fourteenth Congress (Rome, March 1975) – a magnificently orchestrated affair held in the Palazzo dell'Eur – marked a difficult moment of tension with the Christian democrats, but also the final consolidation of Berlinguer's leadership: the politburo was abolished and authority concentrated in the secretariat – a ruling group chosen purely to apply his policy of historic compromise. The congress was marked by three notable events: the ostentatious walk-out of the Christian democrat observers to protest against the banning of the Christian democrat party in Portugal for alleged involvement in an attempted *coup d'état*; Berlinguer's harsh attack on the Portuguese party and on the 'Stalinism' of its leader Cunhal; and his personal denunciation of Fanfani, whom he portrayed as the representative of the Christian democrats' most reactionary wing.

As a result of the congress, Berlinguer was able to install a leadership and a secretariat closely bound to himself. The most striking fact was that Armando Cossutta, hitherto considered the most powerful leader after Berlinguer, was pushed on to the sidelines. In the political secretariat, Berlinguer was joined by Bufalini, Gerardo Chiaromonte (an engineer from Lucania who was to play a dominant role in the party's policy), Giorgio Napolitano, Giancarlo Pajetta and three members coopted from the Executive (*Direzione*), one of whom was the secretary of the Milan branch, Gianni Cervetti, aged forty, a political-science graduate from Moscow university who speaks fluent Russian. Cervetti was to take charge of party organization. Cossutta remained a member of the *Direzione* and was given responsibility for local government.

The regional and local elections were held on 15 June 1975, in spite of Christian democrat attempts to postpone them in the hope of another early dissolution of parliament. (The Christian democrats generally do better in general elections than in local ones.) The result was a major victory for the Left. The PCI came close behind the Christian democrats, with 33 per cent to their 35 per cent. The Left as a whole reached 46·5 per cent (with 12 per cent for the socialists and 1·1 per cent for Democrazia Proletaria – the groups to the left of the PCI). Christian democrat predominance in local and regional government was at an end. The effect of this 'electoral earthquake' was to leave the central government – a pale reflection of the now clearly anachronistic centre-left formula – surrounded by cities, provinces and regions in which the PCI was capable almost wherever it liked of forming an alliance with socialists, social democrats, republicans and liberals to put the Christian democrats in the minority. In many of them it would be possible to set up left-wing administrations excluding not only the Christian democrats but the minor parties and the Right as well.

The repercussions led to a meeting of the Christian democrats' national council, at which Fanfani was forced to resign. He was replaced by the 'honest face' of Benigno Zaccagnini, a former doctor from Emilia who was respected both inside and outside the party. There was talk of 'rebuilding Christian democracy from scratch' – of profoundly transforming a party worn out by thirty years in power and stained in the last few years by scandals and by the parasitical system of *sottogoverno* (roughly equivalent to 'jobs for the boys'). The PCI, too, hoped that Christian democracy would begin a process of regeneration, emerge shorn of its most reactionary and extremist components, and regain its original character as a 'people's party' – that is, become a valid partner for the strategy of historic compromise. Thus, in many cases, the PCI, instead of opting for the 'alternative' urged by the socialists or for alliances with other non-Catholic parties, strove to set up municipal, provincial and regional governments based on broad alliances (*larghe intese*), including the Christian democrats. Already in the past few years it had practised in local government a 'different kind of opposition' which held the door open for collaboration with the Christian democrats. In Sicily, indeed, the historic compromise had been put into practice since 1974. In many local authorities, a *de facto* compromise had already come about. After the 15 June elections, the PCI considered that the march towards the historic compromise could proceed above all in local and regional government, on the basis of agreements on concrete problems and of the slogan of 'good government'. Thus the Sicilian formula of an administration 'open to the left', with communists in the majority supporting it, was extended to other regions: Lombardy, Calabria, Marche, Campania.

In all the big Italian cities – Milan, Venice, Florence, Naples, Turin – left-wing administrations took office. (In Genoa, there was one already.) Bologna continued to be governed by communists and socialists, as it had been for thirty years. In Turin, the new mayor was Diego Novelli, a journalist from the party daily, *L'Unità*, who had always been on good terms with the archbishop, Cardinal Pellegrino (one of the most open-minded Italian bishops), and even with the Agnelli family (owners of Fiat). Even in Rome,[7] where the Vatican had always prevented a 'Red' administration, the new mayor was Giulio Carlo Argan, a famous art critic who had stood as an independent on the PCI list. One of his first acts was to pay an official call on Pope Paul VI. The policy of *grandi intese* succeeded in many regions where the Left had an overall majority (for instance, in Emilia-Romagna, Umbria, Tuscany) and in many provinces and towns. But it did not succeed in Naples, although the PCI there won 40 per cent of the votes – a major victory since it won over a large part of the electorate that for years had voted for the monarchist ship-owner Achille Lauro. The communist Maurizio Valenzi was elected mayor, but his administration remained a minority one, thanks to the unyielding opposition of the local Christian democrat leader. Only in June 1978, after the Moro tragedy, did the Christian democrats agree to join the PCI in the majority in Naples.

Today it is clear, in spite of the great efforts it has made, that the PCI faces serious problems in local government, especially in the bigger cities. In many cases, the accusations and the discontent are now falling on the communist administrators. This results not only from the difficulty of making the historic compromise work, but also from the fact that the cities are burdened with deficits inherited from the previous administrations and sometimes are not able even to pay the salaries of their employees.

The PCI on the threshold of power

Between January and March 1976, the electorate's move to the left received a new impetus. The socialist party considered after the local elections that the period of the centre-left was finally closed. Meanwhile, the 'landmine' of the abortion law resurfaced. An agreement on this with the Christian democrats proved impossible. The radical party had collected the necessary signatures for a referendum which should have been held in the spring of 1976. But, after the publication of an article by the PSI secretary, Francesco de Martino, the Moro–La Malfa government fell. A new Moro government was formed in February, this time of only one party but supported by the social democrats, while the socialists abstained. In the same month, the Lockheed scandal broke, along with that of alleged payments from the CIA to the head of the Italian secret services, General Miceli. The Lockheed scandal appeared to compromise an Italian prime minister referred to in the American documents as 'Antelope Cobbler' who could have been either Leone, Andreotti or Rumor. Also accused were a Christian democrat minister, Gui, and a social democrat leader, Tanassi. The ministerial crisis coincided with the scandal which, after the affair of the subsidies to political parties from oil companies, cast the shadow of corruption, as an acute political scientist Giorgio Galli has put it,[8] 'on the whole governing class and especially on the Christian democrats, by definition the governing party'. In a dramatic congress, the Christian democrat party divided into two camps: one more conservative, opposed to any agreement with the PCI, and including the moderate wing of the party with the followers of both Andreotti and Fanfani but with Arnaldo Forlani as its spokesman; the other, by contrast, prepared for a *confronto* (a type of constructive discussion between opponents) with the PCI, including the left of the party, the followers of Moro, and a part of the old party establishment with Rumor, Taviani and Colombo. The leader of this second camp was the party secretary, Zaccagnini, who was re-elected to his post by the congress, just scraping through with 51 per cent of the votes.

Yet the time-bomb of the abortion law continued to tick. After unsuccessful attempts to reach a compromise, the Moro government resigned. For the second time, President Leone was obliged to dissolve parliament and call early elections. To quote Giorgio Galli again, 'the PCI did not want these but preferred them to a new referendum which would have forced it to oppose the Christian democrats on a moral issue of crucial importance for Catholics, which would have made the final agreement on the historic compromise very difficult'.

The election campaign was fought on two issues: the scandals involving the Christian democrats, and the objective which the

PCI had set itself of 'cutting the Christian democrats down to size'. The Christian democrats realized that the possibility of the PCI entering the government was from now on the central problem, and therefore based their campaign on the defence of freedom against the totalitarian danger within the country and on the international upheaval which would result from a communist victory. The PCI's most effective slogans were 'good government', 'a democratic alternative' and a new definition of the PCI itself: 'party of struggle and of government'. Berlinguer was anxious to convince Italians that voting PCI did not mean switching from the Western to the Eastern camp. He had already stressed the PCI's independence in his speech to the Twenty-fifth Congress of the CPSU in Moscow in February, at which, by contrast, Marchais and Carrillo were conspicuous by their absence. Now, in an interview with Giampaolo Panza of the *Corriere della Sera*, to the question, 'Are you not afraid that Moscow will deal with Berlinguer and his Eurocommunism in the same way that it dealt with Dubček and his "socialism with a human face"?', the PCI leader replied: 'No, we are in a different part of the world and even if it wants to the Soviet Union does not have the slightest chance to obstruct or to dictate our road to socialism. You can argue that the Soviet Union aspires to hegemony over its allies. But there is not a single action to suggest that it intends to go beyond the frontiers fixed at Yalta.' The interviewer asked: 'Then do you feel safer precisely because you are in the western sphere?' Berlinguer replied: 'I feel that because Italy does not belong to the Warsaw Pact, from this point of view we can proceed along the Italian road to socialism in complete independence.' 'So,' the interviewer went on, 'the Atlantic pact could also be a useful shield behind which to build socialism in freedom?' 'Yes,' said Berlinguer, 'that is another reason why I do not want Italy to leave the Atlantic alliance, as well as because by leaving it we would upset the international balance. I also feel safer being on this side of the fence . . .'

As Aldo Rizzo remarked,[9] 'Not only was NATO no longer considered an instrument of aggression, but as a fundamental element in international détente: it now became at least potentially also a politico-strategic cover for the PCI's independent road to socialism.' The communist historian of the PCI, Paolo Spriano, remarks that this statement of Berlinguer's represents 'undoubtedly the furthest point reached by the effective independence of a great western communist party'.

The election results were for the Left the best since 1946: 46·7 per cent of the votes (PCI 34·4 per cent, PSI 9·6 per cent, Democrazia Proletaria 1·9 per cent, radicals 1·1 per cent, joint left-wing lists 0·1 per cent). The PCI, Galli remarks,[10] 'thus gained as much electoral ground between 1972 and 1976 as it had done between 1946 and 1972'. But within the Left the socialists suffered a severe defeat; and the so-called *sorpasso* (overtaking) did not happen.[11] The Christian democrats won 38·7 per cent of the votes, a clear recovery from the 1975 local elections, and remained the largest single party. The new leader of the socialist party, Bettino Craxi, ruled out any possibility of a centre-left majority. It seemed that the Christian democrats had no choice but to allow the PCI into the government. But, after a long crisis, Giulio Andreotti was able to form a one-party Christian democrat government based on the abstention in parliament of communists, socialists, social democrats, liberals and republicans. Thus opened the period which is known, with the characteristic linguistic inventiveness of Italian politics, as that of 'not no-confidence'.

The historic event marked by the elections of 20 June 1976 and by the formation of the Andreotti government is the final collapse of the anti-communist discrimination which had lasted since 1947. From now on, the PCI was potentially a party of government. It was able to reoccupy important positions in parliament. Pietro Ingrao became Speaker of the Chamber, and the PCI obtained besides the chairmanships of several important parliamentary committees. Given that many laws are approved not on the floor of the house but directly by these committees, we can say that the PCI officially participates in the drafting of the laws – to which, in any case, it had during these thirty years been able to contribute in practice, even if it had always voted against them on the floor. The party's penetration of the state was also emphasized by its entry into the state-controlled radio and television networks and its participation in appointments to the boards of certain banks according to the system of *lottizzazione* – the sharing out of executive positions in public and private bodies among nominees of the various parties in power. The communists had to overcome the discrimination which had affected them for thirty years in appointments to executive posts in public bodies. But in some cases they failed to distinguish between this legitimate aim and the sharing out of the spoils of power. In July 1977, after a controversy in the press about certain appointments in the state broadcasting organization and state-controlled banks, *L'Unità* had to admit that a serious mistake had been made and that the party should not in future accept this method of *sottogoverno*.

The PCI's steps towards Eurocommunism

Both during the election campaign and after, the PCI had been concerned – as was shown also by Berlinguer's interview with the *Corriere della Sera* – to reassure the United States about its intentions. One of Berlinguer's chief assistants, Sergio Segre, head of the Foreign Affairs Bureau, who had already been to the US as a member of parliament on a mission led by Andreotti, had frequent contacts with the US embassy in Rome, and, after the elections, with a group of US congressmen and senators who visited Rome.

The march towards Eurocommunism had begun in 1967 with the conference of Karlovy Vary, at which all the communist parties had met. Luigi Longo, who was later to be the first publicly to condemn the Soviet Union over the Czechoslovak crisis, on this occasion emphasized the need to work for collaboration with the socialists, the social democrats, the Christian forces and the progressive forces.

The purpose of this was to justify a project which the PCI then had in hand and whose importance has not yet been sufficiently emphasized. In fact, immediately after this conference the PCI began trying to establish contacts with the West German social democrats. Various missions led by Sergio Segre and Carlo Galluzzi were sent to West Berlin and then to East Berlin. In 1968, the chief advisor of Willy Brandt, Herr Bauer, had a meeting in Rome with the leaders of the PCI. Next there came to Italy an East German delegation led by Werner. Finally, during the official visit of the West German chancellor, Kurt-Georg Kiesinger, there was a conversation between him and Luigi Longo at the Quirinal (official residence of the President of the Republic). The PCI's secret diplomacy was one of the main instruments of the *Ostpolitik* which was to change profoundly relations between the two Germanies, and between the Federal Republic of Germany and the Soviet Union, Poland and the other Eastern countries as a result of the successive negotiations of 1970–72, and thus to put an end to the Cold War in Europe. A German social democrat historian, Heinz Timmerman, has written that these achievements owe much to the new relations between Italian communists and German social democrats.

Before this, in 1969, Berlinguer as leader of the Italian delegation to the Moscow Conference of Communist Parties, had emphasized his disagreement with any position that conflicted with the PCI's independence and its pluralistic approach. And it was in January of that year that, for the first time, nine PCI deputies, led by Giorgio Amendola, had taken their places in the Italian delegation to the European parliament. Here the connection is obvious between internal and international policy. The delegation was chosen by the whole Italian parliament, which thus broke the anti-communist discrimination as far as the European Community was concerned. This was the result of the change in the PCI's attitude towards the Common Market – a change of which Amendola was the chief architect.[12] In January 1971 there was a meeting of West European communist parties in London which reaffirmed the need for popular struggles against the multinationals and for the transformation of the Common Market, thus sketching the future policy of Euro-communism.

In 1971 the PCI's Economic Studies Centre (CESPE) held a conference in Rome on 'the communists and Europe', at which the party began to develop its demand for an independent development of the EEC and launched the slogan of moving 'from Europe of the merchants to Europe of the workers'. In February 1973, Berlinguer declared in a report on international relations: 'We are for a Europe which will be neither anti-American nor anti-Soviet.' The following month he led a PCI delegation to Moscow which signed a document that provoked some controversy because Berlinguer, referring to the European situation, asserted in it that new possibilities had been opened up by, among other factors, 'the realistic foreign policy of the German Federal Republic'. During that year, the PCI continued to spin its network of contacts with other parties of the European Left. Giorgio Napolitano went to London and gave a talk to the Royal Institute of International Affairs while Alfredo Reichlin led a mission to the Scandinavian countries which noted the wide opportunities for working together with the Scandinavian social democratic forces. On his return from Moscow, Berlinguer, in reply to an editorial in *Pravda* harking back to the 1969 Conference of Communist Parties, repeated in an interview the PCI's independent position and spoke of his extensive programme of meetings with the leaders, not only of European communist parties but also with labour and trade-union leaders in the spirit of mutually recognized independence and non-interference in the internal affairs of individual parties.[13]

Also in 1973 the first meeting took place in Rome between Berlinguer and Marchais, so marking a rapprochement between the two parties after a long period of 'fraternal disagreement'. In January 1974, the Conference of West European Communist Parties was held, of which the PCI was the moving spirit. Its positive aspect was the reaffirmation of the need to transform the Europe of the EEC through a joint struggle of communist, socialist, social democratic and Christian forces. In November 1974, preparation began for the Conference of European Communist Parties, proposed by the PCI and the Polish Workers' Party. Setting it up in fact proved extremely difficult. It took a year and a half to draw up a document because the Soviet leaders wanted to take advantage of it to strengthen their own pre-eminence over the other communist parties. But the conference was eventually held in Berlin in July 1976 and Berlinguer took part. In the final document the Italian communists together with the PCF, PCE and the Yugoslav, Belgian and Romanian communist parties succeeded in imposing the principle of 'consensus' according to which there should be no general definition of doctrine without the assent of all the other parties.

While the preparations for the Berlin conference were in progress, there were meetings and joint communiqués between the Italian and Spanish communist parties in July and between the Italian and French communist parties in November 1975. These were the results of meetings spread over several months and showed that a process of revision had occurred in the PCE and the PCF. It was thus possible in the joint documents to proclaim the independence and competence of each party to work out its own line and to build a communist society taking account of national characteristics in independence and democracy. In February 1976, Berlinguer attended the Congress of the CPSU in Moscow, from which both Carrillo and Marchais were absent. In his greeting, he restated the concepts of the independence of each country and each party and explained the PCI's ideas for the construction of socialism in Italy within a democratic and pluralist system. The word 'pluralism' was translated in *Pravda* as 'multiplicity'. This episode provoked controversy in Italy, and *Pravda* explained that in the Soviet Union the word 'pluralism' had a pejorative connotation. In 1977, the PCI extended its diplomatic activity. There was a meeting in Rome with the Japanese Communist Party, with which talks had already been held in Tokyo in 1975. Eurocommunism thus spread beyond the confines of Europe, and in its essentials was adopted also by the Japanese. Less fruitful, perhaps, was the meeting with the British Communist Party, although the latter did align itself on many of the PCI's positions, in spite of maintaining its own opposition to the EEC. Finally, on 4 March 1977, there was the Madrid Conference, described as a Eurocommunist

summit, which brought together Berlinguer, Marchais and Carrillo on the eve of the Spanish elections. Thus, by mid 1977, it
seemed that Eurocommunism had become a common denominator of the three major communist parties of Western Europe.

Party of struggle and of government

In 1977, the PCI managed to oblige the Andreotti government
to carry out at least a part of its programme of bringing moral
rectitude into public life and to take action against the economic
crisis without the whole cost being borne by the mass of the
workers and the poorest classes. This was the objective on which
the PCI had based its election campaign and which had won it
such a remarkable increase in votes. The PCI announced that it
was preparing a middle-term economic programme, and at the
same time tried to put into practice its campaign slogan 'Party of
Struggle and of Government'. But it found that this battle on
two fronts presented enormous difficulties.

Opposition grew on its left, especially among young people
and students, among the *emarginati* and the unemployed. (The
students and the unemployed are the categories which have been
most neglected both by the government and by the trade unions.)
A new student revolt was born, in parts a violent one. In February
1977, the students occupied the faculties and shouted down the
professors, including left-wing ones. (Some had been their
leaders in 1968 and today are front-rank intellectuals of the
PCI.) The Rector of the University of Rome was a communist,
Professor Ruberti. The general secretary of the CGIL, Luciano
Lama, the most distinguished of trade-union leaders, went at the
invitation of the PCI to address a meeting in the university.
Around him was the mass of the students, among whom two
groups stood out: the *autonomi* and the self-styled 'Metropolitan
Indians' who adopted a new form of protest – satire as a weapon
of political controversy. No police were present. Lama was
defended by stewards of the trade union – most of them com-

munist workers. After being disrupted by the barracking of the 'Metropolitan Indians' the meeting was broken up by the violence of the *autonomi*. Lama had to be hurried off the campus. The Rector called the police.

Thus opened not only a breach between the PCI and the young people's revolt, but also a period of serious disturbances of public order. About 50,000 young people from all over Italy took part in a demonstration in Rome. Some of the *autonomi* fired on the police, fortunately without killing anyone, but a few days later a death did occur in Bologna (the town which the communist party had governed for thirty years and had held up to Italy and to the world as the example of 'good government' contrasted with Christian democrat 'bad government'). After a scuffle between members of 'Lotta Continua' – the extra-parliamentary movement with the largest following among the students – and members of 'Comunione e Liberazione' – an integralist Catholic organization accused of being on the extreme right – disorders broke out all over the town. A student belonging to 'Lotta Continua', Francesco Lorusso, was killed on 12 March during a battle with the Carabinieri. For several days Bologna was in a state of siege. The communist mayor, Renato Zangheri, spoke of an 'international conspiracy' against Bologna. In reality, the PCI, too, had neglected the problems of the students in Bologna. A magistrate ordered the arrest of several students belonging to the extra-parliamentary movements. An independent radio station, accused of having fomented the revolt, was closed down.

L'Unità joined the Minister of the Interior in accusing the young people and students of 'fascism' and praised the intervention of the police. These events inspired some famous French intellectuals, including Jean-Paul Sartre, to sign a manifesto 'Against Repression in Italy' – repression supposedly resulting from the historic compromise and the agreement between Christian democrats and communists. On 23, 24 and 26 September, a conference 'against repression' was held in Bologna. It was, in fact, the occasion for a rally which drew tens of thousands of young people from Italy and from abroad – about 80,000, according to *Lotta continua*, the newspaper of the move-

ment which organized the conference, and 40,000 or 50,000 even
by official estimates. At the centre of the conference, which dealt
publicly with the theme of young people's discontent and the
polemics against the historic compromise, was the debate between
the minority, the so-called 'armed party' of the *autonomi*, who
advocated open violence against the state, and the majority who
rejected this. The PCI did not expect such a big attendance at
the Bologna conference. A few days later in Rome, Berlinguer
and the other main leaders took part in a conference at the Eur
where they made their self-criticism and admitted that they had
been caught napping by the problems of the student masses and
the young people. At the Festival di Modena, held only a few
days before the Bologna demonstration, Berlinguer, para-
phrasing Manzoni, had referred to the young students who would
take part in it as 'miserable troublemakers who will not uproot
Bologna'. He now practically admitted that this remark had been
a political error.

At the Eur conference the PCI's number two, Gerardo
Chiaromonte, declared that the problems of young people should
be approached with greater understanding, and those affecting
schools and employment should above all be solved. The leader
of the Young Communists Federation, Massimo D'Alema, also
admitted the delays and difficulties affecting the treatment of the
problem of young people. Intellectuals like Alberto Asor Rosa
and Fabio Mussi argued that the influence on young people of a
culture which was no longer only Marxist had also to be taken
into account. From then onwards, the PCI has tried to win back
the more radical young people by concessions, including
ideological concessions, but on the strict condition that the
common ground must be the rejection of any violence.

Yet, in these same months, other problems and other difficulties were rapidly coming to a head. There was the controversy
with the intellectuals. An ideological debate was opened which
implied a political disagreement with the PSI about the interpretation of Gramsci's thought, to which the PCI referred as the
inspiration of its independence both from the Soviet Union and
from bourgeois ideology. Meanwhile, both the economic

problems and those of public order were getting worse. The terrorism of the Red Brigades showed no sign of diminishing, as the communists and others had hoped. On the contrary, they launched a series of attacks on journalists, culminating in the murder of Carlo Casalegno, deputy editor of *La Stampa* and a highly respected anti-fascist, in Turin on 16 November. The PCI thus had to face many difficulties – within the party, in the factories, in local government and in its relations with Italian society in general. Its attempt to organize demonstrations against the Red Brigades, and in sympathy with Casalegno, was not a great success.

On 16 January 1977, a big conference had been held in the Teatro Eliseo in Rome, to which were invited Italian intellectuals, artists, writers, philosophers, cinema artists and scientists. On 17 January, Berlinguer made a speech in which he argued that the main need was for an austerity policy to confront the crisis but also to change Italy's economic and cultural model based on consumerism. He urged the intellectuals to join in this austerity programme by discussing a medium-term project which a commission of the party was instructed to prepare.[14]

The response of the leading intellectuals was disappointing. Norberto Bobbio, one of the leading democratic philosophers and jurists, replied that Berlinguer's 'theory of sacrifices' had nothing to do with Marxist thought. The controversy became more bitter in June 1977 when Giorgio Amendola, in an interview with *L'Espresso*, accused the intellectuals of 'defeatism' and cowardice because some of them, including the Nobel prize-winning poet Eugenio Montale and the Sicilian writer Leonardo Sciascia, had supported the refusal of some jurors in Turin to serve in the trial of members of the Red Brigades for fear of reprisals. Sciascia answered Amendola harshly, asserting that he had remained a Stalinist and the word 'defeatism' which he had used was typically fascist. Sciascia, who had always been close to the PCI but opposed the historic compromise, chose this moment to break with the party. A few months later it was Napolitano's turn, in an article in *L'Unità*, to urge the intellectuals to 'get their hands dirty'. Meanwhile *Mondo Operaio*, the cultural review of the socialist party, had opened a debate about Gramsci's concept of hegemony, with two essays by Furio Diaz and Massimo Salvadori, a leading student and critic of Marxism. They argued that, for Gramsci, the hegemony of the working class, and of the party which is its expression, is a prerequisite for the dictatorship of the proletariat and not an alternative to it.[15] The PCI's review *Rinascita* at first replied with articles by Alfredo Reichlin and Biagio de Giovanni, one of the most prominent young philosophers in the PCI today: they accused the socialists of trying with absurd controversies to rob the workers' movement of its greatest cultural asset, namely Gramsci.[16] But later the PCI's own intellectuals had to admit that Gramsci's thought, too, was in need of revision. At the conference organized by the PCI to mark the fortieth anniversary of Gramsci's death, Pietro Ingrao admitted that not all the novelties in the PCI's policy and in Berlinguer's statements about accepting the democratic method can be traced back to Gramsci. Thus not even Gramsci could provide an adequate ideological justification for the PCI's new policies. This provoked a very vigorous discussion in the reviews and the daily press about the PCI's ideological problems.

Besides, immediately after the 1976 election the party had realized the need for a reform of its statutes and of its internal organization, as was shown by the report of the organization secretary Gianni Cervetti to the central committee in December 1976. Cervetti recognized that the PCI's internal organization was over-centralized and needed changing even if, up to now at least, it had not renounced 'democratic centralism'. Already in this report he suggested an amendment to Article 5 of the statutes, which states that members must seek their inspiration in the study of Marxism-Leninism. It was now admitted that this was in contradiction to Article 2, which says that party membership is open to all, irrespective of religious belief.

At the end of June 1977, after weeks of arduous negotiations, the six-party agreement was finally approved which brought the PCI to all intents and purposes into the majority and enabled it to take one step further into the area of government. The agreement was signed by representatives of the 'constitutional parties': Christian democrats, communists, socialists, social democrats, republicans and liberals. It involved the communists in concessions on points where they had in the past been in opposition: for instance, they agreed to the strengthening of preventive measures which gave bigger powers to the police, including powers of preventive arrest, and accepted the need for special prisons to house the most dangerous political detainees. Other problems covered by the agreement related to economic policy, policy for the South, state holdings in industry, the implementation of the law on the transfer of powers from the state to the regions, schools and universities, and the laws on the press and television.

In October 1977, Berlinguer made a spectacular gesture towards the Catholic Church. In an interview with *La Stampa* in September, a prominent member of the PCI, Professor Lucio Lombardo Radice, had announced that Article 5 of the PCI's statutes would be changed. He was responding to a challenge from the editor of the Jesuits' review, *Civiltà Cattolica*, Father Bartolomeo Sorge. The announcement caused protest among the communist rank and file, and the PCI's press office published a denial by Lombardo Radice specifying that the decision depended on the next party congress. But on 14 October, *L'Unità* published an advance text of a letter from Berlinguer to the Bishop of Ivrea, Monsignor Luigi Bettazzi, who had written to him eighteen months earlier, putting the same questions about respect for religious freedom which Father Sorge had asked in his articles in *Civiltà Cattolica*. Monsignor Bettazzi had asked him to give up any discrimination against Catholics and Christians, pointing to experiences in communist countries where 'socialist renewal is accompanied by excesses of violence and the suppression of too many freedoms, including that of religion'. Berlinguer took the occasion of the synod, attended by bishops from all over the world for the Pope's eightieth birthday, to make public his answer to the bishop. In his long letter published in *Rinascita*, he stated that

the positions taken and the conduct observed by the PCI through several decades show that in the PCI there is an effective will to maintain in Italy a secular democratic party which as such is neither theist nor atheist nor anti-theist: but also to support, as a direct consequence, a secular and democratic state, which likewise should be neither theist, nor atheist nor anti-theist.

After a first response from the former Vatican Secretary of State (now Archbishop of Florence), Monsignor Benelli, who contested the credibility of Berlinguer's statements, a second one appeared in the *Osservatore Romano* which, while restating all Father Sorge's reservations about Article 5 of the PCI's statutes, none the less left the door open for dialogue. According to the *Osservatore*, which surely reflected the Pope's own thinking,

no one would be more sincerely pleased than us if a great mass party, with the great strength and zeal of the PCI, really succeeded in overcoming both in theory and in practice its Marxist-Leninist, materialist and atheist ideological *parti pris* and in shedding those totalitarian and domineering features that have hitherto placed it outside the category of parties which are democratic even if anticlerical.

The paper went on to say that what was needed was a 'long and difficult process of clarification on the doctrinal level and of reassurance on the level of practice'; and it added significantly: 'we should not wish to discourage any sincere intention since we too are convinced that these are "problems" whose positive solution (where possible, we should add – and let us hope it *is* possible) "is very important for the future of society and of Italy"' – these last being the very words of Berlinguer himself.

Berlinguer's initiative made a notable impact, not only among Catholics but also in anticlerical circles. The historian Giovanni Spadolini remarked that the PCI was not content to wait for a historic compromise with the Christian democrats, but was aiming for 'a privileged relationship with the Catholic world'.

In October, the PSI held a conference in Milan on the theme 'Intellectuals and Politics', clearly intended as a reply to the one held by the PCI in Rome in January at which Berlinguer had launched his austerity plan. The keynote report was delivered by Norberto Bobbio, who contrasted the freedom of intellectuals with Gramsci's conception of the 'organic intellectual'. Meanwhile, in the same month of October, Berlinguer's policy was criticized for the first time at a PCI central committee meeting, especially by provincial branch secretaries voicing the discontent of the rank and file and of the junior party officials who could not see that the agreement with the other 'constitutional' parties was bringing any appreciable results. But the PCI's two guardian angels – Longo and Amendola – made speeches in support of Berlinguer, who was able to reaffirm that the political line would continue as before. Gerardo Chiaromonte, regarded more than ever as the party's number two, had, however, said a few days earlier that more pressure should be put on the Christian democrats to respect their commitments.

Meanwhile, the Red Brigades, under who knows what influence or guidance, launched a series of pistol attacks against regional Christian democrat leaders. By this time (according to a count made by the *Voce Repubblicana*), 1977 had seen seventy kidnappings and an average of nine assaults a day. Terrorism had increased by 400 per cent in six years. The PCI and the unions were worried because, especially in the big factories and in Turin, there was no mass participation in the demonstrations and strikes called in solidarity with the victims of terrorism. Indeed, a certain indifference was noted. To overcome this in Turin, after the murder of the journalist Casalegno, a campaign reaching down to the grass-roots was organized to collect signatures condemning terrorism. Meanwhile, in Rome, a young militant of 'Lotta Continua' was shot dead by the fascists. It was thus in a far-from-tranquil, indeed, in a thoroughly alarming atmosphere for the future of democracy in Italy, that Berlinguer decided to go in person to Moscow for the celebrations of the sixtieth anniversary of the October Revolution.

From the Eurocommunist point of view, the PCI appeared in late 1977 to have taken a few steps backward. Two events gave this impression. The first was the PCI's reaction to the attack launched in June 1977 by the Soviet review, *New Times*, on Santiago Carrillo's book '*Eurocommunism' and the State*.[17] The PCI took a cautious approach to this controversy. It did not condemn Carrillo, but dissociated itself from those of his statements which had provoked the charge of anti-Sovietism. In other words, Berlinguer stuck to his line of 'a Europe neither anti-American nor anti-Soviet'. In July, a PCI mission led by Pajetta went to Moscow, on a visit planned long before the Carrillo controversy broke out. It had meetings with Soviet leaders, including Suslov, and assured them that, unlike Carrillo, the PCI would not dispute the 'socialist character of the USSR'. In return for this cautious attitude, the PCI's own performance was given official Soviet approval.

Luca Pavolini, the PCI's press and propaganda chief, explained:

Unlike Carrillo, we are careful to judge the Eastern Bloc countries in the appropriate historical context, and we take account of the fact that the communist régime in the USSR is based on a broad consensus, even though we have also often said that the problem of dissent does not concern intellectuals only but also relations between the state and the citizen, the fact that the Soviets have lost their sense of purpose, and the one-party system, which cannot solve the basic problems of a society like that of the Soviet Union today.

The second event was Amendola's statement, at the 'Festival dell'Unità' in Modena, that 'Eurocommunism does not exist. As we have rejected the old world centres of communism we do not wish to create new ones.' This statement coincided with the first signs of the breach between socialists and communists in France. Soon afterwards, Marchais broke the alliance on the 'Common Programme', on the eve of an election which should have been decisive for the chances of the Left to come to power. Such was the setting for Berlinguer's visit to Moscow for the October anniversary. Marchais did not go. Carrillo did, but was not allowed to speak at the ceremony in the Kremlin. Berlinguer, by contrast, spoke on 2 November, immediately after Brezhnev himself, repeating all the well-known points of his position: refusal to recognize any other party as a guide, full recognition of democracy, of the multi-party system and of civil, cultural and religious freedom for the construction of socialism in Italy.

This speech had repercussions in domestic politics. The republican leader, Ugo La Malfa, took it as the decisive sign that the PCI was now independent of the Soviet Union, and demanded its entry into the government to help confront a situation that required a stronger executive. Others, however, considered the speech a mere repetition of known attitudes. The Christian democrats rejected La Malfa's proposal. The PCI itself found it premature, and was not in a hurry to bring down Andreotti's one-party government (though Berlinguer was soon to change his mind about this).

In reality, the PCI's policy of reasserting its independence from the Soviet Union but avoiding a complete break in the Carrillo manner is undoubtedly related to the problems and difficulties which the party has encountered since the 1976 election. Many party members have more and more difficulty in accepting the policy of working with the Christian democrats. This policy is not directly disputed, but the results so far achieved are considered very disappointing. It is frequently admitted that the party rank and file has not adopted the Berlinguer line with the same enthusiasm that it has shown for other party lines in the past. 'This opposition,' remarks one PCI leader, 'cannot be identified with greater or less loyalty to the Soviet Union, but with the hope of a complete change of system, a hope which has burned brightly in the party ever since 1944.'

These expressions of discontent and opposition were bound to grow within the party unless it soon reached the goal defined by Chiaromonte: 'the formation of a governing coalition with the PSI and the Christian democrats'. Membership figures for 1977–8 were below those for the previous year, though the organization secretary, Gianni Cervetti, was confident that the target forecasts would be fulfilled. Meanwhile the number of young people on the 'special lists' of job-seekers rose above 700,000, nearly 500,000 of these being in the South.

The PCI in the majority: from the tragedy of Aldo Moro to the election of the new President of the Republic

On 2 December 1977, 100,000 metalworkers marched through Rome, shouting slogans against the government and joining in a mass rally called by their union in the Piazza San Giovanni. In the newspaper *La Repubblica*, Italy's most famous cartoonist, Franco Forattini, depicted Enrico Berlinguer sitting on a sofa in his dressing-gown, sipping a cup of tea and reading *L'Unità*, and listening with irritation to the shouts of the demonstrators, audible through the closed shutters. The communist historian, Paolo Spriano, wrote a letter of protest to the newspaper, thus provoking a controversy about the communists' conception of free criticism.

The metalworkers' demonstration showed the extent of working-class dissatisfaction with the 'abstention' government. On 7 December, the PCI took an initiative which, until a few days earlier, had seemed out of the question. The communist leadership demanded the resignation of the Andreotti administration, which it described as inefficient and inadequate, thus opening one of the longest and most fateful crises in the Republic's thirty-year history. It seems that Fanfani had told Berlinguer that the time was ripe for the PCI to join the government. But whether or not Berlinguer believed in this possibility, the events that followed were to prove that it was not so. Aldo Moro himself concluded that the resistance to the PCI's joining the government was too strong, both within the Christian Democrat party and on the international level. Interfering blatantly in Italy's internal affairs, the US ambassador, Gardner, followed by the State Department itself acting on orders from Carter, pronounced a clear and peremptory veto. This strengthened Andreotti, who became the sole guarantee of Italy's Atlantic fidelity.

The PCI found itself confronted by a stark choice: either agree to vote for the very same Andreotti one-party Christian democrat government that it had brought down, or go into opposition, which meant giving up the 'historic compromise' policy it had pursued so patiently for years – something the PCI's ruling group considered, especially at that time, as equivalent to a catastrophe. In the central committee on 26 January 1978, Berlinguer tried to escape from the dilemma with a report in which he explained that the historic compromise did not rule out changes of government or the alternation of majority and minority, and suggested that a possible solution to the crisis would be a government composed of PCI, PSI and some minor parties, with the Christian democrats abstaining. This was a sensational suggestion, even if put forward in an almost secret way. But no one in the central committee took it up, and when he replied to the debate, Berlinguer said no more about it.

It was useful, however, to Aldo Moro in his task of persuading the Christian democrats to accept the PCI at least within the governing majority. The negotiations to solve the crisis were long and exhausting. The PCI and the trade unions were asked to make much more explicit concessions than hitherto. Luciano Lama responded handsomely. In an interview on 24 January and then on 14 February in the federal assembly of all three unions, he repeated his 'U-turn' and declared that the unions were ready to accept the necessary sacrifices to solve the country's social and political problems.

Aldo Moro was able to complete his political masterpiece. With a famous speech to the Christian democrat parliamentary party, he obtained its consent to the inclusion of the PCI in the governing majority. The PCI did not join the government but achieved its 'legitimization', so ending the discrimination that, as we remarked earlier, had lasted thirty years. But it had to vote in favour of a government almost identical with the previous one, though with a more advanced programme.

On the very day when the government appeared before the Chamber to ask for a vote of confidence, 16 March 1978, Aldo Moro was kidnapped. His five bodyguards were brutally murdered by a 'commando' acting with exceptional speed and efficiency. Responsibility was later claimed by the Red Brigades. Moro was not only the architect of the PCI's entrance into the majority, but also certain to be the next President of the Republic. He was the 'manager' of the historic compromise. From 16 March to 9 May, the day when his body was dumped in a street exactly half-way between the communist and Christian democrat headquarters, it became more and more clear that the Red Brigades' attack was intended to destroy the government pact and to block the historic compromise policy. Right from the start, the PCI set itself against any kind of bargain with the terrorists. The Christian democrat leaders were a little more wobbly, but adopted the same position with the support of La Malfa and his republican party. This attitude created a new solidarity between the leaderships of the two parties: the agreement between them emerged strengthened from the tragedy. By contrast, the PSI, on the initiative of its new secretary, Bettino Craxi,[18] favoured an 'autonomous' gesture by the state to save Moro. This was the first serious breach in the majority, and especially between the PCI and PSI. After Moro's death, it was to have profound repercussions on the political balance and on the prospects of the historic compromise.

On 14 May the first local elections were held since the 1976 general election, affecting more than four million voters. The PCI lost ground throughout Italy, as compared to the 1976 result, but most spectacularly in the towns and villages of the South. It was the first time for many years that the party suffered an electoral defeat. The PSI, which in 1976 had lost votes to the PCI, and which many people expected would be further punished by the voters for its soft line in the Moro affair, in fact did unusually well. The Christian democrats benefited from the emotional impact of the drama in which it had played the central role, and recovered part of the votes lost in 1976.

On 11 June the two referendums were held on the financing of political parties and on the 'Legge Reale' giving the police wider powers for the use of weapons and the detention of suspects. They were held on the initiative of the radical party, which wanted both laws repealed. The PCI opposed this, although it had been against the 'Legge Reale' at the time of its passage in 1975. In both cases, the electorate voted against the proposed repeal, but the percentage of 'yes' votes was much higher than expected, especially for the repeal of the law on state subsidies to political parties. (56·3 per cent 'no', 43·7 per cent 'yes'. On the 'Legge Reale' the vote was 76·7 per cent 'no', 23·3 per cent 'yes'.)

On 14 June, President Leone suddenly resigned at the request of the PCI and the Christian democrats. Before leaving the Quirinal, he recorded a short speech which was broadcast on television the same evening, and in which he rejected the charge of corruption. The socialist party secretary, Bettino Craxi, at once demanded that the new president should be a socialist. The battle for the Quirinal brought to light deep divisions between the PCI and PSI. The PCI would have preferred a president from one of the minor anticlerical parties, but the PSI vetoed the obvious candidate, the republican party leader, Ugo La Malfa, precisely on the grounds that he had come out in favour of the historic compromise. To avoid a spectacular break with the PSI, and to forestall the victory of the real socialist candidate, Antonio Giolitti (whom his party was holding in reserve and whom a section of Christian democrats supported), the PCI decided to support the socialist candidate furthest from Craxi, the veteran anti-fascist and resistance fighter, Sandro Pertini, aged eighty-two, who had sided with the PCI in opposing any concession to Moro's kidnappers. Pertini's election prevented the break-up of the majority, but showed that the PSI had won a political victory against the logic of the historic compromise.

The PSI now put itself forward as a nucleus round which all those favouring an alternative to the historic compromise strategy could gather, ranging from the extra-parliamentary Left to various moderates. Almost every day there were polemics between the PSI and PCI: ideological problems became entangled with those of domestic policy, such as the reform of the state broadcasting organization or the left-wing majorities in municipal, provincial and regional government.

In an interview with the editor of *La Repubblica*, Eugenio Scalfari, published on 10 August, Berlinguer replied to the socialists' accusation that the PCI was still 'Leninist'. The PCI, he said, neither repudiated Lenin nor swallowed him whole. What 'preoccupied' him, he went on, was the 'new vocation of the present ruling group in the PSI' to subject the PCI to an examination in democracy. Craxi replied that the 'attempt to push the PSI to the right smells of Stalinism'.

In his interview, Berlinguer said that the first six months of 1978 had 'been six terrible months'. As autumn approached, two hypotheses became current about the future. Some said that, once the emergency was over, both in the economy and in law and order, the Christian democrats and the PSI would push the PCI back into opposition and a marginal situation. Others, however, were convinced that the PCI's presence in the majority was the first step in an irreversible process which, even if with occasional halts and slippages, would bring the PCI into government, since only in that way could the country overcome the crisis and the Christian democrats manage to hold on for much longer to a good share of power. It is difficult to say which of these hypotheses is correct: the PCI, as the newspapers say, is still 'half-way across the ford', both in its domestic and in its international policy. At the end of May, Berlinguer had gone to Barcelona to meet Carrillo and had made a speech 're-launching' Eurocommunism. Yet the differences between the PCI, PCF and PCE had grown rather than diminished during 1978, both concerning relations with the Soviet Union and on the questions of dissent, of ideological revision and of the evaluation of personalities such as Bukharin and Trotsky in the history of the Soviet Revolution.

Notes and references

1. Umberto Terracini, *Al bando del partito*, Milan, 1976.

2. *The Italian Road to Socialism: an Interview by Eric Hobsbawm with Giorgio Napolitano of the Italian Communist Party*, London, 1977.

3. ibid.

4. Giorgio Amendola, *Una scelta di vita*, Milan, 1976.

5. Franco Rodano, *Sulla politica dei comunisti*, Milan, 1968.

6. From 1971 onwards, there had been rumours of a right-wing *coup d'état*, organized by the former commander of the fascist navy, Valerio Borghese, and of another said to be planned by the head of the secret service, General Raffaele di Lorenzo.

7. The local elections in Rome were not held till 1976, at the same time as the general election.

8. Giorgio Galli, *Opinioni sul PCI*, Rome, 1977.

9. Aldo Rizzo, *La frontiera dell'eurocomunismo*, Bari, 1977.

10. Galli, *Opinioni sul PCI*.

11. In fact, contrary to what some newspapers asserted, the PCI had not set itself the target of overtaking the Christian democrats. Unlike the PSI, the PCI was against the idea of an 'alternative' to Christian democracy.

12. Giorgio Amendola, *I comunisti e l'Europa*, Rome, 1971.

13. *I comunisti italiani e l'Europa: dichiarazioni e documenti 1973–1976*, a PCI publication, Rome, 1977.

14. The drafting and publication of this medium-term project (known as the *progettone*) are highly symptomatic of the difficulties and in-adequacies which the PCI is encountering as it tries to turn itself from an opposition party into a party of 'struggle and of government'. The party was taken by surprise by Berlinguer's announcement. Both in the party and in public opinion there were signs of expectation mixed with distrust because of the disappointing experience of the attempts at planning by the centre-left government.

The drafting of the *progettone*, which should have been the starting-point for discussion of the new austerity policy, was done with materials provided by experts from both inside and outside the party, but these were collected in a very casual manner and suffered both from the fact that the PCI had not independently worked out its own data and from the lack of appropriate methodology for economic and social planning. Though nominally chaired by Giorgio Napolitano, the commission's work was in fact coordinated by Achille Occhetto. It was tormented and agonizing. In the end, the *progettone* dissatisfied not only many of the outside experts and intellectuals who had worked on it, but also the ruling bodies of the PCI itself. The central committee did not en-

dorse the text, on the grounds that it was only a proposal which should
be modified after a debate in the party and in the country – a debate
which in reality scarcely took place at all. There was also an objective
political difficulty. While the PCI was preparing its medium-term
project, it had to pronounce on the immediate economic and social
problems which required very rapid decisions since the party had ended
up by supporting the Andreotti government. The *progettone* was
criticized inside the PCI as well as outside chiefly because it did not contain any real choice. In the end it was forgotten, and today scarcely
anyone mentions it.

15. See the collection of articles, *Egemonia e democrazia*, Rome, 1977.

16. Thus began a polemic which was to grow more and more acrimonious and to develop into a political battle between the PCI and PSI.

17. Santiago Carrillo, '*Eurocomunismo*' *y Estado*, Barcelona, 1977;
'*Eurocommunism*' *and the State*, London, 1977. There had also been
an attack on the PCI's own Eurocommunism in *Pravda* on 12 May
1977, which had drawn only a mild riposte from *L'Unità*.

18. Craxi won a resounding victory at the PSI's congress, held in
Turin at the beginning of April, on a political line of autonomy from
the PCI. He was re-elected party secretary while the factions opposed
to him, including that of the pro-communist Manca, broke up.

Selected bibliography

Giorgio Amendola, *Una scelta di vita*, Milan, 1976.
I comunisti italiani e l'Europa: Dichiarazioni e documenti 1973–1976,
a PCI publication, Rome, 1977.
Il Manifesto (Quaderno No. 5), *Da Togliatti alla nuova sinistra*, Rome,
1977.
*The Italian Road to Socialism: an Interview by Eric Hobsbawm with
Giorgio Napolitano of the Italian Communist Party*, London, 1977
Proposta di progetto a medio termine, Rome, 1976.
Antonio Rubbi, *I partiti comunisti nell'Europa occidentale*, Teti, n.d.
Paolo Spriano, *Storia del PCI*, Turin, 1975.

——, V. *La Resistenza, Togliatti e il partito nuovo*, Turin, 1975.
Giuseppe Tamburrano, *Antonio Gramsci*, Milan, 1977.
XII Congresso del PCI: Atti e risoluzioni, vol. V.
Pietro Valenza, *I paesi socialisti nell'analisi dei comunisti*, Rome, 1977.
Luciano Gruppi, *Il compromesso storico*, Rome, 1977.

Editors' note (May 1979): The atmosphere of national unity created by the Moro affair was short-lived. During the autumn and winter of 1978, dissatisfaction with the results of the historic compromise was more and more openly expressed among the rank and file of the PCI. Finally, in January 1979, Berlinguer was obliged to withdraw his support from the Andreotti government, thereby provoking its resignation. During the ministerial crisis which followed, communist demands for direct participation in government were pressed more firmly than in the past, while the resistance of the Christian democrat leaders was likewise stiffened by pressure from their rank and file. In the absence of any solution, parliament was dissolved on 3 April and new elections called for 3 June. Meanwhile the PCI's Fifteenth Congress, at the end of March, had reaffirmed the basic line of the historic compromise, but for the first time the existence of a substantial dissenting minority was publicly displayed.

4. Un socialisme aux couleurs de la France:
the French Communist Party
Edward Mortimer

The political context: unity of the Left

Whatever criterion one adopts – differences with Moscow,
acceptance of the European Community or of the Atlantic
Alliance, acceptance of pluralism and public debate within the
party, integration into the local 'bourgeois' political system and
culture, abandonment of references to classic Marxist-Leninist
theory, concessions to the bourgeoisie in economic policy and
political strategy – one can say that the French Communist Party
(PCF) lags behind its Italian brother on the Eurocommunist
road; which is not to prejudge whether or not it will in time
advance to the point which the PCI has now reached. What is
clear is that in both cases this road has been chosen not *in vacuo*,
but as the logical and largely inescapable consequence of a prior
strategic choice, which, in turn, was deduced by each party from
an analysis of the national political context in which it had to
operate. While the PCI has sought to rebuild the national consensus based on anti-fascism which was so rudely shattered by
the outbreak of the Cold War in 1947 – a consensus comprising
essentially communists, socialists and Catholics – the PCF since
the mid 1950s has tended to emphasize the distinction between
'right' and 'left' in French politics. The basic purpose was
similar: to escape from the near-isolation (the 'ghetto') to which
the Cold War condemned communist parties operating within the
'bourgeois' democratic systems of the Western camp. The differences between the chosen tactics reflect differences between
French and Italian traditions and circumstances rather than between the two communist parties as such. Alliances going beyond
or outside the left are not at all inconceivable for the PCF, which,

like the PCI, is acutely aware of the need to find a *modus vivendi* with the Catholic Church in order to operate successfully in a Catholic country. The slogan of the 'outstretched hand' (*la main tendue*) to Catholics, first coined by Thorez in 1936, has constantly been recalled and repeated. Another slogan of the same period was the 'French front' (*le Front français*), intended as an extension of the Popular Front to embrace all French patriots prepared to stand up to Hitler's Germany. A similar theme dominated the PCF's participation in the Resistance and Liberation during the Second World War, and was revived in 1953 for the battle against the proposed European Defence Community, in which communists and Gaullists were united against the Christian democratic and fervently pro-European Mouvement Républicain Populaire (MRP), while the French Socialist Party (SFIO) was deeply divided. On similar issues the PCF was prepared to support de Gaulle when he was in power in the 1960s, and in the 1970s it has consistently sought to win over disillusioned Gaullists by emphasizing the dangers to French independence from an American-dominated Atlantic Alliance and a West German-dominated European Community. Since 1974 it has also spoken of the need for a *union du peuple de France* going well beyond the boundaries of the Left.

The PCF has also, in 1945–6, played the card of the three-party alliance between communists, socialists and Christian democrats (*le tripartisme*). This alliance, like its Italian counterpart, was shattered by the outbreak of the Cold War in 1947, but with the important difference that the breach passed to the left of the SFIO rather than through the middle of it. The prime minister who ejected the communist ministers from his government in May 1947 was himself a socialist (Paul Ramadier): and though the MRP played a leading role in many of the subsequent Fourth Republic governments, it never established anything like the hegemony enjoyed by Christian democracy in Italy. Much of its support was drained by the rise of Gaullism as an organized political movement. By the mid 1950s the traditional left–right polarization of French politics had re-emerged, and the MRP, conceived originally as a party of progressive or 'social' Catholicism, found itself included in the right. This was partly because some of its leaders had identified themselves with a hard-line colonial policy, but also because of the resurfacing of old quarrels on issues of church and state – particularly the question of state subsidies to church schools – which might have been thought obsolete. In fact both communists and Gaullists somewhat cynically exploited this issue in order to split the centre coalition (Troisième Force) from which they were both excluded.

Clearly the PCF's leaders sensed very early on that their best hope of regaining power and influence in France lay in the context of 'the Left'. This concept, seldom clearly defined, has a special emotive force in France which is probably without parallel anywhere else. A quite astonishing number of Frenchmen and Frenchwomen feel the need to proclaim themselves in some sense 'of the Left', even – indeed, especially – when professing opinions which by most criteria would appear to belong to the Right. One has to be on the Left, because the Left is the side of the underdogs, the 'small people', the exploited, the oppressed. This vague egalitarian philosophy is shared by many small farmers, professional people, even small businessmen. These social groups formed the base of the 'Radical Socialist Party' which dominated the Third Republic. In fact, its policies were neither socialist nor, in a twentieth-century context, radical. But it was significant that its members and supporters liked to think of themselves as radical and socialist, and that one of its slogans inherited from its founders was 'No enemies on the Left'. The same philosophy pervaded the SFIO, with the added notion of working-class solidarity. In fact even before 1914 this party was attracting voters from the lower middle class as much as from the working class. But, again, the significant fact was that they wished to identify themselves with the working class, and did so by joining or voting for the 'French Section of the Workers' International'. Its other (and more commonly used name before 1920) was Parti Socialiste Unifié, and this too reflected an important element in the mystique of the Left in France. There has to be *unity*. The Left, the 'republicans', the 'small people', the working class – all are potentially stronger than their enemies, if only they can overcome their internal differences and unite against *la réaction*. The need for this was most apparent when elections were held (as they often were under the Third Republic) according to the two-ballot, single-member constituency system (*scrutin d'arrondissement*). The various parties of the Left could then put up their separate candidates on the first ballot, but it was vital that on the second ballot they should observe 'republican discipline', withdrawing the less successful candidates in favour of the one 'best placed by universal suffrage to defeat reaction'.

The PCF in its early years appeared as a spoiler of this system, because of its insistence on a strictly class-based politics which cut across the sentimental egalitarianism of the traditional Left. But in the Popular Front of 1936, when the PCF first emerged as a national party, it fully embraced the tradition of 'republican discipline' and benefited hugely from it.

The victory of the Popular Front, with the spontaneous general strike and the social reforms which followed it, was a moment of intense and euphoric emotion for the Left and has been a focus of left-wing nostalgia ever since. This was perhaps especially true during the grey years of the Cold War, when communists and socialists were ranged on opposite sides and the political initiative, which the Left had somehow failed to seize in 1944–6, passed inexorably into the hands of the Right. This was a frustrating period for the PCF, which, after the heady period of its participation in government, when Thorez had believed himself close to establishing in France a *démocratie nouvelle et populaire*,[1] was brusquely relegated to the margin of French political life – so that, for instance, in 1954 Pierre Mendès France not only refused the offer of communist support for his government, but undertook in advance not to count the communist votes in his favour when calculating whether or not he had a majority in the National Assembly. But it was no less frustrating for the non-communist Left, for no left-wing majority was possible without the PCF, which continued to win more than one quarter of the votes cast in each general election under the Fourth Republic, and oscillated around one fifth even after the inroads made by de Gaulle in 1958. Though widely regarded as the leader of a 'New Left',

Mendès France did not attempt to form a left-wing government in 1954. His government was a centre coalition based on a heterogeneous parliamentary majority brought together by the need to end the war in Indo-China and by hostility to the proposed European Defence Community. Once those two issues were disposed of it soon broke up. Similarly, the Mollet government of 1956, ostensibly a centre-left coalition under socialist leadership and at first enjoying communist support, soon drifted to the Right and eventually fell, being replaced by centre-right coalitions led by right-wing radicals, in part at least because without the communists it had only a relative majority. Many on the non-communist Left deplored Mollet's hard-line policy in Algeria and believed, rightly or wrongly, that such a policy would not have been adopted by a genuine left-wing government based on a united working class. This feeling was strengthened in 1958 by the collapse of the Fourth Republic, which, many believed, a united Left would have been able to avert.

The arrival of the Fifth Republic brought both political and institutional conditions favourable to the revival of a united Left. De Gaulle reintroduced the *scrutin d'arrondissement*. His object in so doing was to weaken the political parties (whose power had been strengthened by the use of proportional representation with party lists since 1945) and to favour the election of independent deputies who would take a lead from the executive rather than from party machines. This tactic succeeded beyond his expectations. What happened, in fact, was that a new Gaullist party came into existence which became the dominant element in a new majority of the moderate Right. The radicals were reduced to a rump, the MRP gradually disintegrated, and the socialists – finding themselves powerless to influence the new government – went into opposition. There was thus now a predominantly right-wing government facing a predominantly left-wing opposition. Then, in 1962, anxious to strengthen the executive still further, de Gaulle proposed to have the President of the Republic elected directly by the people. All the traditional parties (between them still forming a majority in parliament) opposed this, but de Gaulle by-passed parliament and had his constitutional amendment approved by the electorate in a referendum. This was followed by a general election fought largely on the same issue (being provoked by a parliamentary vote of censure on the government for calling the referendum). The socialists, who had been damaged by the new electoral system in 1958, announced that this time on the second ballot they would withdraw in favour of the best-placed opposition candidate in each constituency, even where this meant supporting a communist.

This was the breakthrough the PCF had been waiting for. It quickly announced that it would return the compliment, and in fact even withdrew some of its candidates who were narrowly ahead on the first ballot in favour of other opposition candidates who had a better chance of rallying moderate voters. 'Republican discipline' had reappeared, and though de Gaulle's supporters won the election, both socialists and communists were able to win back many of the seats they had lost in 1958.

Direct election of the President of the Republic (also on a two-ballot system) proved a further stimulus in the same direction. The socialists did not immediately resign themselves to an alliance with the PCF, of whose intentions many of them remained deeply suspicious. They first attempted to construct a centre-left alternative to Gaullism around a socialist presidential candidate, Gaston Defferre. But this attempt broke down in 1965 without being put to the test of an actual election, because a political consensus between the SFIO and the centre parties involved (mainly the rump of the MRP) could not be found. The socialists realized that the centre of gravity of this reconstituted Troisième Force would still be too far to the right, and would prevent them from competing effectively with the PCF as a party of the Left and of the working class.

The implication of this discovery was paradoxical: that the socialists could compete effectively with the communists only by accepting an alliance with them. The man who grasped this paradox earliest and with greatest clarity, and acted on it most consistently, was François Mitterrand – a man who, by a further paradox, came not from within the socialist party but from the ill-structured middle ground of Fourth Republic politics. In the wake of Defferre's failure, Mitterrand put himself forward (after discreetly sounding out both the SFIO and PCF) as candidate of the Left. While ruling out any negotiations on his programme, he made it clear that he would be happy to accept communist support. On 23 September 1965, the PCF central committee decided officially to support him.

Communist and non-communist Left thus embarked on a partnership which, by September 1977, had been in existence for twelve years, surviving many storms and upheavals but without resolving its fundamental contradictions and ambiguities. It is clear that the two partners went into it with different aims and expectations, for whatever the PCF wanted, it was surely not to help Mitterrand to build a new and stronger socialist party that could effectively challenge the PCF's predominance on the Left and its leadership of the working class. The PCF leaders no doubt understood that this was Mitterrand's intention, for he made no secret of it. But they probably calculated that his chances of succeeding were not good. The SFIO in 1965 was a party tired and discredited by its record of participation in Troisième Force governments, riven by internal quarrels and jealousies, deserted in disgust by many of its more talented leaders or potential leaders. Guy Mollet, its general secretary from 1946, was particularly associated in the public mind with the compromises of the Fourth Republic and the Algerian War. Yet his manipulative skills enabled him to remain in control of the party; indeed, Defferre's failure had strengthened his hold. If he supported Mitterrand it was in part at least because a presidential candidate outside the party was unlikely to pose any serious threat to his own position inside it. He could be relied on to resist any attempt by Mitterrand to rejuvenate the SFIO or to absorb it in a broader-based party. It was therefore reasonable to expect that, within a united Left, the PCF would set the tone, and that when such an alliance eventually came to power, France would be able to resume the march towards a *démocratie nouvelle et populaire* so tragically interrupted in 1946–7. Then the PCF's allies in government had been prepared to ditch it on the instigation of the United States. Next time things would be different: the PCF itself and the French people would be on their guard against American imperialism, which de Gaulle himself was now taking steps to resist. The PCF's allies, this time elected on a clear left-wing programme, would not be able to renegue without completely discrediting themselves in the eyes of the voters.

Such, broadly, was the strategy that the PCF pursued from 1965 to 1977, with a consistency sometimes obscured by its abrupt variations in tactics. Periods when no sacrifice was too great to be made for the overriding cause of left-wing unity alternated with periods when the party's militants had to be reassured and its allies firmly reminded about its true priorities. One constant theme was that efforts to reach understanding with the other parties of the Left must be combined with ever-greater efforts to strengthen the party itself. Another was the need for the Left to present itself to the country, not merely united by sentiment or by tactical self-interest, but by a programme of precise commitments which could not be gone back on. Two years before the 1965 presidential election, the PCF was already urging the need for a 'Common Programme of the Left', and declaring that only on the basis of such a programme could it support a non-communist presidential candidate.[2] In fact, its leaders were realistic enough to know that the non-communist Left would not accept such an idea overnight, and that the goal would have to be approached by stages. The first stage was the agreement to support Mitterrand on the basis of a set of essentially reformist 'options' unilaterally announced by him (they included France's continued membership of both NATO and the EEC) and his willingness to accept and publicly acknowledge communist support. This looked very like giving something for nothing, and caused a good deal of grumbling among the party faithful. A section of the Communist Students Union even had to be dissolved, and its leaders (who turned out to be crypto-Trotskyists) expelled.

But the gamble taken by the party leaders paid off. Mitterrand did unexpectedly well in the election, winning 32 per cent of the votes on the first ballot and 45 per cent in a run-off against de Gaulle alone. The morale of the Left rose to its highest point since 1956. Unity seemed indeed to be the recipe for success. The non-communist Left took the bait and embarked, albeit hesitantly, on a process of rapprochement with the PCF. The next stage, in December 1966, was a negotiated agreement for the general election of March 1967. The PCF and Mitterrand's Fédération de la Gauche Démocrate et Socialiste (an umbrella body comprising the SFIO, the radicals and his own Convention des Institutions Républicaines, with a sprinkling of independent left-wing clubs) would each have their own candidate on the first ballot, but on the second there would be only one candidate of the Left (normally the one who had done best on the first ballot) in each constituency. This electoral pact was coupled with a political *constat de convergence* which fell well short of a common programme but still committed the non-communists to such measures as the nationalization of the merchant banks and the arms industry.

Again the bargain proved profitable to both sides. The voters transferred their votes on the second ballot with unexpected discipline in both directions, and the communist and non-communist Left gained thirty-one seats each. De Gaulle's supporters all but lost their overall majority. Thus encouraged, the non-communists agreed to move on to a third stage: a 'Common Platform', published in February 1968. Once again, this fell short of a common programme, for it listed not only points of agreement but also points of disagreement – notably on foreign policy and on the extent of a future left-wing government's nationalization programme. But the agreement was clearly intended as a step towards a left-wing government which would include communists and would be committed to a radical transformation of French society.

At this point the process received a severe setback in the shape of the 'events' of May and June 1968. A student insurrection, led by leftist groups violently hostile to the PCF's gradualist strategy, sparked off a general strike which the PCF had clearly not expected and which it was able only with considerable difficulty to bring under control. As its leaders had always feared, this kind of extra-parliamentary agitation proved detrimental to the Left's electoral fortunes. De Gaulle also foresaw this, called a snap election and inflicted a humiliating defeat on both communist and non-communist Left. This, in turn, provoked a furious bout of recrimination within the non-communist Left. The Soviet intervention in Czechoslovakia did nothing to improve matters. The personality of Mitterrand and the strategy with which he was identified were widely condemned, and the Fédération de la Gauche broke up.

It was soon proved, however, that disunity could be even more disastrous than unity. In April 1969, de Gaulle resigned after being defeated in an ill-judged referendum. This was the opportunity the opposition had been waiting for ever since 1962. But the Left could not have been less well prepared to exploit it. The SFIO had half-heartedly agreed to join Mitterrand's Convention and the various clubs in a 'new' socialist party, but the Radical Party wanted no more to do with it, and neither wished to hear of a joint candidate with the PCF. In the event, the radicals decided to support the centre candidate, Alain Poher (a former MRP man), while the socialists put up Defferre as a specifically social democrat candidate. The PCF was left with no choice but to put up its own candidate, the veteran Jacques Duclos, while Mitterrand refused to endorse anyone. To make matters worse, there were two far-left candidates: Michel Rocard of the 'Unified Socialist Party' and the Trotskyist Alain Krivine. The result was perfectly calculated to make Mitterrand's and the PCF's point for them. The dispersal of the Left's votes made the Right unchallenged masters of the field. The Gaullist and centre-right candidates, Pompidou and Poher, came in first and second, and were thus left to contest the run-off ballot between them – with Pompidou an easy winner. Among the candidates of the Left, Duclos did much the best, with 21 per cent, winning back for the PCF some of the votes lost in 1968. Defferre, the official socialist candidate, won only 5·1 per cent of the votes cast.

The effects took a good deal of time and manoeuvring to work themselves out. But two years later Mitterrand was enthroned as leader of the new French Socialist Party (PS), and three years later that party and the PCF at last signed a 'Common

Programme of Government' (27 June 1972), which was counter-signed a few days afterwards by a movement representing most of the radical members of parliament (the official apparatus of the Radical Party having meanwhile opted for a centrist alignment).

The PCF with good reason hailed this as a major victory: it had, after all, been campaigning for it for nearly ten years. It rushed out the 'Common Programme' in paperback form, and launched a major campaign to sell it to the voters. Opinion polls soon showed, however, that it was the socialists who would reap the main benefit electorally. Against all expectation, Mitterrand was succeeding in his effort to 'rebalance' the Left. There was even speculation that, for the first time since the war, the Socialist Party might win more votes than the PCF. This proved to be premature. In the general election of March 1973, the PCF won 21·34 per cent of the votes, the PS and its 'left radical' allies 20·65 per cent. But this latter figure was a marked improvement on the percentage won by the Fédération de la Gauche in 1967, whereas the PCF had recovered only part of the votes lost in 1968. 'For the first time, unity is to our partners' advantage and not ours, or more to theirs than ours,' commented the PCF's general secretary, Georges Marchais, reviewing the results at a meeting of the central committee.[3]

The PCF's reaction was not to abandon the strategy but to shift the emphasis, stressing its own specific virtues, criticizing various signs of socialist backsliding, but not questioning the basic value or importance of the left-wing alliance. Its big campaign in the latter part of 1973 was for the sale of Marchais's book, *Le Défi démocratique* (*The Democratic Challenge*), which set out in simple language the party's vision of socialism 'in French colours'.

When the sudden death of Georges Pompidou plunged France into a new presidential election in the spring of 1974, the PCF came out without hesitation in support of Mitterrand as candidate of the united Left, and did everything possible to help him in his campaign, notably by stressing the modesty of its own ambitions. Shortly before the second ballot, Marchais made it clear that if

Mitterrand became president the PCF would not expect more than a third of the Cabinet posts, would not seek the prime ministership, and would not even insist on being given one of the three 'big' ministries – Defence, Foreign Affairs and the Interior – as it had tried to do in 1945–7.[4]

Only in the autumn of 1974, it seems, did the PCF leaders become seriously worried by the PS's still-rising score in the opinion polls and by-elections, and by its success in attracting new currents of socialist opinion, notably from the far-left Unified Socialist Party and from the main non-communist trade-union confederation (CFDT) with its strong belief in workers' self-management. (The PCF itself and the largest trade-union movement, the CGT – which it controls – preferred a more classic model of 'democratic management' allowing for a more tightly planned and centralized economy.) For a year after October 1974 the PCF subjected the PS to constant, even carping criticism and there were bitter quarrels between the two – particularly on the subject of Portugal in the summer of 1975. Then, in 1976 and early 1977, the emphasis was again on unity, culminating in the impressive victory of the alliance in the municipal elections of March 1977. Whereupon in the summer of 1977 the PCF's resentment at being treated as a junior partner by the PS burst out in a new quarrel over the updating of the 1972 'Common Programme' for the general election due in March 1978 – a quarrel whose significance will be analysed at the end of the chapter.

Socialism, pluralism and freedom

We have seen that Mitterrand's strategy of using alliance with the PCF as a means to compete with it has been more successful than the PCF leaders can have expected. But that was not the limit of Mitterrand's ambitions. He has never hinted that he hoped to eliminate the PCF, or even to reduce it to a point where its support would no longer be necessary to a left-wing government.

Rather he sought to restore it to what he considered its proper place as *one* of the component forces of the Left, but not one in a position to monopolize or dominate it. He sought to reintegrate the party's supporters into the national community, which meant not only persuading some of them to switch to the PS but also changing the PCF itself, by persuading it – or obliging it – to accept the norms of parliamentary democracy as the price of unity. Thus Mitterrand may fairly be regarded as one of the inventors of Eurocommunism.

In fact the PCF's option for a 'parliamentary road to socialism' dates back to 1944–5 when, following Stalin's instructions, it carefully refrained (like the PCI, and in sharp contrast to the Communist Party of Yugoslavia) from any attempt to transform the Resistance against Nazi occupation into a revolutionary insurrection.[5] Statements emphasizing the parliamentary and non-violent nature of the PCF's strategy can be found in abundance in the party literature of 1944–7 (as in that of most other European communist parties), the most famous perhaps being in Thorez's interview with *The Times* on 18 November 1946:

> It is clear that the Communist Party, in its action as part of the Government and within the framework of the parliamentary system it has helped to re-establish, will hold strictly to the democratic programme which has won for it the confidence of the masses of the people. The progress of democracy throughout the world, in spite of rare exceptions which serve only to confirm the rule, permits the choice of other paths to socialism than the one taken by the Russian communists. In any case, the path is necessarily different for each country. We have always thought and said that the French people, who are rich in great traditions, would find for themselves their way to greater democracy, progress and social justice.

It is true that no more such statements were made for a long time after 1947, but it does not appear that the strategy involved was ever explicitly disavowed. At the founding meeting of the Cominform in September 1947, it was only the Yugoslavs who criticized the French and Italian parties for failing to transform the struggle against Nazism into revolution. The criticism which mattered, that of Zhdanov, concerned only their failure to recognize the role of American imperialism and to denounce its local allies, particularly after their ejection from government in the spring of 1947.[6] There is no indication at any point during or after 1947 that the PCF believed that circumstances in France would allow a revolutionary seizure of power. Although it did organize a series of violent strikes and demonstrations, the object of these was always to weaken the 'imperialist camp', of which France was part, in its struggle against the 'democratic camp' led by the Soviet Union. In fact it is difficult to find any evidence in these years for any PCF strategy for achieving power or installing socialism in France by any means at all – probably because this was not an objective in which Stalin was interested.

Not until 1956 did a clear line again emerge from Moscow on the strategy to be adopted by communist parties in highly developed capitalist countries, and then it was the Khrushchev line, according to which the corollary of the non-inevitability of wars and the possibility of peaceful coexistence between the blocs was a corresponding possibility of a peaceful road to socialism, brought about by an alliance between communist and other 'patriotic forces', in particular the social democrats. Whatever their resentment or embarrassment at Khrushchev's denunciation of Stalinism, the PCF leaders had no cause to quarrel with this aspect of his policies, which was largely a reversion to the Stalin line of 1941–7, the line which had carried the PCF to its peak of power and prestige. It was a line that fitted perfectly with the 'union of the Left' strategy which, as we have seen, the PCF was impelled to adopt by national circumstances. And when the union of the Left became a reality in the mid 1960s, the PCF was able, without inhibitions, to reassure its new partners about its belief in democracy and the parliamentary system, and to argue, by referring to Thorez's 1946 interview with *The Times* and other pronouncements of that epoch, that it was no recent convert to such ideas.

The trouble was, of course, that non-communist politicians were by now well aware that communists are liable to use words like 'democracy' in a rather special sense. The vocabulary used by Thorez in 1944–7 was almost identical to that used at the same period by communist leaders in Eastern Europe. Indeed, while he had spoken of 'other paths to socialism than the one taken by the Russian communists', he had not felt it necessary to stress any difference between the French path and those of the various East European countries under Soviet tutelage. What he had looked forward to was specifically a *démocratie nouvelle et populaire*: a people's democracy. That phrase had acquired a distinctly pejorative connotation in the West as a result of subsequent events, and therefore the PCF avoided reviving it in a French context. But an attentive reader of the French communist press could see that, in the PCF's eyes, not only were the Soviet Union and its satellites 'democratic' as well as 'socialist' countries, but the satellites moreover remained interesting and valid alternatives to the Soviet model. In 1966, for instance, we find the party explicitly quoting Czechoslovakia as an example of the parliamentary road to socialism on which it wishes France to embark:

What happened in Czechoslovakia [in 1948] is . . . a confirmation of the possibilities of making Parliament the instrument of the people's wishes . . . The Parliament elected in 1946 confirmed its confidence in the government formed by the communists, thus consecrating the victory of the socialist revolution by constitutional means.[7]

This was presumably meant to reassure party veterans that there were good communist precedents for what the party was proposing, rather than to warn any French social democrat who might be so unwise as to cast himself in the role of Masaryk. But, in any case, leaders like Mitterrand, who had first-hand experience of communist tactics during the post-war period, needed no such warning. From the moment the union of the Left got under way in 1965, the PCF found itself under constant pressure from its allies to make its commitment to democracy more precise, and each step towards effective unity was achieved at the price of new concessions to the 'bourgeois' interpretation of the word.

A key issue for the non-communist Left was acceptance of a multi-party as opposed to a one-party system. On this a first step was made in 1966 when René Piquet, then a candidate member of the politburo, affirmed the PCF's 'respect' for other political parties and promised 'to each its place in the common struggle but also after the struggle'.[8] This pledge was given more precise form in the manifesto adopted by the central committee at Champigny in December 1968:

> During the passage to socialism and for the construction of the latter the existing democratic parties and formations which will declare for socialism and for the respect of the laws of the new social régime will be able to take a full part in the country's political life and will enjoy all the rights and freedoms guaranteed by the Constitution.[9]

But inevitably the question was asked, what about those parties that refused to 'declare for socialism'? A partial response was furnished in the PCF's 'Programme pour un gouvernement démocratique d'union populaire', adopted by the central committee in October 1971. This included a substantial chapter on the preservation and extension of civil liberties.

> Parties and political groups [it said] will be able to form and to carry on their activities freely provided that they respect the law. Their plurality contributes to the expression of opinion. They will be assured of access to the state information media. The political rights of the opposition will be guaranteed in law, both by the liberties defined above and by the existence of proportional representation. The regular organization of elections under universal suffrage is one of the essential methods allowing the people to express its judgement on the activity of the parties. The parties will respect the people's verdict. There will be no confusion between the parties and the state apparatus.[10]

This also gave at least a partial answer to another question constantly thrown at the PCF by its opponents, the question known as that of *alternance*, or alternation in power: once they attained power, would the communists ever allow themselves to be defeated in an election, or would they hold on to power irrespective of the popular will? For years the PCF wrestled unhappily with this question, to the embarrassment of its allies, for clearly it did present a genuine theoretical difficulty. The PCF claimed to be offering not merely a change of government but a change of society. The 'advanced democracy' it proposed to introduce was 'a step towards socialism'. In other words, it should see at least the beginnings of a transition from the capitalist to the socialist mode of production. Such a profound change in the social structure could hardly be without effect on the political superstructure: indeed, the very advent of a left-wing government would be proof that the contradictions of capitalism in France had reached a point where they could no longer be resolved within the bourgeois political system. To suggest that after reaching a new stage on the road to socialism the majority of the people might voluntarily give back power to anti-socialist parties seemed, at worst, quite unscientific, and at best to cast serious doubt on the communist party's claim to be the unique instrument through which the working class could achieve power.

The PCF was therefore most reluctant to go beyond the general formulation of respect for universal suffrage quoted above. But in the negotiations on the 'Common Programme' in 1972, the socialists insisted on a specific pledge to relinquish power if defeated in an election, since to omit it would inevitably be taken as admitting an intention to hold on to power by undemocratic means if necessary. The PCF eventually agreed, but insisted on inserting a curiously worded rider. The relevant passage in the 'Common Programme' reads as follows:

If the country refused its confidence to the majority parties, the latter would surrender power and resume the struggle in opposition. But the chief task of the democratic government, whose existence implies the support of a popular majority, will be the satisfaction of the toiling masses; and the government will therefore be strong in the ever more active confidence that the masses will place in it.[11]

The PCF thus affirmed in principle its willingness to accept defeat, while hastening to reassure its supporters that it did not expect that the pledge would ever have to be honoured.

The 'Common Programme', in which the PCF also accepted that France would remain a member of the Atlantic Alliance and a full participant in the EEC, was, in any case, a programme for only one parliament. The PCF presented it, like its own 1971 programme, as a blueprint for 'advanced democracy' rather than for socialism itself, which would come later. Would the multi-party system survive in a socialist France? Yes, replied Marchais, in his book *Le Défi démocratique* (1973), but then immediately deprived this assurance of any value by citing as examples of multi-party socialist societies the people's democracies of Eastern Europe and the German Democratic Republic, where, he said, the government was a coalition of five parties and the Speaker of the *Volkskammer* was a Christian democrat!

The PCF was remarkably slow to realize that this kind of explanation was worse than useless, since the French public was not interested in the purely formal pluralism of Eastern Europe, but wanted to see freedom preserved through a genuine pluralism in which parties, trade unions and other corporate bodies were free to oppose each other publicly and compete for popular support. It was not enough to say that socialist democracy in France would be different from the Soviet model. If the word 'democracy' was to carry any conviction on French communists' lips, they had to show that they were aware of the *un*democratic character of society both in the Soviet Union and in its East European satellites. Not until the party's Twenty-second Congress, in February 1976, was this problem tackled at all convincingly.

The breach with Moscow

The origins of the conflict between the PCF and the CPSU have been described in Chapter 1. It should be emphasized that the contradiction between Soviet great-power interests and the PCF's domestic ambition was a necessary rather than a sufficient cause, for this contradiction had been far more glaring at some earlier periods of the PCF's history (most obviously in 1939–41, but also in 1928–32 and 1947–52) than it was in the 1960s, and yet, during those earlier periods, the PCF's leaders had without hesitation sacrificed their party's national reputation and given unconditional support to Soviet policy. What differentiated the

1960s was the legacy of Khrushchev's denunciation of Stalin, the withering of the Cominform and the Sino-Soviet split[12] – events which deprived the Soviet leadership of its unchallengeable supremacy in the world communist movement, and arguably reflected a slackening of Soviet interest in Western communist parties not only as instruments of world revolution (they had been more or less written off on this score since the 1920s) but even as instruments of Soviet foreign policy.

The PCF leaders were certainly embarrassed and irritated both by the denunciation of Stalin in 1956 and by the sudden over-throw of Khrushchev in 1964. On the first occasion they tried for a long time to pretend that they knew nothing about it, referring to 'the so-called Khrushchev report' long after the full text of the secret speech had been published in *Le Monde* and other Western newspapers. On the latter occasion they sent a high-level delegation to Moscow to demand an explanation. Apparently the delegation returned to Paris with reassurances. Only Khrushchev's individualist methods of decision-taking would be changed. His policy of peaceful coexistence (essential if the PCF was to make good its escape from political isolation in France) would be maintained.[13]

Indeed, there is no reason to think that the Brezhnev–Kosygin leadership was unhappy with Khrushchev's general line of en-couraging cooperation between communists and other socialist or 'patriotic' opposition forces in Western countries. But, in the mid 1960s, France was coming to constitute a special case in Soviet foreign policy, because of de Gaulle's various gestures of independence from American tutelage and desire to steer a course of his own between the blocs. The Soviet leaders clearly put a high value on these signs of a breach in the front of Western hostility, and were unenthusiastic about the PCF's willingness to make common cause with a French opposition which was at that time predominantly Atlanticist. Waldeck Rochet's remark in 1962 that withdrawal from the Atlantic Pact or the Common Market should not be a precondition for cooperation between French communists and socialists may well have been received with indifference in Moscow, since at that time there was no serious likelihood of France withdrawing from either. By 1965, when de Gaulle was applying his 'empty chair' policy in Brussels and preparing to withdraw from NATO, the position was rather different, and the Soviet Union could hardly be expected to join the PCF in endorsing a presidential candidate running against de Gaulle on a platform including a pro-EEC and pro-NATO plank. In fact it did the opposite, and gave a discreet endorsement to de Gaulle himself in the form of a Tass report explaining that some opponents of the French régime would probably vote for de Gaulle because of 'certain positive and realistic measures that the Gaullist government is taking in the foreign policy field'. *L'Humanité* ignored this report, and the PCF let it be known that it had protested to Moscow.[14]

Two months later, the PCF was able to get its own back by publishing in *L'Humanité* an article by Louis Aragon, doyen of French Communist intellectuals, which protested strongly against the sentences passed on two Soviet dissidents, the writers Sinyavsky and Daniel. Both sides had thus indicated that there were limits to their solidarity well before the Soviet invasion of Czechoslovakia in 1968 – but this undoubtedly was a traumatic blow for the PCF, as for other West European communist parties. Indeed, perhaps more so, precisely because the PCF had been more thoroughly Stalinized, at any rate than the Italian party, and both its leaders and its militants had till then retained a strong instinctive loyalty to the 'homeland of socialism'. In April 1968, the PCF central committee came out rather gingerly in favour of the 'Prague spring' – a demonstration that democracy and communism were not incompatible was, after all, an electoral argument not to be spurned, especially when the French right-wing press had just been drawing an anti-communist moral from the twentieth anniversary of the 1948 *coup de Prague*. Then, seeing disaster approach, the PCF in July dispatched its general secretary, Waldeck Rochet, first to Moscow, then to Prague, in a desperate but vain attempt to find a compromise. Apparently, like his Italian colleague Luigi Longo, Rochet warned the Soviet leaders that he would have to condemn any military intervention. And sure enough, on the day of the invasion, the PCF's politburo expressed its 'surprise and reprobation'. Next day the central committee announced its 'disapproval'. Many commentators saw this as a significantly weaker expression. What was certainly true was that the party took no pleasure in condemning the Soviet action. For many leaders and militants, doing so meant going against all the mental habits of a lifetime. For Thorez's widow, Jeannette Vermeersch, it was too much: she resigned from both politburo and central committee. Rochet himself, who like Dubček had sought to combine a more liberal version of communism with fundamental loyalty to the Soviet Union, described his party as 'bitter' and 'torn' – implying not that it was about to split, but rather that each French communist must find himself torn by conflicting loyalties.

Undoubtedly the condemnation was as sincere as it was electorally indispensable. But, having made the gesture, the party's immediate instinct was to try and limit its scope, and to find a way out of a psychologically unbearable situation. It at once welcomed the 'agreement' imposed on the hapless Czechoslovak leaders in Moscow. The party's leading philosopher, Roger Garaudy, a member of the politburo, was censured by his colleagues for attacking the Soviet leaders in an interview with the Czechoslovak news agency: he was accused of an 'inadmissible interference in the internal affairs of brother parties'. In November, a further PCF delegation travelled to Moscow and held long discussions with the Soviet leaders. They agreed to differ, but at the same time reaffirmed their 'fraternal sincerity and friendship'.[15] The PCF was thus the first of the communist parties which had condemned the invasion to resume formal contacts with Moscow: and it went on to accept the successive stages of 'normalization' imposed on the Czechs – never questioning the legitimacy of Gustav Husak and his colleagues as genuine leaders of a genuine communist party. At the Moscow world conference of June 1969, the PCF, while reaffirming the independence of each party, was one of the very few West European communist parties (along with those of Ireland, Luxemburg and Portugal) to give total support to the CPSU in its condemnation of China,[16] and to avoid making any reference to Czechoslovakia.

While in Moscow to attend that conference, Waldeck Rochet
fell victim to a stroke. It was soon apparent that he would be able
to play no further part in the party's affairs. (In fact, he is said
to have remained in a virtual coma ever since.) The role of party
leader was taken over by Georges Marchais, who was named
assistant general secretary in February 1970 and full general
secretary in December 1972. Marchais had since 1961 held the
key post of organization secretary, but was not well known outside the party. He was neither a member of parliament nor a
noted public speaker, and had not been publicly involved in the
party's attempts to forge links with other opposition forces or
to endow itself with a more liberal image. As his rise to the leadership coincided with the period of 'normalized' relations with the
CPSU, he was at first identified as 'Moscow's man', and bitterly
attacked by those, like Roger Garaudy and Charles Tillon, who
had hoped to see the party develop a more radical opposition to
Stalinism both at home and abroad. (He was also attacked for
not having a wartime Resistance record, and has had repeatedly
to rebut the accusation that he volunteered to work in a German
aircraft factory in 1942.) Both Garaudy and Tillon were expelled
from the party in 1970, and it seemed at first that a period of
re-Stalinization had set in.

By the end of 1970, however, Marchais had consolidated his
position within the party and was able to show that it would be
at least as independent of Moscow under his leadership as under
his predecessor. In December of that year, Étienne Fajon, editor-
in-chief of *L'Humanité* and a veteran member of the party
secretariat with the reputation of being an unreconstructed
Stalinist, was chosen to express the PCF's criticism of the
'mistakes and insufficiencies in the working of socialist democracy' which led to the strikes and riots in Poland (culminating
in the fall of Gomulka). Marchais himself confirmed the criticism
in a speech to the central committee; and, the same month, the
PCF publicly protested at the death sentences passed in Lenin-
grad on two Soviet Jews who had attempted to hijack a plane,
joining in the (successful) international chorus of appeals for
clemency. Marchais expressed his dislike of 'barracks communism'; and the following month the PCF made a further public

protest when the 'normalized' central committee of the Czechoslovak party retrospectively justified the Soviet invasion.

A 'Marchais line' was thus established which remained fairly
consistent until the autumn of 1975: a line which combined
freedom to criticize specific actions by the Soviet Union and its
satellite régimes with acceptance of East European society as
genuinely socialist (and therefore, in the last resort, preferable to
existing capitalist society in the West) as well as *de facto* acceptance of Soviet leadership in the international communist movement. It could be defined as a centrist position between the
uncritical pro-Sovietism of, say, the Portuguese and the 'auto-
nomism' of the Yugoslavs, Romanians, Italians and Spaniards.
Thus, up to and including October 1975, the PCF supported
Soviet efforts to convene a conference of European communist
parties which would reaffirm the essential unity of the international communist movement; and during the summer of 1975,
it expressed its solidarity with the Portuguese Communist Party
(PCP), then under attack from both French and Portuguese
socialists, and criticized also by Italian and Spanish communists,
for disregarding election results and trying to gain power through
the armed forces. But the PCF was careful to add that solidarity
did not mean 'alignment' and could not be 'unconditional'.
Clearly, the tactics applied in Portugal were very different from
those which the PCF proposed for France. But, as it sought
respect for its own right to work out its own tactics in France,
so it was prepared to defend the PCP's right to choose its own
tactics in Portugal. And when Konstantin Zarodov, writing in
Pravda, sought to use the Portuguese context as the basis for a
general criticism of the strategy of relying on electoral alliances
and 'arithmetical' majorities, Marchais bluntly recalled that 'our
policy is decided in Paris, not in Moscow'.

A number of factors must have combined to convince the
PCF's leaders of the need for a more radical change of policy in
the autumn of 1975. Marchais himself, who had suffered a slight
heart attack earlier in the year, regained his health and resumed
full control of the party. The relatively tough line, combined
with carping criticisms of the French Socialist Party, the PS,

which the PCF had taken during the previous twelve months had served only to strengthen the PS's support as revealed in by-elections and opinion polls. Support for the PCP had clearly damaged the PCF's liberal image, while the PCI, after its triumph in the Italian local and regional elections in June 1975, became an ally hardly to be spurned. Finally the Soviet leaders had annoyed the PCF not only by publishing Zarodov's article, but also by welcoming President Giscard d'Estaing in Moscow in October and publishing an incomplete version of the PCF's statement on the visit (which stressed that détente did not imply acceptance of the social and political *status quo* in France).[17]

Whatever the relative importance of these various aspects, the fact is that in November 1975 the PCF suddenly aligned itself with the PCI. The two parties published a joint statement which stressed a general 'concordance of solutions' for situations having a 'common character' in highly developed capitalist countries. In the discussions on the proposed conference of European communist parties, the PCF now changed sides and joined the 'autonomists' in rejecting a draft document considered to go too far in the direction of a unified world communist strategy. Then, in January 1976, Marchais came out with statements on the 'French road to socialism', indicating that the PCF would now drop the term 'dictatorship of the proletariat', which no longer accurately expressed its policy, and, after restating the PCF's attachment to democracy, pluralism of political parties and freedom of speech, went on to say:

We consider that the principles which we enunciate concerning socialist democracy are of universal value. It is clear that we have a dis-agreement with the Communist Party of the Soviet Union about this problem.[18]

This statement is clearly crucial, and may be said to mark the PCF's true ideological breach with Moscow. Up to then the 'French road to socialism' had been different from the Soviet one, but leading essentially to the same goal. Now it was pro-claimed to embody principles of universal application, which the Soviet Union was condemned for failing to observe.

Already at the end of 1975 the PCF had signalled this new approach by publicly calling on the Soviet Union for an explanation of scenes said to have been filmed in a Soviet labour camp and shown in a documentary on French television. (Earlier, such a film would either have been ignored or denounced as anti-Soviet propaganda serving the interests of the French bourgeoisie.) In January 1976, the arrival in France of Leonid Plyushch – whose internment in a Soviet psychiatric hospital the PCF had earlier denounced – provided the occasion for a further demonstration of hostility to Soviet repression and, for the first time, positive solidarity with its victims: PCF leaders appeared alongside Plyushch at a press conference and associated themselves with his struggle for democracy in the Soviet Union.

The PCF showed a certain insolence, too, in scheduling its Twenty-second Congress for the same month as that of the CPSU (February 1976), at which Marchais was conspicuous by his absence. This congress was the occasion for the PCF to set out in detail its conception of political democracy and its strategy for achieving socialism in France. The dictatorship of the proletariat was jettisoned and replaced by a *union du peuple de France* – union of all 'non-monopolist' social classes. As summarized by the communist historian Jean Elleinstein, 'the *union du peuple de France* can be realized around the working class which is its driving force and on the basis of the union of the Left, but what is important is to see clearly that the new political power thus constituted will not only be that of the working class but also that of all the social forces which will have worked to transform society and bring the new political power to birth'.[19] The PCF thus adopted an essentially Gramscian vision of working-class hegemony (though without the word) in a class alignment apparently indistinguishable from the 'new historic bloc' which Garaudy had been condemned for proposing in 1970.

As in Italy, so in France, the circumstances of advanced industrial capitalism were seen to make both possible and necessary a combination of socialism with political democracy and 'public freedoms' which, so far from being obstacles, were presented as instruments of social and economic transformation;

whereas the bad name given to socialism by Soviet practices was frankly acknowledged as an obstacle to be overcome. 'We cannot allow,' said Marchais in his report to the congress, 'the Communist ideal, whose object is the happiness of mankind, and on behalf of which we call upon the working people to struggle, to be besmirched by acts which are unjust and unjustified.'[20]

But the limits of the change were equally clearly set. Internationally, the Soviet Union remained a socialist state under which 'great historical progress' had been accomplished, and with which the PCF was still involved in 'the common struggle against imperialism and for our great common goals'. Nationally, the hoped-for union of the French people still depended on 'the irreplaceable role of the party of the working class'. So describing itself, the PCF implicitly relegated the socialists of the PS to the role of representing some of those secondary social forces over which the working class was to exercise its 'guiding role' (*rôle dirigeant*). In retrospect, one can perhaps see this as serving notice that the PCF would not agree to play second fiddle in a left-wing alliance where the French Socialist Party had become dominant.[21]

Image, self-image and essence

It is generally accepted in France that the PCF 'has changed' in some important respects since the time of the Cold War. We have already seen that the content of its public pronouncements has changed in two highly significant ways: it is willing to give assurances in detail about the maintenance of individual freedoms and pluralist democracy in France during and after the 'transition to socialism'; and it has formed the habit of publicly criticizing the policies and actions of communist governments in the Soviet Union and Eastern Europe, and of publicly alluding to the shortcomings of those countries as models of a socialist society.

There has also unquestionably been, since the late 1960s, an important change of style. The party has made a very serious effort to get away from its previous image as a closed society holding itself deliberately apart from and in opposition to not only the existing political system but the whole range of social and ideological activities associated with the existing capitalist order, a society speaking its own mysterious jargon and imposing a rigid ideological conformity on its members. This change can be dated roughly from 1970, the year when Georges Marchais officially assumed the leadership of the party, and when its head-quarters were moved from their forbidding pre-war fortress in central Paris (44 rue Le Peletier) to the resplendent and un-mistakably modern glass-and-concrete palace in the place du Colonel Fabien, designed by Oscar Niemeyer. Since then it has been a clear priority for the party to project a 'modern' image: the image, that is, of a party free from left-bank trendiness but in close touch with all the social and cultural changes affecting French society in depth; a party fully integrated into the France of today, whose members are not colourless prototypes of working-class virtue but three-dimensional human beings from all walks of life, whose common commitment to the party's ideals does not prevent them from having the most varied tastes or even, on many subjects, the most varied opinions. Marchais himself, who at the 1970 congress appeared a thoroughly colour-less *apparatchik*, an expert in organization who read out a five-hour report virtually without expression, managed within a year or two to turn himself into a jovial and approachable public figure, fully at ease in public question-and-answer sessions and television and radio interviews. Even his complexion underwent a notable improvement. But this was only part of a rapid adapta-tion of the party to modern techniques of communication and of public relations, which ranges from offering a glass of whisky to visiting journalists to securing internationally famous pop groups to entertain the masses at the annual Fête de l'Humanité.

Perhaps the most keenly debated question among those in France who study the PCF from outside, is how far this dramatic change in the party's presentation of itself to the world corre-sponds to a more profound change in its internal nature. The leaders of the party who gave the impulse to the change of style are necessarily people who were already members of it and worked their way up through its apparatus during the preceding period. In other words, they were people who accepted the conformism, the tight ideological discipline and the close identification of the party with the Soviet Union which characterized the party in the 1950s and early 1960s, and it may be assumed that their motives for imposing a change of style were essentially tactical. But the question has been asked[22] whether a party can 'remain unchanged when its system of relations with French society, with the other parties, with the French political scene, with the international system, is modified'? More particularly, can a party integrate itself into an essentially pluralist society without itself acquiring a more pluralist character? And can it present a democratic image of itself to the outside world without encouraging its own members to acquire democratic habits and expectations? There was a time, not fifteen years ago, when a good French communist militant would have avoided reading any book or newspaper not recommended by the party. Today, when as an earnest of its liberalism the party allows the works of Solzhenitsyn to be sold at the Fête de l'Humanité, it must be difficult for its militants to avoid forming their own opinions and particularly their own judgements about the credibility or the efficacy of their party's policies and statements. This is especially true when one remembers that something like two thirds of the present party's members have joined it since 1968, and at least one third since 1972.[23] In other words, a majority of French communists has been attracted to the party since it adopted its democratic and 'open' image. It may therefore be supposed that, even internally, the party leadership cannot act in a way completely inconsistent with this image without provoking a grave internal crisis and the departure of many party members. The transformation undertaken in the last ten years might not be easily reversible, and the longer the party's present image is maintained, the truer that will be as militants of the new generation rise to higher positions in the apparatus.

On this point, however, the experience of the past must teach us caution. Reintegration into the national political mainstream and adjustment of style and language as well as policy to the contemporary political context were features of two previous periods of the party's history: the period of the Popular Front (1934–7) and that of the Liberation (1944–7). These were also periods when party membership increased very rapidly. In both cases the period ended abruptly (in 1939 and 1947) with the return to class-war politics and complete political isolation. In 1939, the volte-face following the German-Soviet pact was so abrupt that it did indeed provoke a major crisis within the party and the departure of numerous members. In 1947 the leadership held together, but the rise in membership came to an end and a decline set in. In both cases the crucial factor was the instinctive obedience of party cadres, most of whom had been trained in the period of extreme sectarianism before 1934. Those who had been attracted only by the broad anti-fascist programme of the periods of expansion had not risen high enough to have any real role in the party's chain of command.

The same is probably true today. In the 1970s, the PCF, traditionally a Leninist 'vanguard party', has taken to describing itself as a 'mass party' (as its Italian sister has done ever since the 1940s). In practice, this reflects a reversion to the recruitment practice, current during the immediate post-war period but abandoned in the 1950s, of accepting and indeed encouraging new members without any attempt to test the depth of their political and personal commitment. To take out a party card is a gesture easily made in a moment of enthusiasm at a party meeting or fête. Often the same enthusiasm will not sustain the new member through the routine but time-consuming activities of the party cell in his workplace or neighbourhood. After a year or two he may drop out: the party reckons to lose about 10 per cent of its members every year.[24] But even of those who stay, only those who show themselves not only zealous but disciplined and ideologically sound are likely to rise to positions of responsibility. To take a simple example, the party encourages non-Marxists, and especially Christians, to become members. But at the same time it defines itself as a Marxist party, and specifies in the preamble to its statutes that it 'founds its action on Marxism-Leninism which generalizes the most advanced philosophical, economic, social and political knowledge'. It follows that those who fail to embrace Marxism-Leninism at least verbally are not likely to rise very high in the party. But more important is the 'democratic centralist' structure, which ensures that the candidates for responsibility at one level are always vetted (and usually proposed) by those who already hold responsibility at the superior level.

Undoubtedly the rank and file of the party are now encouraged to discuss general political problems to a much greater extent than used to be the case. But decisions, once taken by the appropriate party organ, are still not supposed to be questioned, and discussion at the base of the party takes place within the framework of the cell, a group of about twenty people. The cells do not normally communicate directly with each other but with the section to which they belong, the sections with the federation and the federations with the central committee. A democratically organized opposition to the leadership or the prevailing line within the party remains something unthinkable; and the leadership in recent years has continued to decide on and announce important changes in policy with little or no public discussion. A famous example was the decision to abandon the concept of the dictatorship of the proletariat, announced by Marchais in a radio interview and voted by a unanimous party congress a month later. Another was the decision to support continued development of France's nuclear strike force, taken by the central committee in May 1977 virtually without debate after hearing a single report from a politburo member, Jean Kanapa.

The crisis of 1977–8

But by far the most striking example of this phenomenon, one which has profoundly altered the terms of the debate about the nature and destiny of the PCF, obliging almost every French

politician to reconsider his strategy and every observer of French
politics to reconsider his analysis, has been the party's behaviour
towards its socialist 'ally', during and since the 1978 election
campaign. This is certainly not the place to attempt a defence of the French Socialist Party against the PCF's accusations. Indeed, it can readily be admitted, with hindsight, that the
performance of the PS and its leaders became, by the summer of
1977, subjectively as well as objectively, a source of irritation to
the leaders of the PCF. Not only had the PS's electoral support,
according to opinion polls corroborated by by-election and local
election results, dramatically outdistanced that of the PCF – a
development which, as we have seen, the PCF can hardly have
expected, still less intended, to be the result of its united-left
strategy – but this had encouraged Mitterrand and other socialist
leaders to treat the PCF with a certain condescension. Concentrating on the task of winning over floating voters in the centre of
the political spectrum, and assuming no doubt that the PCF was
by now committed to the union of the Left beyond recall and
without alternative, they tended to stress that the communists
were now the junior partner in the alliance, with no chance of
dominating a future left-wing government. Seeing themselves
close to power and responsibility, some of the PS's economic
specialists sought to reassure businessmen by putting a reformist
gloss on the 'Common Programme', and to inject a note of
'realism' into the Left's short-term economic proposals. Yet their
concessions to classical 'bourgeois' economics did not go as far
as those of the Italian communists, nor, indeed, as far as the PCF
itself had done during its 'productivist' phase in 1944–6.

It had been generally expected that the negotiations to update
the 1972 'Common Programme' for the March 1978 elections
would be difficult, but also that the prospect of victory would
create a mood in which such difficulties could be overcome. Perhaps the socialist leaders assumed a little too easily, from past
experience, that the communist leaders would share their anxiety
to reassure middle-of-the-road voters, and would therefore agree
in the end that any changes in the 1972 text should be in the direction of moderation and realism.

At first, indeed, it seemed that the PCF might be trying to out-flank the PS by moving further and faster into 'realism', when in May 1977 it suddenly announced its conversion to the French nuclear strike force – a decision which the PS had been manoeuvring towards for some years in spite of strong internal resistance. Later in the summer the PCF embarrassed the PS by its robust defence of France's civil nuclear-energy programme, which had run into strong opposition from the 'ecologist' lobby – the newest and most vigorous form taken by youthful protest in France. The 'ecologists' were generally closer to the PS than to other conventional parties in their outlook, and their candidates were thus a potential threat to the PS on the first ballot. Accordingly, Mitterrand tried to hedge on the nuclear issue, suggesting that it might be dealt with by a referendum after the election. The communists were not inclined to let him off so lightly, and the referendum suggestion was greeted with outraged scorn by Marchais as well as by the parties in power.

But it was not until September that the full scope of the communist campaign became clear. The main issue on which negotiations finally broke down was the extent of the nationalization programme. The communists insisted that the 1972 programme implied the complete nationalization, not only of the groups named, but of all companies in which they had a holding of more than 50 per cent. This claim was resisted by the socialists and the small, often-forgotten third party to the alliance, the Mouvement des Radicaux de Gauche (MRG). The socialists pointed out that the state would gain indirect control of the subsidiaries anyway, and that to mark them down for full nationalization would mean taking over well over 1,000 firms – a figure which could easily be used by the Right to intimidate the floating voter.

It rapidly became apparent that the PCF leaders did not want to reach agreement. The final session of negotiations was broken off without any serious discussion of socialist counter-proposals, which included some significant concessions, and almost simultaneously an edition of *L'Humanité* was on the streets including a cartoon which showed President Giscard d'Estaing thanking Mitterrand and the MRG leader, Robert Fabre, for their alleged betrayal of the union of the Left. This has been the constant theme of PCF propaganda ever since: the PS had 'veered to the right' and was secretly preparing to do a deal with Giscard for a new centre-left government which would exclude the PCF and would maintain the economic and social *status quo*. The socialists replied by protesting their fidelity to the programme of 1972, even without updating if necessary, and their determination to go into government only as part of a union of the Left, rejecting any reversion to the strategy of the 'Troisième Force'.

The communist accusations lacked credibility, and had manifestly issued from some secret decision of the politburo. (Many believed that Marchais, hitherto strongly identified with the policy of left-wing unity, must have been outvoted and now be applying a policy with which he did not really agree.) The rank and file of the party had had nothing to do with the origins of the campaign, and were clearly bewildered by it. The leadership had to embark on a series of intensive explanations to make it clear that the breach was the fault of the socialists, and these appear to have been only very partially successful.

Some observers were inclined to see the change as resulting from a victory for pro-Soviet forces within the party, and intended to serve Soviet interests by avoiding a left-wing victory in France and so preserving the European *status quo*. It seems more likely, however, that the campaign was a reaction of self-defence against the PS's success. The strategy of the union of the Left had been predicated on the ability of the PCF to hegemonize the Left and to remain the uncontested 'party of the working class'. A left-wing government in which the PCF would be reduced to the role of junior partner (*force d'appoint*) was of little interest. The risks involved were too great: the economic circumstances (world depression) and the constitutional circumstances (a parliamentary election, leaving the Right in control of the all-important presidency of the republic) were both unfavourable to the Left in 1978. A predominantly socialist government would be likely either to collapse quickly or to pursue an essentially reformist policy, rapidly resorting to classic deflationary measures to stabilize the economy. (The examples of Britain and Portugal have been cited.) The PCF leaders may well have calculated that the result was more likely to be a setback than an advance for their own strategy of initiating fundamental changes in French social and economic relations – that *démocratie avancée* which was to be a form of transition to socialism. The priority for them was to reassert their own party's image as the party of the working class, the poor and the underprivileged, in contrast to the reformism, technocracy and opportunism of the PS. Thus one of the main planks in their election platform was the immediate raising of the minimum monthly wage from 1,700 to 2,400 francs – a plank which the PS soon felt politically obliged to endorse against the advice of its own economists.

From this point of view, the PCF's campaign may be considered a half-success. The PCF's own share of the vote did decline by comparison with 1973, but not dramatically (from 21·4 to 20·6 per cent). The PS did overtake the PCF for the first time in a national election since 1936, but much less dramatically than it had hoped. Instead of the 27 or 30 per cent predicted by opinion polls, it obtained 22·6 (24·7 if the MRG votes are included). And the Left did not win the election. The perils of governing in un-favourable circumstances were thus avoided. The PCF acquired more time: time in which the PS might be weakened, if it did not disintegrate, under the pressure of mutual recriminations about responsibility for failure and the emergence of contradictions hitherto contained by the strong personality of Mitterrand and the strong expectation of success. Time too, perhaps, in which the PCF could continue its own evolution towards Euro-communism.

For it is by no means certain that the events between September 1977 and March 1978 mark a definitive halt in that evolution. Even at the height of the anti-socialist campaign the decisions of the Twenty-second Congress were recalled and reiterated. The specific policies put forward by the PCF were clearly very differ-ent from those currently proposed by the PCI (austerity, Euro-pean integration and so on). But it could be argued that the objective of the PCF is to reach the position which the PCI already enjoys – that of being the dominant force on the Left. To reach that position it might be necessary to reintroduce, temporarily and somewhat artificially, an atmosphere of cold war in order to divide and discredit the socialists. But once the objective was achieved, it might well be as necessary in France as in Italy to propose a 'historic compromise' in order to obtain for a communist-dominated Left a share in power.

Such may or may not be the dreams of Marchais and his colleagues. But, at the same time, their tactical manipulation of their party (reminiscent of some of the clumsiest manoeuvres imposed in the past by the Comintern) is in such glaring contrast with their proclaimed belief in liberalism and democracy that it appears to have provoked a genuine crisis not only among the rank and file (who are liable to 'vote with their feet' simply by not turning up to cell or section meetings) but also among the cadres. The extent of this crisis is as yet (in the summer of 1978) difficult to gauge. If it is quickly contained and the façade of unanimity restored, the rest of the world will conclude that the PCF has not, after all, changed in its fundamental nature. If it is allowed to run its course, it is just possible that a genuinely democratic communist party may at last emerge.

Notes and references

1. Interview in *The Times*, 18 November 1946.

2. Jacques Fauvet, *Histoire du Parti Communiste français 1920–1976*, Paris, 1977, p. 523.

3. Quoted by Jacques Ozouf in *Esprit*, February 1975, p. 187.

4. *Le Monde*, 16 May 1974, p. 44.

5. See F. Claudín, *The Communist Movement from Comintern to Cominform* (English translation), Harmondsworth, 1975, pp. 316–79.

6. ibid., pp. 381–5.

7. Institut Maurice Thorez, *La Marche de la France au Socialisme*, Paris, 1966, p. 71.

8. Fauvet, p. 532. Even before this, the Seventeenth Congress of the PCF (1964) had rejected the notion that a one-party state was necessary for the construction of socialism. See Jean Elleinstein, *Le P.C.*, Paris, 1976, p. 15.

9. Quoted by W. Rochet, *L'Avenir du Parti Communiste français*, Paris, 1969, p. 117.

10. Parti Communiste français, *Changer de cap: programme pour un gouvernement démocratique d'union populaire*, Paris, 1971, p. 128.

11. *Le Programme commun de gouvernement* (supplement to *L'Humanité*, 28 June 1972), p. 10.

12. Possibly there was also a growing financial independence of the PCF, whose business enterprises, at first heavily dependent on Soviet and East European concessions, were by now able to stand on their own feet.

13. Fauvet, *Histoire du Parti Communiste français*, p. 523.

14. ibid., p. 529.

15. ibid., p. 562.

16. Ronald Tiersky, 'Le PCF et la détente', in *Esprit*, February 1975, p. 224.

17. Ronald Tiersky, 'French Communism in 1976', in *Problems of Communism*, 1976, p. 41.

18. *L'Humanité*, 15 January 1976 (quoted by Tiersky in art. cit. n. 17, p. 42).

19. Elleinstein, *Le P.C.*, p. 19.

20. *L'Humanité*, 5 February 1976 (quoted by Tiersky in art. cit. n. 17, p. 47). All these decisions of the Twenty-second Congress were bluntly recalled by Marchais in his speech at the Berlin Conference of European Communist Parties when it finally met in June 1976. He even questioned the utility of such gatherings, and said he did not expect to take part in any more.

21. See *Le Monde*, 5 October 1977: 'M. Poperen (PS): l'objectif du PCF est de détruire la social-démocratie'.

22. For instance, by Georges Lavau in *Esprit*, February 1975, p. 175.

23. Elleinstein, *Le P.C.*, p. 111.

24. ibid., p. 98.

Select bibliography

Jean Elleinstein, *Le P.C.*, Paris, 1976.
Jacques Fauvet, *Histoire du Parti Communiste français* (new one-volume edition), Paris, 1977.
André Harris and Alain de Sedouy, *Voyage à l'intérieur du Parti Communiste*, Paris, 1974.
Annie Kriegel, *Les Communistes français* (revised edition), Paris, 1970.
——, *Un Autre Communisme?*, Paris, 1977.
Georges Marchais, *Le Défi démocratique*, Paris, 1973.
Jean Montaldo, *Les Finances du P.C.F.*, Paris, 1977.
Ronald Tiersky, *French Communism, 1920–1972*, New York, 1974.

5. El pacto para la libertad: the Spanish Communist Party

Jonathan Story

For nearly forty years after General Franco's victory over the Spanish Republic in 1939, the Communist Party of Spain (PCE) was torn between its ties to Moscow, its political roots in Spain and its internal rivalries. As long as loyalties to Moscow predominated, the party's existence posed few difficulties: Franco's caricature of the party as an agent of Soviet imperialism needed no denying and provided free propaganda. But, as relations between Moscow and Madrid became more cordial in the 1960s and memories of the Spanish Civil War faded, so loyalty to the Soviet Union became a less rewarding policy. There was the suspicion that if Franco could be brought to offer Moscow an adequate prize, perhaps in the form of Soviet access to Spanish ports, the Soviet Union would be tempted to deliver the party's militants to the régime. There was also the realization that, following Franco's eventual death, few Spaniards would be eager to exchange his dictatorship for the dictatorship of the proletariat.

This process of questioning the received canons of a faith defined in Moscow was accelerated by the split in the communist movement with the break between Moscow and Peking, and by the transformation of Spanish society as the country industrialized. Millions of Spaniards flocked from the countryside into the major industrial agglomerations around Madrid, the Basque country and Catalonia. Far from collapsing, the Spanish economy boomed as it had never done, growing at a rate only slightly less than Japan's. Greater economic freedoms along with the declining influence of the state syndicates and the régime's policy of centralization ignited national sentiment, particularly among the Basques and Catalans. In these conditions, it became increasingly meaningless for the PCE to toe the Moscow line: the Kremlin knew even less about what was going on in Spain than the exiled party leadership in Prague. The Warsaw Pact's invasion of Czechoslovakia in 1968 therefore set a seal on the party's development: to play a major role in Spain after the dictator's death, the party had to establish its own independence, to develop a separate ideological identity and integrate more closely into Spanish society. In the early 1970s, the party's protection seemed to stretch out to cover the protagonists of armed violence; but it also itself appeared as a viable interlocutor to conservatives. Carrillo has presented moderation as a revolutionary platform, but he has not allayed the suspicions in the party that he may be a reformer at heart, nor has the party yet convinced the country at large that it is as Eurocommunist as it claims to be.

The PCE diverges from Moscow

Carrillo's frequent appeals to his fellow-countrymen to forget the past are not explained solely out of his desire to avoid provoking the sensitivities of the armed forces, or out of his commitment to install a more democratic system in Spain. The party has never conducted a public appraisal of its policies during the Civil War, and has sought to avoid any discussion on the many bloody intrigues that punctuated the long years of its clandestine operations against the Franco régime. Little may be gained by resuscitating old passions, and, as Carrillo indicated in January 1978, when a former party member, Jorge Semprun, published his autobiography,[1] insinuations of the leadership's treacherous carelessness only provide grist to the mill of the PCE's enemies. The fact that Carrillo lumped the Soviet Union with the United States as objectively interested in avoiding a Western communist party's participation in government is less significant, perhaps, than the fact that the book touched on one of the party's more sensitive spots. General Franco's decision to execute Julian Grimau, a member of the central committee, on 20 April 1963 marked a decisive turning-point in the PCE's relations with Moscow.

One of the most prestigious parties of the Comintern in the 1930s was the PCE. The general elections of February 1936 had provided a working majority for the political parties of the Popular Front, a name suggested by the PCE in pursuance of Stalin's policy of promoting alliances between communists and social democrats against 'fascist' parties. The National Front of conservative parties took fright, and violence mounted as revolutionary proclamations were countered by plottings and murders. On 13 July 1936, Calvo Sotelo, the monarchist deputy, was taken from his home, pushed into the back of a car and shot twice in the back of the neck. His murderers, associated with the young Santiago Carrillo's Socialist-Communist United Youth Movement, deposited the body at the Madrid cemetery. On 18 July, General Franco pronounced against the Spanish Republic. That evening, Dolores Ibarruri, known as 'La Pasionaria', delivered an impassioned speech, urging Spaniards to violent resistance against the insurgents. 'It is better,' she cried, 'to die on your feet than live on your knees! *No pasarán!*' [2]

As the war intensified, the PCE became the predominant party in the republic. Small property-holders, terrified by the more numerous anarchists, looked to the party as a bastion of law and order, and communist control over training assured a steady stream of new recruits. The party's importance in the republic's war effort was magnified by the arms, advisers and International Brigades sent by the Comintern, and its primacy was assured through the overthrow of the socialist leader, Largo Caballero, the liquidation of the anarchists, and the crushing of the breakaway party associated in Stalin's mind with Trotsky, the POUM, at the height of the purges in Russia. But the republic's fortunes waned, and after the Munich conference of 1938 between Hitler and Chamberlain, Stalin wrote the Spanish Republic off and turned his efforts towards an arrangement with Germany. With victory assured, Franco laid the foundations of his régime. Communists and freemasons were outlawed; class war was 'abolished' and Spain declared a 'vast syndicate of producers'. Repression was fierce, as many as 200,000 people being shot, many communists among them. The communist leaders in exile in Latin

America, France or the Soviet Union were completely dependent on Stalin. This dependence was not regretted by Carrillo, who has recalled thinking of British and French political leaders of the time, 'those swine deserve what they get'.[3]

Little is recorded of the PCE's reaction to the momentous news of the Stalin–Hitler Pact. But the rancours of defeat left the PCE isolated from other anti-Franco forces, who hoped for Allied intervention in Spain once the world war against Hitler was won. In Moscow, the party's leaders were wracked by recriminations, while scores in Spain were allegedly settled through betrayals to the Spanish police. For a brief moment, the PCE joined the National Alliance of Democratic Forces set up by republicans and socialists in 1944. But then the Cold War, with the slow rapprochement between the United States and the Franco régime, led to a split in the alliance over relations to the monarchists and the PCE. Communist guerrillas, operating from south-west France, met with an indifferent peasantry, while the urban proletariat was cowed by the police and by hunger. Grass became a staple diet, and Spain's population of cats and dogs dwindled. Enrique Lister, the party's military expert, later admitted that up to 15,000 communists lost their lives in the guerrilla war with Franco's Civil Guard between 1944 and 1949.[4]

Stalin was the first to propose an abandonment of the armed struggle in Spain and an accommodation to the realities of Franco's rule. Carrillo records the following meeting with the Spanish communist leaders in the Kremlin in 1948 and describes his and La Pasionaria's sentiments on being ushered into Stalin's quarters in the Kremlin.

We were very excited. The day after our arrival, in the afternoon, we were told: 'Comrade Stalin is waiting for you.' We went ... to his office. Molotov and Suslov were present. Stalin received us cordially, and impressed us by asking us news of each one of our companions, calling them by their names. 'It seems,' said Stalin, referring to the communist guerrilla leader, 'that Lister feels little affection for the Soviet Union.' I did not know what he was referring to; but Dolores did. 'He is becoming more prudent.' He asked us: 'Continue your guerrilla activities in Spain, but why not work in the legal organizations of the masses? Your work in these organizations is weak. The Bolshevik experience proves that it can be done. You must have patience. Then, when you are strong, strike.' The essential question was that we work in the fascist syndicates and organizations. We had a very spirited discussion. How were we going to work in the fascist organizations, so discredited with workers? But the truth is [Carrillo concluded] our position was sectarian and leftist.[5]

Stalin's realism marked the beginning of a long march through the Franco régime's institutions. The failure took twenty years to realize. But, initially, the policy met with some success. As the PCE began the arduous task of infiltrating Franco's official unions, penetrating the universities and entering the Church's Catholic Action, the Soviets returned prisoners from the Blue Division, sent by Franco to fight on the Russian front in 1941, and in 1955 voted for Franco Spain's membership in the United Nations. After Khrushchev's denunciations of Stalin in 1956, Carrillo – already affirming his leadership in the party – announced his policy of National Reconciliation. The policy stood for cooperation with other opposition parties in exile, or outlawed in Spain, and cooperation with Franco's disaffected followers. Khrushchev's overtures to the Western powers thus complemented Carrillo's proposals for class collaboration. The party's Stalinists had little option but to follow suit – especially in view of the policy's paternity.

Franco's appointment of a new cabinet in February 1957 represented a major turning-point in the régime's history. A new economic policy was required to cure the country's endemic inflation, and the task of the new cabinet – strongly backed by the United States – was to dismantle controls and open Spain's frontiers to foreign investment. A harsh austerity policy followed, leading to bankruptcies, higher unemployment and mass migrations. Carrillo considered the régime on the verge of collapse, but police powers were strengthened. An apathetic population ignored the party's appeal for a 'Day of National Reconciliation' in April 1958, and for a 'National Peaceful Strike' in June 1959. To boost the party's flagging morale, the leaders turned their attention to foreign affairs.

The Spanish-American base agreements of 1953 had firmly established United States influence in Spain. Franco was thereby committed to a policy of trade liberalization, and America to propping up the régime with loans and military equipment. But as the arms race between the great powers developed, so American nuclear weapons were stockpiled on Spanish soil. A West German effort to develop a missile system in collaboration with the Franco régime only served to strengthen the Kremlin's view of the Western alliance as inspired by West German 'revanchist' policies. So, in October 1961, the PCE central committee opened a vigorous campaign against the American bases and Spain's eventual association with the European Economic Community (EEC). The base agreements were coming up for renegotiation, and in February 1962 Spain applied for associate status with the EEC. Spain's outlawed political parties, assembling in Munich as guests of the European Movement, passed a motion in the absence of the communists – who were not invited – requesting member states to reject the régime's application until Western democratic institutions had been introduced.

The Munich meeting effectively barred Spain's association with the EEC. But the Spanish outlawed opposition's demands for democratic change at Madrid, as a prerequisite to Spain's membership in the community, embarrassed the PCE in its relations with the Soviets. Opposition to Spain's membership isolated the communists from other Spanish democratic groups, and identified the party with Moscow's hostility to the Community. The Soviets preferred Franco in power, and Spain as a diplomatic pariah in the Western alliance, to an eventual democratic government at Madrid with the credentials to bring Spain into the EEC. To the Soviets, the EEC had to be stopped; acquiescence in Franco's order was not considered too high a price in Moscow.

There was more trouble in store for the PCE in its relations with the Soviets, this time over Julian Grimau. Grimau, a central committee member wanted by Franco's police for crimes allegedly committed during the Civil War, had been sent to Madrid for clandestine work. Semprun, in his autobiography, has written that, in the summer of 1962, he reported to the central committee that Grimau's methods were dangerously careless: in particular, he went to meetings in Madrid without checking whom he was going to see. Grimau, Semprun proposed, should be withdrawn immediately.[6] His advice was not heeded. In September 1962, Grimau was betrayed, and the police surprised to find that such a senior party official, with such a price on his head, had fallen into their hands. Carrillo was immediately accused by the régime of knowingly sending Grimau to his death, and the suspicion preyed on the minds of party members that the party needed a martyr to deflect attention from the inadequacies of its analysis of the domestic situation in Spain. Furthermore, the Soviet Union, in the aftermath of the Cuban missile crisis, wanted to improve relations with Madrid but to exclude Spain from membership in NATO or the EEC. So Khrushchev sent Franco a note on 19 April 1963, appealing for clemency in the case of Grimau for humanitarian reasons. Franco replied, explaining his reasons for the execution, and signing himself 'Chief of State of Spain'.[7] Both states thus achieved their immediate objectives: the outcry in Europe against Grimau's execution assured the Soviets that there would be no membership for Spain in NATO or the EEC; Franco resumed diplomatic negotiations with the Kremlin, facilitating Madrid's rapprochement with Castro's Cuba. In other words, there is sufficient circumstantial evidence to suspect that Grimau was a victim of *raison d'état*, and that the PCE central committee was aware of it.

With Spain excluded from NATO, Moscow's next priority was to have the US nuclear base at Rota, on Spain's southern Atlantic coast, closed to America's Polaris submarines. In May, the Spanish government received a Soviet note proposing the Mediterranean's denuclearization, and responded by adhering to the Test-Ban Treaty. The base agreements were signed in September, but Franco Spain launched its campaign against Gibraltar as an Anglo-Saxon base in Iberia. In December, Sergei Vinogradov, Soviet ambassador in Paris, toasted the 'establishment of diplomatic relations this year between Spain and the Soviet Union'. Khrushchev also sent a note to Franco as 'Chief of State', inviting Spanish diplomatic support for recognition of post-war boundaries, especially East Germany's. This courtship was interrupted by President Johnson early in 1964 with hints of a cut in military aid and a reduction of American investments in Spain. In February 1964, the American Department of Defense posted Polaris submarines at Rota harbour, apparently without Spain's permission. Thus, as Soviet nuclear weaponry expanded in range, American warheads stockpiled on Spanish soil became a viable target for a Soviet nuclear offensive, placing further strains on the PCE in its relations to Moscow. It was with 'considerable emotion'[8] that the PCE recorded Khrushchev's deposition by the more conservative Brezhnev, Kosygin and Podgorny.

As relations between Madrid and Moscow improved, so the PCE's subservience to Soviet foreign policy became increasingly harmful to its reputation in Spain. Closer ties were established with the Italian communists, and more overt support given to Romania. Meanwhile, Franco's foreign minister, Castiella, openly wooed Soviet support on Gibraltar and attempted to restrict Western overflight rights after an American plane had accidentally disgorged an atomic bomb near the village of Palomares, Almería; fortunately, the bomb never detonated. Consular relations were resumed with Romania in January 1967, and a shipping convention was concluded with the Soviet Union in February. Madrid supported the Palestinian cause in the June 1967 war between Israel and Egypt, and at the United Nations in December secured Latin American, Moslem and Eastern Bloc votes on Gibraltar.

That October, Ibarruri, on the occasion of the fiftieth anniversary of the October Revolution, praised the Red Army as the backbone of revolution in Eastern Europe.[9] But the strains between the Soviet and Spanish communists were not so easily glossed over. The Soviet newspaper, *Isvestia*, at that time featured an article favouring the Spanish monarchy. The PCE strongly objected, and *Isvestia* retracted. But the incident left its mark: the PCE withdrew its previous support in favour of full diplomatic relations between Moscow and Madrid.[10] Spain's communists were no longer willing to subordinate policies to the dictates of Soviet foreign policy.

Towards a new policy

By 1964, it was becoming evident that the political situation in Spain no longer allowed for a comfortable dialectic of loyalty to the Soviets and enmity to the Franco régime. For years, the party leaders had boosted the militants' morale with optimistic predictions of the régime's imminent collapse. But the régime endured. Franco began to appear *inmorible* – 'undiable'. After the austerity policies of 1959, the bankruptcy rate rose along with unemployment, and Spain's trade account moved to surplus. Wages were frozen. But the inflow of money from tourism stimulated the economy towards the end of 1961, leading to a series of strikes in April and May the following year. Contrary to communist expectations, the workers were primarily concerned with wage levels and prices, not with unattainable revolutionary ideals. Franco soon recovered his composure, reshuffled his cabinet ministers, proposed more press liberties and had state-planning techniques imported from France. The Bank of Spain was nationalized and a Four-Year Plan drawn up. The régime began to secrete its own legitimacy.

What was the PCE to do? It could continue to preach revolution in the desert: that policy had proved barren. It could advocate the régime's transformation to a Western-style system with free parties and trade unions, as proposed by other Spanish opposition leaders; but the risk of a break with the Soviets was high. Finally, the PCE could work for the régime's 'democratization', preserving the single-party state and the official syndicate.

In March 1964, Fernando Claudín, a prominent member of the central committee, raised the problem of party policy in Franco Spain from the obscurity where others may have preferred it to remain. Claudin argued[11] that Franco's 'Prussian state' was revolutionizing Spain's society and economy with its vigorous interventions in every aspect of the country's life. The armed forces and police provided ample guarantee that this change would not lead to collapse. Smaller capitalists were dependent on monopolist business, either through subcontracting or by their need for external financing. Consequently, the chances of winning over the middle classes to a broad alliance with the workers against the régime were minimal. Smaller capitalists were locked into a para-statal system, where the central authorities were no longer content to act as nightwatchman to the 'laws' of the market, but were themselves active participants. The new industrial working class constituted the main agent of revolutionary change. Their task – the 'seizure of power in this state' – was facilitated by the convergence between monopoly capitalists and Spanish opposition leaders towards agreement on the need for a régime of political liberties. In this more relaxed atmosphere, the party could afford to loosen central discipline and not claim sole possession of the truth. Such claims, Claudín argued, were the fundamental cause of the grave 'deformations' in Eastern Europe.

Claudín was ousted from the party, but over the coming years the party absorbed some of his ideas. The process was slow, delayed by internal struggles invisible to the outsider. Carrillo's first public response came in the form of a book, *After Franco, What?* (1965). Contrary to Claudín, Carrillo argued that Spain was still afflicted by uneven economic development between an archaic and a modern sector. The state's actions only served to aggravate contradictions, thereby promoting constant crises in Spain. Consequently, the party had to retain strict central discipline in order both to infiltrate the state syndicates and to forge a broad alliance between the workers and other classes for the establishment of a parliamentary state. Thus, Carrillo proposed an evolution of the régime's state syndicate into a democratically elected organization as the vehicle for a régime of social and economic democracy in Spain. But he urged a fundamental break with the single-party state and a return to 'bourgeois parliamentary liberties'. Political parties represented class interests, and these had to find expression in an open political system. The instability attributed to parliamentary systems, Carrillo argued, flowed from the lack of social and economic democracy, not from any inherent defect of the parliamentary system.

To some, both Carrillo's and Claudín's arguments smacked of revisionism. A Maoist party was set up late in 1963, leading to a complex proliferation of Chinese, Marxist-Leninist and Trotskyite factions over the coming years. But the party remained firmly under Carrillo's control. A declaration was published in June 1964, advocating Italian parliamentary tactics 'for the effective liquidation of fascist forms of government'. In September, the first officially recognized worker commission was elected in the presence of the state syndicate representatives. Police operations against communists were attenuated, prison sentences reduced, and union officials from Moscow invited to Spain. But the commission leaders – whose communist affiliations were publicly revealed in 1976 – overplayed their hand, alienating both syndical officials as well as anarchists and socialists. In October 1966, elections to the syndicates none the less resulted in a massive victory, with an 80 to 90 per cent turnout of the workforce. At the same time, the authorities became disturbed at communist cooperation with sympathizers in Catholic Action. The organization was purged, rigorous censorship was imposed on Catholic publications, and a highly restrictive Law on Religious Liberty was passed.

Thus, by the time of Franco's December 1966 referendum on the Organic Law, designed to perpetuate the Generalissimo's state beyond his grave, the PCE's strategy of infiltration of legal institutions, as recommended by Stalin in 1948, was played out. The party called for abstention, and a 'Day of National Action' in January 1967. This marked the end of the régime's truce with the PCE. The worker commissions were outlawed in March, and representatives elected in the October 1966 syndicate elections were dismissed. Anarchists and socialists left the commissions in the summer. The régime's police apparatus was further strengthened, and Admiral Carrero Blanco was appointed Franco's vice-president of the Council of Ministers. He replaced General Muñoz Grandes, who had done much to promote a policy of national reconciliation from within the régime. The admiral's views were reminiscent of the 1940s. Carrillo addressed himself to these adverse developments in the PCE's Spanish and international affairs in a book whose title translates into English as *New Aspects of Today's Problems* (published late 1967).[12] Significantly,

Carrillo recognized a common interest for representative government in Spain between the PCE and the 'evolutionists' in the régime, anxious for Spain's eventual membership in the EEC. This argument was elaborated and repeated with increasing frequency over the coming years, as the party came to appreciate the European Community cause as favourable to political liberalization in Spain. But, in the context of 1967, it may also be read as Carrillo's realization that little was to be hoped for from Stalin's strategy of infiltration. Simply, Franco's state and syndicates were not suitable to Spain. Spain had to reject 'what was purely Russian in the revolution': a single party and the lack of liberties. Spaniards, he wrote, felt 'a deep demand for liberty and democracy'. The various class interests had to be represented in political parties, competing for votes in an open political system rooted in universal suffrage. As the mass of Spaniards were now salary earners, the dictatorship of the proletariat would emerge spontaneously, leading to 'government of the people, by the people and for the people'. There was no reason why the communists should be sole executors of that dictatorship, nor for the dictatorship to negate the political laws of the bourgeoisie.

The sophistry was painful. But so was Carrillo's predicament as his control over the party became less secure. After the split with the socialists and anarchists in late 1967, a new central organization of the worker commissions was set up in Paris, with parallel powers to Carrillo's party secretariat. It benefited by the patronage of the PCF, with its strong ties to Moscow. Moscow may have been disturbed at the direction Carrillo seemed to be taking, judging by the *Isvestia* article already referred to, and the many Moscow loyalists in the party made intervention by the Soviets a relatively easy matter. Dolores Ibarruri, decorated in 1965 with the Order of Lenin, lived in Moscow. Enrique Lister, a legendary figure among the rank and file, had worked for the Soviets in Eastern Europe and Latin America. He received a pension from the Red Army. Another Moscow loyalist was Eduardo García Lopez, who had commanded a brigade at the Ebro at the age of nineteen; his younger colleague, Agustín Gómez, had played football for the Soviet Union. Many less exalted party members had returned to Spain from the Soviet

Union, some with Russian wives. The party secretariat was located in Prague, and most financing came from Eastern Bloc countries.

Carrillo's own reputation as a Stalinist was second to none. He had established his position in the party through his deft handling of Lister in the guerrilla campaign waged from France against Franco's Civil Guard. Khrushchev's revelations on Stalin's persecution of communists came, he argued in 1975, as a 'shock' to him, but he was none the less unwilling to abandon 'democratic centralism' – the ideological justification for his authority in the party – 'as long as fascism exists'.[13] Furthermore, he always assured himself of Ibarruri's support, thus legitimizing his real power exercised through the secretariat. With a handful of friends, he controlled promotions, finance and the flow of information. An executive committee was supposed to control the secretariat between the central committee meetings, which received instructions theoretically from the party congress. But meetings were few and far between. Militants found attendance risky, and there was the ever-present danger of the police stooge.

Another reason for the rigid authoritarian structure of the party was Carrillo's fear that the other communist parties might exploit rifts between the PCE hierarchs. Conversely, to avoid confrontation, the party leadership was willing to reach compromises on policy between internal factions at the cost of ideological consistency. Claudin's exclusion in 1964 may be explained in this manner. A clearer ideological line risked splitting the party, in particular in the sensitive matter of relations to Moscow. But the price paid was continued ambiguity, which the pressure of events in Spain and in the world communist movement refused to tolerate. This became particularly evident as a younger generation of communist worker leaders came to the fore in Spain. Their Marxism was, in many ways, more sophisticated than the older generation's, though it would be rash to assume that these younger communists were necessarily opposed to policies identified in official circles with Stalin. Their main characteristic was impatience with the older generation. In 1967, Carrillo had to chide younger party members to pay greater respect to their elders.

This, then, was the condition in which the party confronted

the news of Antonin Novotny's overthrow in Czechoslovakia in January 1968. Members of the secretariat, located in Prague, observed events at first hand; Moscow's rendering of events therefore proved difficult to credit. Furthermore, the Soviet Union's priorities in foreign affairs, and especially on the German problem, seemed to contradict the PCE's priority for a parliamentary régime in Spain. Moscow had to secure Franco's support as an additional vote in favour of a European settlement; amicable exchanges were therefore essential. In return, Franco demanded reduced Soviet support for the Spanish communists.

The PCE and the Soviet invasion of Czechoslovakia

Spanish communist party leaders were greatly relieved at the turn of events in Czechoslovakia early in 1968. At last the Soviets had an opportunity to grant greater autonomy to local communist parties, and thereby – as Carrillo wrote – 'to recover the initiative in the ideological struggle against imperialism'. Santiago Álvarez, a senior party official, writing in April, expressed the PCE's 'great sympathy' for Dubček's reforms, and described the new Czechoslovakian Action Programme as outlining the 'type of socialist society we think we must have in Spain'.[14] Spanish communist exiles living in Prague witnessed the enthusiastic worker demonstrations of 1 May, while the PCE stressed Czechoslovakia's success in introducing measures 'to democratize the party and the state'. The parallel to Franco Spain's failure to democratize between 1963 and 1966 was patent. All the more disturbing, therefore, were the Soviet Union's evident preparations to crush Dubček's experiment. What would Spaniards – with their 'deep demand' for liberties – think of a pro-Soviet communist party which had once again condoned the suppression of liberties in Eastern Europe?

Moscow's invasion of Czechoslovakia on 21 August 1968 forced Carrillo to take the plunge. On 22 August, he and Ibarruri, with the Italian communist leaders, met Mikhail Suslov, the Soviet ideologist. Suslov had attended the meeting with Stalin in 1948.

'The talks were most painful,' Carrillo records.[15] 'At one instant
Suslov brushed aside PCE objections with the remark: "After
all, you are only a small party." '[16] No agreement was reached,
and on 23 August Radio España Independiente declared the PCE
executive committee's 'contrary opinion to the armed invasion in
Czechoslovakia'. The statement was strengthened in an article in
Mundo Obrero on 15 September, when the PCE declared that
any military invasion in Spain of the type undertaken by the
Warsaw Pact in Czechoslovakia would meet with 'the most
energetic resistance'.[17] This was ratified by the central committee
by 65 votes to 5. Lister later recorded his dissent.

By comparison with the Claudín affair, and with the leftist
splits of the 1960s, a clash with Lister was a very serious matter.
Lister was number three in the party hierarchy, enjoyed much
prestige among the rank and file and had powerful friends in the
Soviet Union. His challenge represented a direct attack on Carrillo's leadership in the party. So Carrillo first edged Lister's lesser
supporters out of the central committee, and then secured the
backing of Ibarruri. Lister's publication of an open letter in January 1970 denouncing Carrillo seems to have roused the old lady's
ire. 'Splittism' was a sin she could not forgive. Thus a fragile
peace was established between Moscow and the PCE on the basis
of a joint communiqué signed in Moscow in April between Ibarruri and Carrillo on the one hand and Suslov on the other. The
communiqué declared each party's intention to 'reinforce the
combined struggle of both parties ... against political and military
revanchism, fascist foci, and the intangibility of post-war frontiers, especially the recognition of the German Democratic Republic as an independent state'.[18] The communiqué deprived
Lister of full Soviet support, and he was eased from the party in
September 1970. The step was taken by the central committee,
which Carrillo had expanded for the occasion from 82 to 111
members.

Soviet diplomatic wooing of Franco, however, led to a straight-
forward conflict of interest with the Spanish communists. The
Soviets needed the United States' consecration of the German
Democratic Republic, and appeared willing to trade that for

acceptance of the *status quo* in Spain. In the longer term, the Soviets and the PCE as Marxists could anticipate a new convergence of interests as the Western economic crisis deepened and the differences between the EEC and the United States became more acute. Franco's Spain was condemned by the 'laws of history'. In the meantime, contradictions between Soviet state interests and Spanish communist party needs in Spain could be discounted as inherent to a still imperfect world. But such augmentation seemed peculiarly inappropriate in the circumstances, with Franco praising the Soviet Union and Polish coal being imported to break Asturian coal strikes. Consequently, Carrillo, in a series of statements between 1968 and 1970, elaborated on his ideas on autonomy for individual parties within the world communist movement.[19]

In essence, Carrillo argued that relations between communist parties in Eastern and Western Europe had to be conceived on an entirely new basis. Communist parties outside the Soviet sphere of influence had to detach themselves from Soviet state policies and to develop revolutionary strategies suited to national conditions. The world communist movement had to be organized anew, with no new centre claiming a monopoly on truth. Each party had to enjoy 'creative capacity', to wage the ideological struggle which lay at the heart of Khrushchev's policy of peaceful coexistence between states of different social systems. If the communists were denied these liberties, the capitalists would retain the ideological initiative, thereby increasing the risk of war innate in capitalist states. A European peace had to be secured, not so much by the deterrent effect of nuclear weapons as by the transformation of capitalist states from within. Communist parties had therefore to emerge from the ghetto into which conservative governments had banned them, because of their loyalty to Moscow, by paying closer attention to national problems. 'Life,' Carrillo declared, 'shows that vitality of national sentiment is a factor of enormous force.' Western communist parties, in short, needed a free hand to pursue the class struggle in their own countries.

The PCE, Carrillo argued, was ready to conclude a Pact of

Liberty with all Franco's opponents to reinstall a parliamentary system in Spain. The PCE viewed socialism 'as a régime in which the political, cultural and individual liberties that the bourgeois revolution won in its struggle with feudal society . . . are developed, and merged with fundamental liberties, that only socialism can assure men, ending capitalist exploitation, oppression and inequalities . . . Our vision of socialism considers pluripartism . . . as one of the characteristics peculiar to the Spanish revolution.' 'Political liberties,' Carrillo added in September 1970 at the time of Lister's dismissal from the party, 'are a great conquest of the working class and the people, the most favourable platform in a capitalist régime to organize and prepare forces capable of realizing the socialist revolution.' The ultimate objective was the 'radical democratization of the apparatus of the state and all institutions in society'.[20]

Carrillo's renewed emphasis on parliamentary liberties and union freedoms led inevitably to a more critical attitude to Eastern European states. Early in 1970, a number of articles appeared in *Nuestra Bandera* attacking Stalin's 'despotic authoritarianism'. Manuel Azcárate, a prominent personality in the PCE, wrote an article entitled 'What is Going On in Socialist Countries?'[21] The Poznan riots in Poland that summer were caused, wrote Azcárate, by insufficient decentralization in the economy, by too much authoritarianism and by abuse of the Red Army. Such hostile remarks redoubled when Lister, financed by the Soviets, the Czechs and the Poles, held his own party congress in April 1971, and attempted to seat his supporters, along with an official delegation, at the World Peace Council in Budapest in May. Simultaneously, Soviet press comments on the Franco régime became more favourable, stressing Spain's 'independent' line in foreign policy. After President Nixon's visit to Moscow in July 1972, the Soviets signed a trade agreement with Spain in September, and pointedly ignored Carrillo's request at the PCE Eighth Congress in the same month by accepting the Franco government's delegation at the Helsinki talks on security in December – 'without protest', as the communist Radio España Independiente pointed out.[22] In January 1973, East Germany's resumption of diplomatic relations with Madrid were condemned by the PCE as 'unacceptable', and Poland's invitation to the falangist general Iniesto Cano – head of the Civil Guard and veteran of the Blue Division – as an 'abandonment of traditional friendship'.[23]

For all these conflicts with Eastern European states, party leaders kept their close friendships among the communist parties in power, especially in East Germany. French and Italian comrades also volunteered to mediate in the PCE's differences with the Soviets. In the last resort, neither wanted a break: for the Soviets, the PCE represented the best-organized force for revolution in Spain; for the PCE, Soviet détente policy was an essential complement to its political strategy in its own country.

The party's attitudes on Western Europe also changed. All member states of the EEC, with the exception of France, categorically rejected Spain's association in the European Community without prior changes in the régime. This was taken by Spanish business interests, particularly in Catalonia, where the communists are strong, as a major threat to their export markets. An Assembly of Catalonia met in November 1971, and was attended by the Catalan wing of the PCE as well as by Christian democrats and socialists. A joint platform was drawn up, demanding regional autonomy, liberties and a union of all democratic forces. Similar if less spectacular fronts were organized in the rest of Spain. Support came from political parties and unions in Western Europe, where over 600,000 Spanish workers were employed. Western European communist parties took tentative steps to coordinate their policies, and in the summer of 1972 the French socialists and communists signed their 'Common Programme'. European heads of state and government met in October 1972 in Paris, and agreed on an objective of European Union by 1980.

It was no coincidence that the PCE's Eighth Party Congress – the last party congress had been held in 1965 – coincided with the Paris summit. The congress marked the party's official recognition of the EEC as an 'objective force' in the overthrow of the Franco régime.[24] The European Community, Carrillo argued, was 'irreversible', and the task of communists was to prevent its development as a 'holy alliance' of capitalists directed against the Soviet Union. In return, the PCE would cooperate with the Spanish bourgeoisie for Spain's association in the EEC, and therefore for the installation of a democratic state in Spain. Closer ties between Western European communist parties were essential. 'Among these parties,' Azcárate stated, 'there exists a common vision on basic problems of democracy and socialism; a concept of socialism as the development and full application of democracy, giving power to the workers; a socialism which recognizes political, cultural and scientific liberties; that attributes no official ideology to any state; that accepts the plurality of parties and the autonomy of unions.'

The Franco régime's declining years

After the Lister affair, the party launched a recruitment drive to explain its policies at meetings held throughout Spain. The affair had interrupted the flow of funds from Moscow, leaving the party dependent on donations from rich sympathizers and on its own fund-raising activities. Subscriptions came from migrant workers in Western Europe, where mass meetings were held at Paris and Frankfurt in emphasis of the party's new political orientation.

But the party's cultivation of a moderate image in preparation for a democratic Spain after Franco posed certain problems for the militants in Spain. On the one hand, they were accused of class collaboration by non-communists, who boycotted elections to Franco's state syndicates in 1971 in order to force employers to bargain directly with worker representatives in the factories. Communist trade-union leaders were then arrested near Madrid in June 1972, and the strike weapon passed into the hands of more extremist groups. On the other hand, the PCE regularly sprang to the defence of the various Marxist-Leninist, Trotskyite or Maoist advocates of armed struggle against the régime. This was not surprising. Many of the rank and file sympathized with the radicals; the régime's oppression of Basque nationalists enabled the PCE to champion minority rights and to present communist policies as a moderate alternative to the extremes of fascism and nationalist violence. But many of these leftist groups were infiltrated by the police, and it may have been caution rather than lack of sympathy that inspired the PCE's official moderation.

The radicals, not the PCE, dealt the régime two severe blows from which it never recovered. The PCE's relations with the military branch of the Basque nationalists, the Euskadi Ta Askatusana (ETA), had cooled since the late 1960s, with the ETA's rejection of the PCE's Marxist analysis of the armed struggle. The Anti-fascist and Patriotic Revolutionary Front (FRAP) was associated with the PCE (Marxist-Leninist), which had broken away from Carrillo's party at the time of the Sino-Soviet split. On 1 May 1973, FRAP activists murdered a policeman, Juan Fernández, causing a demonstration by the police, headed by Iniesto Cano, in the streets of Madrid. The demonstrators called for Franco's resignation and a change of government. Franco retired to Head of State, appointing Admiral Carrero Blanco as prime minister and a police chief, Arias Navarro, as minister of the interior. The admiral was to guarantee the régime's continuity in the event of Franco's death, and Prince Juan Carlos's succession to the throne. This separation of powers crossed lines of police authority, formerly concentrated in Franco's hands. After a short premiership of unprecedented violence, strikes, church hostility and regional antagonism to Madrid, Carrero Blanco was assassinated. ETA claimed responsibility. The régime's decline was now irreversible.

Meanwhile, President Nixon's policy of rapprochement between the United States and the Soviet Union bore fruit in Mr Brezhnev's visit to Washington in June 1973. To many in Europe, the visit symbolized entente between the great powers to consolidate the *status quo* in Europe. For the PCE, the visit offered an unrivalled opportunity to place the Soviets in the same boat as the Americans, and thereby facilitate talks with Spanish business representatives, who saw the PCE as the only viable worker party.

A step away from Moscow would ease the dialogue with Spanish capitalists without unduly alienating party militants. Consequently, in September, talks were opened with a group of Spanish businessmen. Azcárate, at a central committee meeting that month, in a speech otherwise supporting the general aims of Soviet foreign policy, delivered a blistering attack on Moscow's domestic régime. The Soviets, Azcarate stated, suppressed democracy in Russia while promoting business deals with the 'greatest sharks of world capitalism' – the American multinationals.[25] Western European communist parties had 'to elaborate together an image of what socialism can and ought to be in this part of the world'. His ideas were included in the party's manifesto, thereby becoming official party policy.

Thus the PCE had already elaborated the doctrinal underpinnings of its own 'historic compromise' before the overthrow by General Pinochet of Premier Allende in Chile. After that event, the PCI abandoned any idea of a 'left alternative' in Italy, based on a communist-socialist alliance, and began actively to search for a working relationship in government with the Christian democrats. The parallel policies of both Spanish and Italian parties extended further: each saw their country's membership in a democratic Western Europe as a guarantee for democratic institutions, threatened in Italy by the inadequacies of the Christian democratic state and impeded in Spain by Franco's rule. Hence the PCE's support for the PCI's demands at the conference of West European communist parties at Brussels in January 1974 for a 'democratic and multinational Europe', independent of either the United States or the Soviet Union.[26] It was the prospect of this independent Western Europe, challenging Soviet leadership of the world communist movement, that triggered the first explicit Soviet outburst against the PCE. In February, the Soviet journal, *Party Life*, criticized Azcárate's September report to the PCE central committee on five points: its 'absurd thesis' of contradictions between the interests of the socialist states and the world revolutionary movement; the idea that East-West economic cooperation hindered the chances of the socialist movement in Western Europe; Azcárate's unjustified

attack on the Soviet domestic order; his 'nationalistic' ambitions
for an independent Western Europe; and his opposition to the
new communist party conference, at which the Soviet ideologue,
Suslov, continued to hope for a condemnation of China.[27]

Thus, by early 1974, Carrillo's road had led from acceptance of
Stalin's advice in 1948 to infiltrate the Franco régime's mass
organizations, through the policy of national reconciliation of
1956 and the ambivalent collaboration and opposition of 1963–7
to a renewed emphasis on parliamentary democracy as the best
way of reconciling socialism with liberty. The PCE's Pact of
Liberty, announced after the Soviet invasion of Czechoslovakia in
1968, represented the Spanish version of Secretary-General
Berlinguer's 'historic compromise' between communists and
Christian democrats in Italy. With the rapid decline of the Franco
régime, the problem was no longer one of theory but of the
theory's enactment in practice.

The PCE and the Portuguese revolution

A few months after Admiral Carrero Blanco's assassination on 20
December 1973, the neighbouring autocracy in Portugal was overthrown and the communists entered a government of national
reconciliation. On 26 April 1974, Carrillo enthusiastically
broadcast over Radio España Independiente that Caetano – the
Portuguese prime minister – fell as the result of pressures 'similar
to the Pact of Liberty which we advocate to liquidate the fascist
dictatorship in Spain'.[28] A plan of action was quickly drawn up
by the central committee, proposing that Don Juan, the son of
Alfonso XIII and heir to the Spanish throne, should replace
Juan Carlos, Franco's appointed heir. This implicit acceptance of
a democratic monarchy flowed from the communists' deal with
opposition monarchists. The party's revolutionary credentials
were preserved through an appeal to the 'workers' – the communists – to lead 'an offensive against the cost of living' and to
reject austerity from a government with no legitimacy. A party
conference was hastily convened at Geneva, attended by 30,000

militants. 'Even the cats,' Carrillo declared, 'would be republican', if Franco's succession plans for Juan Carlos were implemented.[29]

Early in July, the ageing dictator fell gravely ill. At the end of the month, Carrillo, with Calvo Serer – one of Don Juan's advisers – announced the formation of the Democratic Junta at a press conference in Paris. The junta's programme included amnesty for political prisoners, a provisional government, legalization of all political parties, free trade unions, a free press, an independent judiciary, regional autonomies and separation of Church and state. It was signed by a small social democratic alliance, the worker commissions, and the Popular Socialists of Professor Tierno Galvan, who favoured a common front in Spain in the manner of Mitterrand's socialist-communist alliance in France. Two hundred businessmen also joined, but the presence of the Catalan communists – the PSUC – and the Spanish Workers' Party (PTE) convinced other opposition forces that the junta was a front organization.

Carrillo was convinced that the régime's days were numbered. But two disturbing developments clouded his horizon. General Antonio de Spinola fell from power in Lisbon in September as the revolutionary whirlwind gathered force. Then West Germany, France and the United States encouraged the Spanish Christian democrats and socialists to organize as a counterweight to the Democratic Junta. The Spanish Socialist Workers' Party (PSOE) took its first step to leadership of the outlawed Spanish opposition, with the election of Felipe González as secretary-general in October. Shortly after, the socialists began to build up their strength in the clandestine unions, with powerful backing from the West German Confederation of Unions.

Autonomy from Moscow was now imperative for the PCE: Spain's communists could not afford to compromise their freedom of action through close identification with the Soviet Union. Franco was dying, and far-reaching changes were obviously imminent in Spain. Consequently, an agreement was signed with the Soviets in October 1974.[30] The Soviets, especially Suslov, who was present, no doubt hoped events in Spain would develop as in Lisbon.[31] Both sides agreed to term the régime 'an anachronism which poisons the climate of Europe', and the communiqué appealed to all anti-Franco forces to join the Democratic Junta. In return, the PCE expressed broad agreement with the thrust of Soviet foreign policy – the Soviets had recently made known their view that the main threat to Western Europe in the economic crisis was a return to fascism – and both parties approved the results of the January 1974 conference in Brussels of Western European communist parties. The squabble over the *Party Life* article was buried.

Relations with the Soviets none the less remained cool. Cunhal's methods in Portugal met with growing hostility throughout Western Europe and ran contrary to Moscow's own preference for alliances between conservative and Left parties. Probably there was no unanimity over what to do with the Portuguese situation; Ibarruri – hardly suspect of revisionism – thundered in Moscow against 'sectarianism' in patent allusion to the PCP.[32] After the PCP's nationalization of credit institutions and the creation of a single union – the Intersindical – under communist control, the PCE hurriedly disassociated from Cunhal. Delegates from the Democratic Junta were received by EEC luminaries in Brussels and Luxemburg, and Carrillo sought to shore up his relations with Georges Marchais, the French communist leader, who was also dismayed at the general unpopularity in France of Cunhal's activities in Portugal.

The crunch came in April 1975, when the Portuguese communists clung to power, despite the electoral verdict against them. Immediately the Western Powers turned to an active policy in Spain. Franco was urged to resign, and hand over the reins of power to Juan Carlos. But the Caudillo withdrew into his 'bunker', accompanied by his most fanatical followers. Violence ensued. In this Wagnerian setting, Carrillo launched a 'Manifesto of National Reconciliation', declared the citizen's right to overthrow a government 'which flaunts the people's will'[33] – a reference to the Franco régime as well as to Cunhal in Portugal – and told the American press that Cunhal was a 'narrowminded man, who has spent too long in jail'. In July, Carrillo and Berlinguer – the Italian leader – signed a common statement at Leghorn on socialism and liberty in Western Europe.[34] When in August *Pravda* inveighed against 'right-wing deviationists' among Western communist parties,[35] Carrillo declared, 'I am a heretic, and glad to be one. The future has always been on the side of heretics.'

Relations with the Spanish socialists, however, were slow to improve. Both parties claimed victory in the elections to the state syndicates in June, and the socialists formed a Democratic Convergence with the Christian democrats to rival the Democratic Junta. But rivalries were submerged in the last months of Franco's life. Late in July, the Caudillo cursed 'dogs who bark for change', and introduced a decree law against terrorism, withdrawing the suspect's right of defence. Five alleged terrorists were executed in September; Western European ambassadors were withdrawn from Madrid and anti-Franco demonstrations staged in European capitals. The Soviet Union charged that the executions flouted 'universally recognized standards of humanity', contradicting the agreements on European Security and Cooperation, signed by the Spanish prime minister, Arias Navarro, at Helsinki in July.[36] So, on 30 October – as Franco sank into his last, prolonged coma – Junta and Convergence published a joint communiqué, rejecting the régime's continuity and demanding amnesty for political prisoners, political and union liberties and a 'democratic rupture' – meaning a broad interim government in Spain, including the PCE.

The PCE and King Juan Carlos's first government

Franco died on 20 November, counselling his Spaniards to remain 'alert against Spain's enemies',[37] and Juan Carlos was crowned king a few days later. After much in-fighting, a new government was appointed, with Arias Navarro as prime minister. Areilza – an old colleague of Castiella's, – was appointed to the Foreign Ministry, and Fraga Iribarne to the Ministry of the Interior. Fair words on reform flowed freely. But the new government stumbled from one mistake to another. On 28 December, the new finance minister, Villar Mir, announced an austerity policy to bring down prices and improve the country's balance of payments, strongly in deficit since the fourfold increase in oil prices in November 1973. All opposition unions called workers out on strike, refusing to accept austerity and unemployment from a government appointed by 'Franco's son' – as Carrillo had called Juan Carlos. Early in January, Navarro, describing himself in *Newsweek* as a 'classical conservative', announced national elections by 1977, followed by Spain's entry to NATO. The PCE was not to be legalized. The interview coincided with the meeting of European socialist parties at Elsinor, Denmark, at which the US Secretary of State, Kissinger, and Chancellor Schmidt of Germany made known their hostility to alliances between communists and socialists. Navarro's policies thus complemented American and West German government priorities; but they were incompatible with the new political realities in Spain.

This soon became clear as a wave of strikes lamed the Spanish postal services, and Navarro declared his intention to crush subversion. The government's proposals for constitutional reform, he declared, were 'such as Franco might have desired'. Negotiations opened immediately between the communists, socialists and Christian democrats to draw up a common political platform, based on the opposition's combined demand for legalization of the PCE. Everything hinged on this crucial concession, from labour's acquiescence in an austerity policy to the resumption of diplomatic relations with Moscow. Areilza had, as foreign minister, started negotiations with the Soviets after concluding a treaty with the United States that met Soviet demands, namely, the withdrawal of American Polaris missile submarines from Rota base by 1979. But Carrillo interposed his veto.

The régime was trapped. It dared not resort to full-scale violence, but was unwilling to make more than tepid reforms. Some steps were taken towards altering existing legislation on parties, unions and the press. The communists emerged to semi-legality, holding a number of press conferences and sneaking

Carrillo into Spain, probably with Areilza's knowledge. But in Vitoria the police opened fire on demonstrators, mainly to the left of the PCE, killing seven and wounding 150 others. Fraga Iribarne, in Bonn, denied knowledge. Meanwhile, the Spanish opposition parties assembled in Rome at a meeting of the Italian-Spanish Committee, presided over by the veteran Italian socialist leader, Pietro Nenni, who had fought in the Spanish Civil War. A new strategy was devised for a 'negotiated rupture' with the régime, and at the end of the month the junta and the Platform formed a new unitary body – the Democratic Coordination of Platajunta, as it was called. Its object was 'to open a period of constitutional reform that ends in a popular consultation to determine the form of state and government'.[38] Both the PCE and the PSOE dropped their hostility to the monarchy. Carrillo declared that the PCE had long ago abandoned the notion of 'dictatorship of the proletariat' as understood in Eastern Europe, criticized the lack of liberties there, and pronounced the PCE in favour of the American bases in Spain, as long as the Soviets retained their troops in Czechoslovakia.

The Platajunta was not joined by some Christian and social democrats, nor by the smaller Spanish liberal parties. But it marked the end of the Navarro government. Juan Carlos began to take initiatives on his own account. He publicly declared Navarro a 'disaster', received conservative opposition leaders, and had Areilza – with the Finance Ministry – draw up preparations for his forthcoming visit to the United States. As the workers had refused austerity and Spain's external debts were rising, the transition to democracy in Spain had to be financed from abroad. For that, the blessing of the United States was necessary. On 2 June, the king declared, to a joint session of the United States Congress, his commitment to the 'creation of a society ever more prosperous, more just and authentically free'. But what was 'just', and who was to be 'free'? The government had placed before the Cortes an amendment to Franco's Penal Code, legalizing all political parties except those 'subordinate to an international discipline'. The amendment was debated on 9 June. The PCE published a denial of any subordination, but the American

Embassy in Madrid – and the régime diehards – thought otherwise. Mr Wells Stabler, President Ford's ambassador, declared disapproval of the Spanish opposition's demands for the PCE's legalization. The reform was duly blocked. King Juan Carlos, however, dismissed Navarro on 1 July, following rumours of a tank *putsch* led by the falangist general, Milans del Bosch. The next day a petition calling for liberties was signed, covering the full political spectrum from monarchists to communists.[39]

While Juan Carlos was affirming his power in Madrid, East Berlin played host to the Pan-European Conference of Communist Parties. Preparation had been going on for over a year, with the Soviets seeking to have their authority over other communist parties defined on a piece of paper, while the Italians, the Yugoslavs, the Romanians and the Spaniards insisted on their autonomy within the world communist movement. Carrillo was most outspoken. Comparing the militant Marxists of the early twentieth century to the Christians of the catacombs, who considered Moscow as the Rome of a new Marxist Church, Carrillo stated

... those were the days of our infancy. Now we are grown up. We communists have no leading centre, no international discipline which can be forced upon us. What unites us are bonds of affinity ... We accept no return to the structures and concepts of an internationalism of former times.

Azcárate later added that there was no prospect of a common strategy with the Soviets because of their 'deep ideological weakness' and the 'non-existence of a real democratic régime there'.[40]

Towards the PCE's legalization

Meanwhile, the new prime minister, Adolfo Suárez's, announcement early in July that 'sovereignty resides with the people' was taken by the PCE as marking the king's will to push through major institutional reforms. The radicals in the Platajunta disagreed, terming the government's policies 'reactionary'. Indeed, resistance among the régime's barons to the party's legalization remained strong, and the PCE had to hold its first public central committee meeting in Rome rather than in Spain. Ibarruri presided, and the meeting was attended by leading Italian and Spanish politicians.

Spaniards learnt for the first time the composition of the central committee. It transpired that the party's leadership was relatively young, with an average age of forty-five. Fifty-seven of the 133 members of the central committee were workers, 22 were white-collared employees, and 54 were 'intellectuals' – doctors, lawyers, writers, professors. This varied composition reflected – as the party economist, Ramón Tamames, pointed out – the complexity of a developed economy, where the old bipolarity between bourgeoisie and proletariat had been surpassed.[41] An ambitious goal was set for 300,000 party members by the end of 1977.

Emergence from clandestinity ended the PCE's privileged status as the Franco régime's principal enemy and reduced it to one among a number of political parties and unions. The process was painful, particularly for the worker commissions. At their clandestine conference in Barcelona in July 1976, a Coordination of Syndical Organizations (COS) was set up, with the PCE central committee member, Marcellino Camacho, as head of the national secretariat. Camacho visited the Soviet Union in August. Twenty out of twenty-seven COS officials were members of the PCE. A majority voted for a single union structure, but the anarchists, socialists and Maoists insisted on retaining some degree of autonomy. A similar blow was delivered to Ibarruri when she wrote in the French communist newspaper, *L'Humanité*, the the PCE formed the vanguard of the popular movement in Spain. 'Mme Dolores Ibarruri,' said González, the leader of the PSOE, 'has lost a feel for the dimension of Spanish political reality. I think the PCE is not, and cannot be, the main force of the opposition, especially in this moment of transition.'[42]

The PCE's dependence on the PSOE was borne home in the subsequent manoeuvres with the régime. Suárez's political agility in introducing reforms caught the Platajunta by surprise.

After so many years of political immobility, where the opposition's main task was to propose in the certain knowledge that nothing would result, the experience of an active government shattered the Platajunta's cohesion. As the PCE's greatest fear was isolation, and its principal hope a status of legality, the PSOE had little difficulty in confirming its primacy. Matters were brought to a head by the worker commissions' efforts to replace the official syndicates by a single union under communist leadership. But González threatened to leave the Platajunta and the communists backed down. The COS dragged on until March, and was effectually dissolved after it had become clear that the socialist unions would not allow the worker commissions to parade as sole representatives of worker interests. On the problem of the parties, a negotiating body was created in November 1976 to promote the PCE's legalization as the main plank of the opposition's platform for relations with the government.

Legalization of the PCE destroyed the régime's mythology of the single-party state as the best bulwark against communism, as well as the PCE's privileged status as the main opposition party. It also meant confrontation between Suárez and the falangist generals, the prize being reform of the armed forces, eventual entry to NATO and the renewal of diplomatic relations between Madrid and Moscow. Carrillo, fearing isolation, held a semi-public press conference in Madrid on 10 December 1976.[43] Repeating his ideas on socialism and liberty, Carrillo made clear that he expected his party to be legalized. Liberty, he told the journalist, is indivisible, and therefore the PCE should be legalized like all other political parties. The Penal Code had been amended by Franco's Cortes in July 1976, specifically to exclude the communists on the grounds of their membership of a totalitarian state. But the PCE advocated pluralist politics and belonged to no International. Meanwhile, he proposed abstention in the referendum on the government's reform plans. But he withdrew the PCE's veto on diplomatic relations with Moscow, offered a three- to four-year pact with capitalists to overcome the economic crisis, and declared the PCE's willingness to participate in a government presided over by Juan Carlos.

This interview gave the signal for the government's final struggle with the falangists. The next day, a member of the traditionalist Urquijo family was kidnapped. Orders were given to the police to seek both Carrillo and Urquijo. Carrillo was arrested on 22 December, but – fortified by its overwhelming victory in the referendum – the government released him, launched on the reorganization of the police and armed forces and started dismantling the special courts set up by Franco at the time of the Grimau affair in 1963. Suárez conceded that the PCE could put up candidates for the forthcoming general elections, on condition of their running on individual tickets. But the occasion for the final showdown with the falangists was tragically offered in January 1977, when communist labour lawyers were machine-gunned in their office in Madrid. Three hundred falangist terrorists were arrested, but so were radicals to the left of the PCE. In other words, Suárez drew the line of legality past the PCE.

First to react to Suárez's move was Moscow. Relations were resumed with Madrid after forty years, less because the PCE enjoyed greater freedoms than because Moscow was concerned at Spain's eventual membership in NATO. Furthermore, the Soviets were highly displeased with Carrillo's utterances, and appointed Sergei Bogomolov – reputed for his hostility to Eurocommunist ideas – as ambassador to Spain. His clumsy efforts to create a dissident faction in the party came to nothing, and Carrillo pre-empted any remaining doubts as to his party's official views in his book '*Eurocommunism' and the State*.[44] The book appeared on Spanish bookstalls in March 1977, in time for Spain's general elections, held in June. The book may be taken as the party's manifesto after forty years of clandestinity. The party, Carrillo wrote – taking up some of the themes alluded to at the Eurocommunist 'summit' between the PCI, PCF and PCE in Madrid in March 1977 – 'does not aspire to conquer power for itself as a monopoly, but seeks to conquer power in which other political forces cooperate and participate, according to their real weight'. This meant anchoring the state's legitimacy in universal suffrage, and in the principle that 'the masses must have the right to throw out incompetent governments, and elect new ones'. After four decades of dictatorship, Spanish communists set too high a value on freedoms to duplicate in Spain the Soviet single-party state, with its 'deficiencies and degenerations'. Though the PCE was unlikely to enter government in Spain, 'the victory of socialist forces in Western European countries will not augment Soviet state power by one iota, nor will it mean the extension of the Soviet model of a single-party state; it will be an independent experience, with a more aggressive socialism that will exercise a positive influence on democratic evolution in existing socialisms of today'.

The forces of the Left in Western Europe, Carrillo declared, had to intensify cooperation in order to protect political democracy against the depredations of capitalism. Given the close economic ties with Western Europe, Spain had to become a full member of the EEC. The PCE's objective was a Europe independent of the United States and of the Soviet Union, and rooted in a political system of parties, the separation of powers and defence of human rights. NATO was an instrument of political, military and economic control of the United States over Western Europe, so an essential aspect of the region's independence was cooperation between national armed forces in a regional defence. 'We are not,' wrote Carrillo, 'opposed to a phase of European defence.'

On 9 April 1977, the PCE was legalized. Falangist generals in the Supreme Council of the Land Army declared that the government had 'blackened the image of the king'. There were dark rumours of a *putsch*. But the government disciplined the offending officers. The PCE was legalized, Suárez declared, 'because its behaviour was compatible with the law'.[45] Carrillo got the party to adopt the monarchy's gold and red flag, and for the short three weeks of the election campaign reiterated its commitment to parliamentary democracy, called for a 'socialization' of credit and proposed a Constituent Cortes. Large crowds attended the party's meetings in tribute to the moral capital accumulated by the communists during the dictatorship, and also out of curiosity to see in the flesh men whom the régime had until recently depicted as adorned with tails and horns and reeking of sulphur.

It was the rapidity of the PCE's legalization as much as the weight of the past that in part explains the party's modest success in the June 1977 elections. The PCE received only 9·6 per cent of the total vote, with nineteen seats in the Chamber of Deputies and none in the Senate. The Catalan communists, the PSUC, provided the communists with their greatest victory, recording 19 per cent of the votes cast in Catalonia. But the communists won no seats at all in the Basque country where the socialists were strong, as they were in Madrid. The PSOE received 118 seats in the Chamber and 31 seats in the Senate, second to the loose coalition of parties that formed around the prime minister, Suárez. As Carrillo admitted to the central committee in a report on the election, the results were disappointing.

Caciquism, failings in the censure, the obstacles to emigrant votes, the failure to extend the vote to eighteen-year-olds, the electoral system, the delays in the process of democratization, the tardy legalization of the PCE and the fear that a vote for the communists might serve as a pretext for a *coup d'état*, and the attitude of the press, which exaggerated the prevalent fears and sought distance from us ... are so many reasons for the poor electoral result of the PCE in the recent elections.[46]

There was much truth in Carrillo's assessment. Intimidation of the voters no doubt occurred, but many of these fears were widely held and needed no stimulation. Fraga Iribarne, leader of the Francoist Popular Alliance, inflamed his hearers' imaginations with images of communists in power turning churches into garages. Then, interests that had profited under the régime also sensed the end of an era: the electoral reform, voted by Franco's Cortes in November 1976 and on which the elections had been held, were the work of the Popular Alliance, and it was weighted heavily in favour of the countryside against the cities. The police, also, anticipated violence from extremists: the security measures for the election, which they dubbed 'Operation Battering Ram', were perhaps designed to inspire confidence in voters, but the presence of armed police in the voting booths may not have been felt as a comfort by all voters. Above all, the voting papers and results were manipulated: voting papers to working-class areas in Madrid were not distributed until three hours after voting was officially supposed to have begun. Results from the wealthier areas came in almost immediately, while returns from working-class areas were still not in one month later. In the meantime, Juan Carlos reconfirmed Suárez as prime minister.

Whatever the disappointment, the immediate concern of the PCE was to dispel fears of its intentions and cooperate to the full in establishing the newly emergent bourgeois democracy in Spain. The tone was set by the state: on 13 July, the anniversary of Calvo Sotelo's murder in 1936, the new Cortes was opened by the king. Before the inaugural speech was delivered, Dolores Ibarruri was introduced to Adolfo Suárez. The meeting, which was immediately attributed symbolic significance by the press, was seen as representing the reconciliation between the Spanish Communist Party and the new régime. Old grievances were laid aside, and rivalries between parties representing different interests were to be conducted in an open polity. 'The various ideologies represented here,' said Juan Carlos in his inaugural speech, 'are nothing more than different ways of understanding peace, justice and freedom, and the historic reality of Spain. In the same ideal . . . they are motivated by the same impulse: love for Spain.' [47]

No doubt Carrillo would have chosen different words, but all his actions have been informed by a consistent policy to persuade the party faithful and the country at large to accept that the PCE intends to play a responsible role in the democratic process. A communist deputy was elected to the committee of nine that drew up the proposal for the Constitution, and the party collaborated in the Moncloa Pact between all parties that was concluded in October 1977 after two weeks of negotiations with the Suárez government. The pact spelled out the economic policy of Spain for the following eighteen months, and the permanent negotiations on its enactment ensured Carrillo innumerable occasions to present the PCE in a reassuring light. To criticisms from party members that the PCE was helping the capitalists administer the crisis, the reply was that the democratic system in Spain was still fragile and that neither conservative nor socialist parties held sufficient seats in the Cortes to put through the necessary political and economic reforms. As Carrillo was well aware, socialism in Spain could not be identified with the Soviet model and held no chance without a strong infusion of liberty.

Carrillo's influence in the PCE has not been seriously challenged, though the series of party debates leading up to the Ninth Congress in April 1978 showed considerable diversity of opinion. The Basque and Catalan parties both held their congresses in October 1977. At the Basque congress, the heart-searching over the electoral results ended in the nomination of a new secretary-general, and the confirmation of the Carrillo line. But innumerable amendments were submitted to the proposals for party statutes, and though the party condemned the continued violence in the Basque country, an electoral front with the nationalists was favoured. At the Catalan congress, the Euro-communist line also triumphed with the election of Antoni Gutiérrez to the post of secretary-general, but the struggles of at least four identifiable tendencies in the party ranging from the former Maoist group identified with the most moderate wing, the 'pure' Eurocommunists, the 'historicals' to the 'Leninists' in the worker commissions may have caused Gutiérrez to state afterwards that the party had not rejected democratic centralism and would not tolerate sectarianism. Significantly, some resentment was caused by one speaker from the PCE central committee who referred to the communist parliamentary group in the Chamber of Deputies in Madrid without distinguishing between the PCE and the PSUC – the Catalan branch. In other words, the emerging federal constitution of the Spanish state inevitably modified the authoritarian structures of the PCE that had, perhaps, been appropriate under the Franco régime but seemed ill-suited to the new Spain.

In January, the new PCE statutes were published for prior discussion within the party before their submission to party congress in April. The principal points were the definition of the party as 'Marxist, democratic and revolutionary': the word 'Leninist' was dropped because of its connotations of recourse to armed force, the dictatorship of the proletariat, the exclusive alliance of peasants and workers, and the party as an *avant-garde* to lead the revolution. The PCE was declared a lay party, respectful of religious faiths and accepting people with religious beliefs in its ranks. The communist parties of the Basque country and Galicia were defined as belonging to the PCE, but with their own autonomy and central committee. Deference was paid to Catalan nationalist susceptibilities in the description of the PCE and the PSUC as defining jointly a general line of policy. The party was promised complete liberty of discussion, but democratic centralism was maintained on the grounds that unity of action had to be assured. At the Ninth Congress the debates were lively, but Carrillo's new line was not seriously challenged. Perhaps the strong Leninist faction in the PSUC was held back by the knowledge that their party had in October voted to call itself both Marxist and Leninist.

Thus, the question as to whether or not the PCE is genuinely Eurocommunist misses the mark. The PCE has no other option than to adapt to the new political conditions in Spain, whatever the personal views of party members. The Spaniards are not likely to vote heavily for a party proposing dictatorship, with Moscow as a model, nor are they likely to favour proposals for a further concentration of powers at Madrid that would diminish the powers that have been acquired by the nationalities. The new Spain is highly diverse, with a plurality of power centres, more similar in its constitution to West Germany or Italy than to a centralized state like France. Its political diversity encourages a permanent weaving and undoing of alliances on particular issues, and places a premium on political dexterity with a minimum of ideological baggage. Had the PCE failed to distance itself from Moscow over Czechoslovakia, or clung to the old gods, it would have been condemned to irrelevance. Spanish politics reward flexibility, whereas the peculiarities of French domestic politics have tended to reward the communists for consistency.

The PCE's relations with Moscow are shaped first and foremost by these domestic considerations. Indeed, the affinity that Carrillo proclaims with other parties in the international communist movement, and the solidarity that party members express with other parties and 'progressive' movements, are expressions of their conviction of diversity in the world. Spain is seen more as a microcosm of the global arena than as a future testing ground for a decreasingly relevant Soviet experience. On repeated occasions, PCE officials have argued that conditions in Spain in the late 1970s are light years away from those prevailing in Russia in 1917. And as Semprun and Claudín, and then Carrillo, realized, the party could not hope to champion freedoms in Spain, and continue to describe the Red Army as the *avant-garde* of the proletariat in Eastern Europe. So the party developed its own ideas on autonomy within a world communist movement, denying Moscow's claim to infallibility in the Marxist Church and logically resisting the temptation to set up the Eurocommunist ideas as a rival catechism. The real thrust of Carrillo's significance is rather different: he must proclaim communism as adaptable to the peculiarities of Spain.

It is this that makes the PCE such a thorn in Moscow's side. Whatever Carrillo may state about his maintaining affinity with the Soviet Union, or however close some of the Spanish communists may be to this or that faction in the Kremlin, the Soviet dilemma is acute: the PCE, and its regional parties, can on occasion be relied on to represent Soviet interests in Madrid, though the resumption of diplomatic relations has created more official channels. But the emergence of the PCE from clandestinity, and its daily participation in the politics of the new Spain, takes place in a country stamped by a thirst for Western liberties and by diversity of nationalities. The PCE has developed an ideology to accommodate that reality, and furthermore has declared, through its secretary-general, that the Soviet Union may have much to learn from the experience of the Spanish communists. Hence the frequent attacks on the PCE in the Soviet press, though it is not so much the fear of the PCE breaking away from the international communist movement that worries the Soviets as the knowledge that the PCE is more likely to stay in. Carrillo was not allowed to speak at the sixtieth anniversary of the October Revolution in Moscow in 1977

186 The Spanish Communist Party

because what he had to say as a Spanish communist many of his hearers may also have wanted to say, but would not be able to because their political base fell within the Soviet empire. In other words, the real change, and it is one of degree rather than of essence, is that the Communist Party of Spain has become primarily a Spanish communist party; its ties to Moscow are secondary.

Notes and references

1. Jorge Semprun, *Autobiographia de Federico Sánchez*, Barcelona, 1977.

2. Quoted in Hugh Thomas, *The Spanish Civil War*, London, 1961.

3. Santiago Carrillo, *Mañana España*, Paris, 1975, pp. 93–4.

4. Enrique Lister, 'Lessons of the Spanish Guerilla War, 1939–1951', *World Marxist Review*, VIII (February 1965), pp. 53–8.

5. Carrillo, *Mañana España*, pp. 124–5.

6. Semprun, *Federico Sánchez*, p. 206.

7. Benjamin Welles, *Spain, the Gentle Anarchy*, New York, 1965, pp. 297–8.

8. *Mundo Obrero*, 15 October 1964.

9. Dolores Ibarruri, *De Febrero a Octubre 1917*, Paris, 1967.

10. See Fernando Claudín, 'Las relaciones Sovietofranquistas', *Horizonte Español 1972*, Paris, 1972.

11. Fernando Claudín, *El subjetivismo de la politica del Partido de España (1956–1964)*, Madrid, 1968, cited in Guy Hermet, *Les Communistes en Espagne*, Paris, 1971, p. 82. Also, Fernando Claudín, 'Dos concepciones de "La via española al socialismo"', *Horizonte Español 1966*, Paris, 1966, pp. 59–100.

12. Santiago Carrillo, *Nuevos Enfoques a problemas de Hoy*, Paris, 1967.

13. Cited in Hermet, *Les Communistes en Espagne*, p. 95.

14. This attitude was complemented by Álvarez's insistence on greater autonomy from Moscow of communist parties. See *Nuestra Bandera*, No. 58, second quarter, 1968, pp. 75–9.

15. Carrillo, *Mañana España*, p. 174.

16. *Le Monde* (Paris), 23 October 1970.

17. *Mundo Obrero*, 15 September 1968.

18. *Nuestra Bandera*, No. 64, second quarter, 1970, p. 76.

19. *Nuestra Bandera*, No. 59, third quarter, 1968, pp. 41–53; *Nuestra Bandera*, No. 63, second quarter, 1970, pp. 63–70; *Nuestra Bandera*, No. 65, third quarter, 1970, pp. 11–17.

20. Santiago Carrillo, *Libertad y Socialismo*, Paris, 1971.

21. *Nuestra Bandera*, No. 66, fourth quarter, 1970, pp. 51–6.

22. *Radio España Independiente*, 27 January 1973.

23. *Nuestra Bandera*, No. 70, first quarter, 1973, pp. 81–3.

24. VIII Congreso del Partido Communista de España (Bucharest, 1972).

25. Manuel Azcárate, 'Sobre la Politica Internacional del PCE', *Nuestra Bandera*, No. 72, fourth quarter, 1973. This talk comprised four parts, the second of which was not published until after the Soviet criticism of it in February 1974. The offending part was then published by the PCE, together with the Soviet critique in *Party Life*. It became a basic text in the growing liturgy of Eurocommunism. See Editorial Cambio 16, *El PC Español, Italiano y Frances cara al Poder*. The liturgy leaves out the other three parts, where Azcárate's views generally support Soviet foreign policies.

26. Santiago Carrillo's speech at the Brussels conference is reproduced in *Mundo Obrero*, 13 February 1974, pp. 4–7.

27. *Le Monde*, 23 February 1974.

28. *Mundo Obrero*, 8 May 1974.

29. *Mundo Obrero*, 3 July 1974.

30. *Pravda*, 16 October 1974.

31. This was not the PCE's view. As early as October 1974, the party's press voiced concern at Cunhal's tactics in Portugal.

32. *Mundo Obrero*, first week in May 1975.

33. *Mundo Obrero*, third week in April 1974.

34. Editorial Cambio 16, *El PC Español*, pp. 27–31.

35. *Pravda*, 6 August 1975.

36. *Pravda*, 4 October 1975.

37. *ABC*, 21 November 1975.

38. *Cambio 16*, 29 March 1976.

39. See Pedro Calvo, *Juan Carlos, Escucha*, Madrid, 1976, pp. 86–8, 131.

40. 'Debate Claudín-Azcárate: Eurocommunismo', *Triunfo*, 3 July 1976, pp. 26–31.

41. Editorial Cambio 16, *Ramón Tamames*, pp. 57–8.

42. *Le Monde*, 15–16 August 1976.

43. *Mundo Obrero*, 20–26 December 1976.

44. Santiago Carrillo, '*Eurocommunismo*' *y Estado*, Barcelona, 1977; English translation, '*Eurocommunism*' *and the State*, London, 1977.

45. *La Vanguardia*, 4 May 1977.

46. *La Vanguardia*, 30 June 1977.

47. *La Vanguardia*, 14 July 1977.

6. The Alternative: Portuguese Communism
Diana Smith

1. The party and the nation

The Portuguese Communist Party (PCP) has spent forty-three of
its fifty-seven years of life underground. The political police of
the Salazar and Caetano régimes – the PIDE (International and
State Defence Police), subsequently renamed DGS (Directorate-
General of Security) – systematically persecuted the party from
1935 to 1974 but failed to dismantle it.

When the PCP emerged into legal life on 25 April 1974 in the
aftermath of the military *coup* that overthrew Marcelo Caetano
in a new climate favourable to the Left, instead of adapting itself
to the fresh mood of democracy, it made a bid for power as
totalitarian and intolerant of dissident opinion as the régime in
the USSR.

The speed and vehemence with which the PCP rose to a
dominating position in Portugal alarmed the Western world.
The PCP's conduct also raised doubts about the credibility of
the 'gradualist' French, Italian and Spanish communist parties.

The chasm between the PCP's repeated protestations of respect
for democracy and pluralism, and its psychological or physical
aggression in 1974–5, crystallized European fears that any
communist party given the opportunity to come close to, or
share, power would elbow out all opposition and, against the
wishes of the public, install a régime of tightly controlled state
capitalism, first destroying the structures of private enterprise and
individual representation. The PCP failed in its bid for power
when disciplined army officers, led by General Ramalho Eanes,
proved on 25 November 1975 that left-wing agitprop and determination were no match for military precision and planning.

Subsequently the PCP had to accept a secondary role in politics, concentrating on retaining its footholds in industry – through the CGT/Intersindical Trade Union Confederation, which it dominates (and which represents about one third of Portugal's labour force), and in the Alentejo farming region, where it still holds sway over a number of collective farms and some parish or town councils.

In many respects, its power is putative: it can still influence government decisions with the threat of what it *might* do to destabilize the situation rather than by its numerical weight, either in parliament, among the electorate or with the totality of workers.

In the 1976 general election, the PCP took about 12 per cent of the vote (650,000) in an 85 per cent turnout. In the June presidential elections that year, while General Eanes received 61 per cent of the vote, the PCP candidate, Octavio Pato, came in fourth with 7 per cent. In the December municipal elections of 1977, the PCP-dominated United People's Front took 17 per cent of a lower poll – winning council seats in the Alentejo and Lisbon belt but not increasing its nation-wide impact.

The party claims about 125,000 members – more than the Portuguese Socialist Party (PS), which has about 80,000 paid-up members.

Essentially, the PCP maintains a large paid-up membership, not only because it holds regular, well-organized recruitment drives, but also by default of the PS which has been largely unable to attract the working class into its ranks or to satisfy its needs while in government.

The PCP's conduct from 1976 on became respectable, and the industrial performance of its militants has been generally constructive and low in profile. However, it has not followed the example of Santiago Carrillo in Spain, first loosening ties with Moscow then abjuring Leninism. The PCP still preaches democracy, respect for election results and civil freedoms; its criticism of Portugal's bid to join the EEC is made on justifiable economic rather than ideological grounds, but its secretary-general, Alvaro Cunhal, has made it clear that there will be no renunciation of loyalty to the USSR, or of Leninism. The term 'dictatorship of the proletariat' has been dropped from the PCP's programme, because of the pejorative connotations of the word 'dictatorship' in Portugal – but there is, at this stage, little doubt that, whatever the semantics, the PCP's long-term strategy is still revolutionary not gradualist.

As long as General Eanes is President of the Republic, Portugal's climate will not favour another PCP upsurge, nor can the PCP venture into widespread industrial or agricultural upheavals without the risk of massive military retaliation: therefore even its putative might as a disruptive force must, in present circumstances, be taken with a pinch of salt.

Nevertheless, the examinations of conscience the PCP has made since its 1975 defeat have not induced a will to test, however timidly, the merits of Eurocommunism, above all at the level of the central committee. There are gradualists and potential experimenters in the PCP, especially among younger militants, but today's PCP brooks no internal dissent and the innovators are shouted down at cell meetings.

The question is obvious: why does the PCP maintain absolute allegiance to Moscow and continue to believe that collective farming, nationalized, centrally controlled industry, stifling of freedom of thought and the imposition on the collective will of the ambitions of the vanguard could be viable in an individualistic Western nation like Portugal?

Why, moreover, has the PCP leadership been unable to exercise the soul-searching of French, Italian or Spanish communists and, like Jean Elleinstein, the PCF historian, admit that, 'There is a moment in history when eyes must open'?

The answers cannot be clear-cut: it is not in the communist or Portuguese tradition to be clear about motives or goals. But there are innumerable clues, and I would suggest that most of them hinge on the Portugueseness of the PCP: by-product of the country's geographical, political and psychological particularities which cannot be accurately reconciled with the distinctive natures of Spain, Italy or France.

Arguably, Portugal is the most geographically isolated and

psychologically insecure nation in Western Europe. For the first 500 years of its existence as a kingdom it expended most of its efforts warding off Spanish territorial ambitions. For reassurance and prosperity, overshadowed by its self-assertive, large neighbour, Portugal turned to its overseas empire, neglecting its domestic material and human resources. Even when the Spanish threat waned, this neglect persisted.

Portugal looked first to Brazil. When it lost Brazil, it looked to Africa for wealth, identity and a sponge for its excess domestic manpower. The identity never truly emerged. While a Spaniard has a powerful sense of national or regional persona and, at best, barely tolerates outside notions or philosophies, the Portuguese have remained amorphous, prone to scavenging foreign theories for home consumption but generally failing to find practical applications for them.

In the nineteenth century, as Europe began to modernize, Portugal lagged behind, fragmented politically, more fascinated by parliamentary debates than by building roads, railways or mills, or rationalizing agriculture, and compelled to struggle harder and harder to retain its overseas empire at high financial, political and human cost.

In our century, Portugal's atavistic compulsion to retain absolute control of its African colonies first weakened then toppled the Salazar/Caetano dictatorship. Once the ties were forcibly severed it became clear how perilously dependent the country had been on resources gathered thousands of miles away. With the props removed, inherent domestic weaknesses became glaring – only sketchy industry, much of it under foreign control, minimal foreign trade, heavily weighted in favour of essential imports, and slumbering agriculture.

In 1974 Portugal was exposed as what it had always been, out of step with the continent on which it was located, politically bankrupt and moderately financially solvent only because Salazar had amassed a stockpile of gold and Caetano had encouraged tourism – but devoid of durable stocks of skilled labour and management, political structures or understanding of the responsibilities of government.

2. Between Salazar and Stalin

It is too simplistic to blame all Portugal's woes on forty-six years of Salazarism and Caetanism: one must remember that Salazar was brought in by a military triumvirate, not to combat nascent communism but to untangle absolute financial chaos.

Inheriting the backwardness and political confusions generated in the nineteenth century, the forty-two governments that operated in the sixteen years of the First Republic, from 1910 to 1926, dealt a death-blow to Portugal's hopes of catching up with the outside world. Successions of squabbling élitists, oblivious to the country's needs, spent and borrowed money abroad with no effort at control while Portugal degenerated into a degree of anarchy where the rising anarcho-syndicalists had no need to set a pace – they merely occupied ground left open to them.

It was in this chaotic climate that, in 1921, the PCP was formed from no more than a handful of zealots struggling to make their voices heard in the general uproar – dedicated theorists in a country obsessed by political theory. So the party remained until the early 1930s, after Salazar had completed his original task – balancing Portugal's books – and turned his mind from an obsession with wheat production to Mussolini's brand of corporativism and Hitler's anti-communism.

At that stage, apart from the Corporative Constitution – framework for Portuguese politics for the next forty years – Salazar introduced a repressive Labour Law, tying workers' syndicates to state control, banning strikes and, essentially, giving individual management or managers' guilds a free hand to exploit labour without redress.

Protests and strikes ensued, either spontaneously or with the backing of the anarcho-syndicalists and the embryonic PCP. In 1934, when a general strike was attempted, Salazar's National Republican Guard cracked down so brutally that the anarcho-syndicalists were decimated and the small PCP was given the *raison d'être* it needed – resistance to persecution.

Declared illegal, forced underground and besieged by the

PIDE (formed in 1935 with a cadre of officers trained in Nazi Germany), the PCP thrived on adversity. Deportations of its leaders to the concentration camp of Tarrafal in the Cape Verde islands, where many died of malnutrition, disease or brutal treatment, failed to weaken the party. Indeed, the PIDE's assault on the PCP merely weeded out the 'softer' leaders, and hardened the revolutionary determination of the more resistant. Alvaro Cunhal (born in 1913), who first made an impact as a Young Communist in the early 1930s and became one of the PIDE's main targets, was one of those who developed his resolve under PIDE torture and in PIDE solitary-confinement cells.

In its earlier stages, the clandestine PCP concentrated development of cells on Lisbon's ports and shipyards, and Portugal's one industrial complex, the CUF (Companhia União Fabril), which had factories scattered around the country. Even more intensively, it worked on the Alentejo – the only stretch of land where large-scale agriculture was possible but not practised. Most of this land was owned by generally absentee *latifundiarii*, who ignored Salazar's exhortations to produce more wheat and preferred the easy revenue of cork and olives, using miserably paid seasonal labourers.

The Alentejo was a cliché breeding-ground for communism: the realm of injustice, unemployment or under-employment where a labourer stood little chance of feeding his family properly, let alone bettering himself.

In other rural areas, the land was worked by smallholders or medium-sized farmers, as fiercely independent as any farmer anywhere in the world. There, communist promises of the day of reckoning and a share for all in the riches of the land fell on deaf ears.

While the PCP laid the groundwork for a revolutionary future, Salazar and the omnipotent PIDE forced the country into a political and productive coma – preferring docile rural poverty to industrialization, spreading the repressive net from the original target, the PCP, to all forms of opposition, however moderate.

Portugal's geographical isolation from Europe intensified when

Franco dominated Spain. The PCP, apart from expressions of solidarity, contributed little to the Spanish Civil War: a few militants fought on the side of the Republicans and, ironically, some of them – who fled after Franco's triumph to Soviet Russia – became, eventually, the most outspoken opponents of the Soviet system. They discovered that the USSR was not the utopia they had expected, but an alien, brutal land where modest workers had no say and living conditions were intolerable.

Since Portugal remained neutral during the Second World War, the PCP had no chance to earn credits through involvement in international resistance as its French or Italian comrades had done. It was as isolated from the changes in Western Europe as Portugal itself was. Operating in a comatose country where its militants earned abysmal wages and were unable to contribute more than a pittance to party funds; periodically seeing its leaders imprisoned; cut off from Portugal's mainstream, let alone that of the outside world, the PCP on the one hand relied on financial and ideological lifelines tendered by Moscow and, on the other, grew increasingly introverted, romanticizing the future since it could do little more than organize clandestinely and resist police assaults in the present.

After the Second World War there was no way the PCP could test its impact out in the open as Italian or French communists could, joining in the tensions and exchanges inherent in democracy. Everything had to be done in the conspiratorial shadows, heightening the introspection and intolerance endemic to orthodox communism.

Masquerading behind unitary opposition façades, the PCP worked in Portugal's periodic, heavily rigged election campaigns for the presidency or National Assembly, perhaps most significantly in 1958 (the last direct presidential elections until the dictatorship fell), backing the candidacy of a bombastic but popular general, Humberto Delgado, whose 'loss' of the election will remain open to question for ever. Even in those clandestine days, the PCP was known to non-communist members of the opposition as prone to impose its wishes, but the fragmented, confused opposition needed the PCP's gift for organization, ability to keep clandestine printing presses running one step ahead of the PIDE, and contacts among the working classes to press its case.

General Delgado's flight into exile and subsequent attempts to mount *coups* proved useful to the PCP. His military supporters were rounded up by the authorities and imprisoned. In PIDE jails, they came into contact with PCP militants and proved sympathetic to PCP philosophies, forming a military nucleus that assisted the party's bid for power in 1974–5.

The PCP's allegiance to the USSR was cemented in the early 1960s when Alvaro Cunhal, after a particularly long, brutal bout of torture and imprisonment, escaped and fled, first to Prague, then to Moscow. There he remained until 1974, PCP secretary-general *in absentia*, an honoured guest, living in comfort, impervious to the complaints and requests for help of lesser PCP militants in the USSR.

Cunhal did not condemn the Soviet invasion of Czechoslovakia: indeed, he praised it, thereby setting the first distance between his PCP and the PCI, PCE and PCF. His subsequent guidance of the PCP, out in the open, indicates that he was not merely paying tactful lip-service to his generous Soviet hosts, but that he believed absolutely in the need for totalitarian authority and the right to crush even mild liberalization.

It is not difficult to conclude that the PCP's physical and psychological distance from the softening influences of Western democracy made it develop a particularly utopic, authoritarian and unworkable brand of communism. Only Cunhal himself can say why, unlike Santiago Carrillo, he remained obstinately blind to the USSR's shortcomings and, indeed, the agricultural and industrial failures of Soviet policies – but blind he remained.

Furthermore, there are two extremes inherent in the Portuguese character: anarchy and authoritarianism. The structures and life-styles of orthodox communism obviously eliminate anarchy and, in the case of Cunhal and other senior PCP militants, served to heighten inborn authoritarianism.

Portugal's social injustices, ferocious police system, concentration of wealth in a few hands, lack of political or administrative structures, cult of mediocrity and haughty disdain for the basic needs of its people were classic fields for totalitarian communism to plough. The meek, superficial liberalization introduced by Caetano after Salazar's death in 1970, as the country blindly pursued the costly, impossible African wars started in 1961, served simply to throw some of the innate tension to the surface, putting unbearable strains on intrinsically weak structures, ensuring that it was only a question of time before major upheavals occurred.

3. From 25 April to 11 March

The dictatorship worked its own destruction, mobilizing hundreds of thousands of young men to fight a hopeless war.

Only a minority of the Portuguese armed forces subscribed to the government's calls for death or glory: the rest were visibly reluctant to fight, seriously under-trained for bush combat, equipped with obsolete weapons, paid only a pittance and horrified by what they found in Africa – not least the massacres of women, children and old people instigated by the PIDE, which did far more to terrorize and brutalize the Angolans and Mozambicans than the army did.

The collective guilt of the Portuguese military at their participation in a losing, dirty war was another fertile breeding ground for the PCP and Portugal's *gauchistes* – as was their collective naïvety about politics.

The young officers who planned and made the 25 April 1974 *coup*, however, were neither clandestine PCP militants nor sympathizers. They were tired idealists, with a childlike faith in the healing powers of democracy. Made scapegoats by Lisbon for the failure to win the war, they gradually realized that the only way to end their and the African colonies' suffering was to end the dictatorship.

The *coup* was quiet and bloodless – only the PIDE, besieged by jeering crowds in its Lisbon headquarters, caused death and casualties, firing on the people in the streets below. But the expectations aroused in those first, euphoric days, when there was widespread conviction that, miraculously, true democracy would implant itself because that was what Portugal deserved after forty-six years of stifling paternalism and backwardness, were excessive, and the tools at hand were faulty.

First, innate Portuguese anarchy exploded back to life; factionism manifested itself when no less than fifty-seven political parties were formed. Instead of forcing itself on to the job, keeping up production and office work, thus preventing justification for right-wing cries of imminent chaos, Portugal took a holiday from its responsibilities and, often, its reason.

Inheriting structures that existed more on paper than in reality, the new military leaders had little material to mould into democratic shape: what they found, and what the exhilaration and irresponsibility of the immediate aftermath of the *coup* generated, was a vacuum.

Inevitably, as the only tightly organized body with a notion of what it wanted or powerful ideological motivation, the PCP stepped into that vacuum before moderate forces could understand what was happening.

Mário Soares, leader of the PS (a party then still in an embryonic stage of organization, only formed, in exile, in 1973 and without back-up structures in Portugal), understood the dangers. He knew Cunhal from his Young Communist youth and, as a lawyer, had defended many communist militants at their trials. As a long-standing member of the opposition to Salazar and Caetano, he had direct experience of the PCP's tactics in election campaigns, and had little reason to think that, emerging from clandestinity, the PCP would instantly convert to democratic methods.

However, Soares and the PS, mistakenly believing that willpower minus organization could superimpose democratic aspirations on totalitarian ambitions, first tried to work with, not against, the PCP. They had a common purpose – to see that the far Right should not regain a foothold – but they had too little common ground.

Quickly sensing the PS's structural weaknesses, the PCP, calling for order and discipline among workers and an end to the wildcat strikes sweeping the country (many of them, it was soon discovered, fomented by the far Right), forced recognition of its well-organized and hitherto underground trade-union confederation, Intersindical, as 'sole representative of the workers'. While Intersindical must be given credit for trying to call the celebrating, striking workers to order in those early days, its later role as the vanguard of revolutionary take-overs of factories, and, subsequently, of private land, epitomized the first stages of the very dictatorship of the proletariat which the PCP had sworn to abjure.

The PS was left with no option but to protest at the PCP's peremptory tactics and to set about finding the kind of public support that could stem the PCP tide while also ensuring that it had a place in government.

The moderate military began to lose steam. Saddled with political responsibilities for which they were unprepared, operating on fuzzy ideals rather than practical policies, they were gradually nudged out by PCP sympathizers – most importantly Brigadier Vasco Gonçalves, who became prime minister in July 1974.

Many early PCP advances, it must be said, were made easier by the personal ambitions of General Spinola and his taste for intrigue. Appointed as President of the Republic by the military junta on the grounds of his latter-day questioning of the feasibility of a military solution to the African wars, Spinola reacted to Portugal's euphoria in tones and terms that uncomfortably echoed the authoritarian past, haranguing the public while, behind the scenes, he formed plans to install a government of his choice, weighted towards the Right. The ousted Portuguese far Right enthusiastically supported Spinola and, throughout the summer of 1974, bunglingly and noisily made plans for a counter-*coup*, thus giving the PCP every justification for issuing warnings of a right-wing *putsch* and for using aggressive counter-tactics.

Spinola's first attempt, in July 1974, to alter the government, angered the moderate military and gave the left-leaners a chance to introduce Vasco Gonçalves as prime minister; his second attempt, in September that year, through a 'silent majority' demonstration covering a right-wing movement, led to his fall from grace and the introduction of the ambiguous, wavering, General Costa Gomes as president.

Western governments and Western businessmen with interests in Portugal also unwittingly helped the PCP along; in the first instance by removing a suave, low-profile American ambassador early in 1975 and replacing him by Frank Carlucci, later number two in the CIA, who, on the basis of his previous record, was immediately labelled as a CIA plant by the PCP and brandished as 'proof' that the West was out to sabotage Portugal's new democracy. In the case of businessmen, too many shut their factory doors and departed rapidly after 25 April – thus providing excuses for accusations of 'sabotage' or 'capitalist imperialism', and leaving thousands of bewildered, previously loyal workers without employment or means of keeping the factories running.

Time and again, in 1974 and 1975, it was as if those who could have helped to consolidate Portugal's new democracy, by refraining from ambiguous conduct and concretely supporting, financially or otherwise, men like Mário Soares and the social democratic PPD leaders (who included some of Portugal's most competent and open-minded businessmen or liberal professionals), were inadvertently dropping the country into the lap of the revolutionary Left.

In innumerable cases, the PCP did not have to force down doors: it walked into space abandoned by people whose sense of national responsibility or international solidarity appeared to have deserted them. The PCP's 'conquest' of factories and the Alentejo was often as much by default of fleeing proprietors as by use of psychological or physical violence. In many cases, the flight came before the threat had materialized. The proof that the PCP need not have been allowed to go so far lies in the fact that, where it met with resistance – in factories in the strongly anti-communist north, in Alentejo areas where local farmers set up armed guards – it backed away.

Furthermore, when businessmen or farmers negotiated peacefully with their employees, the PCP's vanguard was unable to make a dent and persuade workers to turn on their employers. But, in the early days, cooler heads were in the minority and the consequences are part of history.

Least cool of all, General Spinola's coterie fell for a classic piece of communist scarifying: the hint of an 'Easter massacre' list of 1,500 prominent civilian and military personalities slated for 'elimination'. This led Spinola's military supporters, on 11 March 1975, to try a *coup* destined to wipe out the Portuguese Left – PCP or otherwise. The military Left, however, with little difficulty found out the plans and, masquerading as Spinola sympathizers, actively helped the *coup*, manipulating its timing and location so that it would occur in broad daylight and be visibly crushed by loyal revolutionary forces. Thanks to the coterie's naïvety, the military Supreme Revolutionary Council took power on 11 March, heavily weighted with revolutionary officers. Three days later, in response to 'popular appeal', it ordered the nationalization of the banks and, since these were major holding companies, 51 per cent of the fixed capital formation and most of the newspapers of Portugal.

4. From 11 March to 25 November

The gift to the PCP that 11 March offered was not absolute, however. Although they were cocksure in some ways, pro-PCP members of the Revolutionary Council did not dare to cancel the promised 25 April elections: instead, over-estimating their acceptance by the people (who were beginning to recover from their euphoria and notice that their incomes were shrinking and their freedoms threatened), they tried to sway the results.

That was the first in a series of major gaffes caused by the revolutionary military's and PCP's dwindling grasp of Portuguese realities. When the military appealed to voters to cast blank ballots signifying their rejection of civilian politicians and endorsement of the Armed Forces Movement (MFA) as true representative of the people, the Portuguese were appalled. After four decades of restricted, rigged elections, attempts at further interference with their right to a free choice disgusted them. Only 6 per cent of over six million ballots were either spoiled or blank. As a party, the PCP came in third place with 15 per cent, and all hopes of a revolutionary landslide election victory were dashed. Deprived of voter consent for a revolutionary utopia, the PCP and their friends in the armed forces took up blunter methods.

On the assumption that they had sewn up industry, the PCP and the MFA set about the 'Cultural Revolution' – inundating state-controlled media with interminable revolutionary propaganda and catch-phrases (apparently unaware of the fact that sales of newspapers were plummeting downward and a nation of former television addicts was switching off *en masse*), and going out into remote rural areas in the north and north-east to 'educate' the people with performances of Bertold Brecht and hours of half-digested, garbled Marxist theory. Not only did these efforts not make converts, they swelled the ranks of anti-communist forces and began to make laughing stocks of the MFA and civilian 'educators' who, once they came into close contact with uneducated but shrewd country people, were seen to be not omnipotent wizards but fallible, pompous and confused human beings.

In the Alentejo, having forced through a revolutionary Agrarian Reform Act against the wishes of PS and PPD ministers, the PCP sought to implant the linch-pin of its revolution: take-over and collectivization of the land, with an immediate goal of intensive wheat production – proof, they believed, of communist perfection.

However, the raw materials were faulty. The arid Alentejo soil was not favourable to intensive farming, and the rural labourers, on whom the PCP had worked for decades and who followed instructions to swoop on the land, had only rudimentary understanding of the complexities of farming. Furthermore, the PCP had no agronomists or competent farm managers to give them technical help – it had only its ancient conviction that collectivization equalled full production by (apparently) magic transformation.

The Agrarian Reform, agriculturally, socially and politically, was an unqualified disaster. After an initial spurt of energy and one reasonable crop, the labourers grew lethargic, or frightened of the huge responsibilities imposed on them. When, in 1976, the government began to restore part or all of the seized land to private owners, despite PCP sabre-rattling and threats of a holocaust in the Alentejo, thousands of labourers meekly walked off the farms and back into unemployment. Exploited first by the *latifundiarii* and later by the PCP, they seemed doomed to be always victims.

In mid 1975, while those with sharp eyes could spot the cracks in the PCP's 'achievements', the myth-making was such that the party seemed unstoppable. It needed to move fast – keeping the general situation unstable and confused, trying to discredit the PS and the moderate military, labelling centre-left or centre parties as 'fascist' – to forge a mood where it could push in a puppet government. That government, apart from 'cementing the conquests of the revolution' by rubber-stamp legislation, had a broader purpose: to proclaim the Marxist-leaning Angolan MPLA as sole, legitimate representative of the Angolan people, by independence day on 11 November 1975, so that Angola could become a 'legitimized' base for Soviet operations in Africa.

By mid July the PCP had its puppet government, headed by Vasco Gonçalves. A month later, both government and Gonçalves were out in the cold. By then the PS was rallying anti-communist forces nation-wide, the moderate military had shaken themselves from their stunned silence and Gonçalves himself was on the verge of mental collapse, ranting at public and rambling in cabinet meetings. The PCP, realizing he was no longer an asset, abandoned him and let the moderate military strip him of his position, military and political.

Having lost its chance to control Portugal from the government palace, the PCP stepped up its disruptive tactics and street theatre, as well as the media barrage, hinting at another right-wing *coup* in the making, but focusing its main propaganda guns on the PS with ever-dwindling effect.

Among the PCP's many oversights – proof that it was too

fascinated by its myths to notice what was really happening –
was the party's underestimation of the fury and force of white
Angolans, caught up in the civil war between the Marxist
MPLA, the thuggish Zaire-backed FNLA and the strongly
representative, middle-of-the-road UNITA. If the USSR was
using the PCP to try and walk through the front door of Angola
once the MPLA was given the blessing of Lisbon, while both the
USSR and PCP misjudged the Portuguese mood, the West was
no less erroneous in its judgement of Angolan realities. With the
CIA covertly backing the FNLA – a group that had next to no
real support in Angola – and the US administration either
deliberately or accidentally failing to exploit non-Marxist gaps
in the persona and pronouncements of the MPLA leader
Agostinho Neto and so help him to become non-aligned, rather
than Cuba and the USSR's puppet, the historical errors in
Angola were monumental.

In 1975, the FNLA was the most bloodthirsty of the Angolan
movements, and, on a heightened level, like the tactics of the
Right in Portugal, gave the MPLA justification for retaliation.
Caught in the cross-fire, Angolan whites of Portuguese origin
fled to their native land.

The tidal wave of refugees that poured into Lisbon was the
ultimate weapon non-communists needed in their struggle to
weaken the PCP. The PCP, because of its support for the
MPLA, was roundly blamed for the plight of the refugees, who
were far more militantly and, indeed, violently anti-communist
than the tired, confused Portuguese. It is no coincidence that
organized, systematic attacks on PCP headquarters in the north
and centre gained momentum as the number of refugees in
Portugal swelled, or that demonstrations called by the PS in
protest at revolutionary military and PCP tactics drew ever-
larger, more strident crowds as the summer and autumn wore on.
The plight of the refugees was the factor needed to galvanize
Portugal. Increasingly, the PCP was backed into a corner and
into the company of the fragmented, vociferous *gauchistes*, whom
it hoped to manipulate to its advantage.

The *gauchistes*' major military supporter was the equally

vociferous Otelo Saraiva de Carvalho, whose political peregrin-
ations had ranged from right to centre-left, to communist
sympathies, to pro-Fidel Castro 'people's revolution', to a
decidedly confused urge for revolution more total than even the
PCP contemplated. As commander of the country's security
forces, Otelo was a key figure. The *gauchistes* assumed he was
fully under their control, together with a handful of junior
officers at key Lisbon and suburban barracks.

Indulging in media hyperbole, operating running performances
of street theatre, besieging the government and deputies in
parliament, using handicapped war veterans to block roads and
take over radio stations, the *gauchiste* actors in the last stages of
the 1975 revolutionary drama, as well as the producers and
directors (the PCP) waiting in the wings, were convinced they
had a captive audience.

The grand finale was scheduled for 25 November 1975 when,
using the paratroops as puppets, the *gauchistes*, their military
friends and the PCP would take over Lisbon's main barracks
and topple the two-month-old middle-of-the-road government
that had supplanted the stillborn PCP cabinet.

Just as the Left, in March, had helped Spinola's supporters to
believe the way was open for a successful *coup*, so the moderate
military, led by Ramalho Eanes (who spent three months in
back rooms at the army high command, planning the overthrow
of the Left), helped the *gauchistes* to believe they would have
little trouble succeeding with their plans.

The PCP sensed trouble, however. On the eve of 25 November,
when it found that thousands of armed private farmers had
blocked access routes to Lisbon and that the doggedly anti-
communist Lisbon Commando Regiment was oiling its tanks and
guns, the PCP pulled out of the *coup* plans, leaving the *gauchistes*
to rely on their 'revolutionary' military friends. Once the Eanes-
controlled tanks came out, however, revolutionary zeal melted.
A deflated Otelo Saraiva de Carvalho offered himself to his
superiors for instructions, and was sent home in disgrace.
Supposedly reliable revolutionary units failed to respond to
increasingly shrill *gauchiste* appeals for action. By the time the

state of emergency imposed by the moderate military was lifted three days later, Portugal had turned its back on the revolution and opted for tranquillity.

5. The lessons of failure

Having tried to prove that a Leninist revolution was possible in Portugal – and having failed, once the people on whom that revolution was being imposed found their wits and stamina – the PCP opted for pragmatism. It did a deal with the new powers headed by General Eanes: it would behave itself, fight a clean fight in the forthcoming 1976 elections, as long as its name was kept out of the 25 November fiasco, and its militants were not arrested (indeed, only *gauchistes* and *gauchiste* military went to jail).

That was the first backstage deal of many: after that, the PS, which won the 1976 general election, gritting its teeth accepted that the price of industrial peace with the PCP was slower returns of land to private hands in the Alentejo, and as a result was forced out of government by its Christian democrat coalition partners in July 1978. Such deals are one of Portugal's major problems; they arise from the fact that too many prominent socialists were briefly communists (and some have skeletons in their closets), and that the PCP, like any efficient communist party, keeps files on ex-members just in case there is an opening for blackmail. But the deals work both ways: the PCP is known to have played an ambiguous part in the PIDE's murder of General Delgado in Spain in 1965, and to have had an ambiguous relationship with the PIDE from the beginning of the 1970s onwards, when arrests of Maoists or *gauchistes* vastly outnumbered those of PCP militants. One might even say that Portuguese politics hinge, to a large extent, on which side can present the greater threat of blackmail.

The PCP's public condemnation of past activities of the PIDE was greatly diluted by the common knowledge that, to protect its own operations, the PCP betrayed other opposition elements to the PIDE; that, to cover its tracks, it spirited away all files covering PCP militants from the PIDE archives once these came into public hands after April 1974, and that it did not offer its leading members to testify at eventual PIDE trials, thereby making it possible for the courts to ignore the confused, half-apologetic testimony of other PIDE victims and pass light sentences.

It is doubtful whether the PCP, because of either past ambiguities or overweening practices, can ever bridge the credibility gap it created for itself in Portugal: its protestations of democratic principles are greeted either with a shrug of the shoulders or scornful laughter by millions of Portuguese, and its claim that, 'like all communist parties', it is autonomous, free to develop a Portuguese variety of 'true socialism', does not stand up to the test set by its silence in the face of Soviet persecution of dissidents, or its criticism of Eurocommunist leaders.

Its conduct, in the seventeen months of revolution between April 1974 and November 1975, serves as an object-lesson for other communist parties and for moderates. Moderates learned that when a country's political situation alters abruptly, every effort must be made to fill all gaps quickly with solid, self-disciplined, practical elements – King Juan Carlos's conduct of the Spanish transition was a clear example of how disastrous mistakes could be avoided. Spain, above all, benefited from the Portuguese disaster, watching its next-door neighbour leave all the loopholes a determined, revolutionary force needed to slip into prominence.

Other communist parties had it made clear to them that, although there may be momentary success for an aggressively superimposed artificial process, the will of a Western people eventually rejects this incompatible transplant.

Only the PCP, at this time, appears not to have learned the object-lessons, continuing to see and proclaim the Soviet Union's version of 'socialism' as a crime-free workers' paradise where the Gulag Archipelago is an invention of 'Western imperialism'.

The ageing PCP leadership has only a limited life-span in

which to keep its eyes closed to the march of history. Cunhal grew up under repression, motivated by dreams and hatred, while Carrillo spent time in democratic Paris, and Berlinguer learned – as a true Italian – that the secret of survival lies in compromise.

Portugal is not given to voluntary political or personal compromise as a pragmatic principle, nor is it comfortable with power-sharing – witness the PS's refusal to share government in a time of crisis until this was forced on it by a pragmatic president of the republic. It is an atavistic, idiosyncratic nation, which gave birth to an atavistic, idiosyncratic communist party. If Portugal matures politically, the PCP is likely to follow suit. If it lets either its anarchic or authoritarian instincts prevail in its present financially weak state, then one can expect a lengthy cycle of right-wing/left-wing repression waged on the fringe of modern Europe and at the everlasting expense of the Portuguese people, impervious to the lessons of other nations while remaining a case-study for them.

7. The New Communist Economics[1]
Stuart Holland

During one of his periodic and voluble television appearances,
early in 1978, Henry Kissinger warned that the Western European
communist parties still were Stalinist wolves, whatever their new
democratic clothing. They were out to grab power, and precedent
showed that they rarely handed it back. Moreover, he claimed,
their analysis of history was based on economic determinism.
They held that capitalism was bound to collapse and be super-
seded by a communist economy and society. Thus they had a
one-way view of economic forces underlying the political world.
The idea that they would allow themselves to be turned back
from entry to government by commitment to 'advanced democracy' or pluralism was a myth.

At best, Kissinger's warning shows an ignorance of the new
economic analysis of what have become known as 'Eurocommunist' parties. At worst, it misrepresents both differences between
them, and differences from the fatalist and determinist elements
in their previous economic ideology. A closer look at their
economic theory and its bearing on their political strategies indicates that the older theories on the inevitability of a capitalist
crisis have been modified in significant ways since the inter-war
years. During those years, the communists argued that the inherent crisis of capitalism could not be offset by a capitalist state,
and that increasing instability in the economic base would be
reflected in political and economic superstructures. Good communists were bidden by Moscow to sit back, and prevent social
democrats from tampering with the iron laws of economics.
After January 1933, and the National Socialist seizure of power
in Germany, the burden of the argument shifted somewhat:
communists were told to cooperate with anti-fascists, but there

was to be no doubt that the capitalist contradiction of over-production and under-consumption had been resolved, not by domestic economic management but by armaments production.

After 1945, just as there was a change in the rationale and extent of state intervention, based partly on economic doctrines associated with Keynes and partly on the necessity of government intervention for reconstruction, so there was a change in the economic philosophies of leading communist parties. The change came fastest in Italy, where the reconstruction programme of the communist party was markedly Keynesian in character, and slower in France and Spain. It rested on a fundamentally new admission of the capacity of the modern capitalist state to intervene in and affect the behaviour of capitalist economies. In turn, this implied a new political strategy, as might be expected of Marxist parties steeped in the materialist tradition: the assumption that the economic collapse of capitalism would create the conditions for mobilization of the working class for its overthrow gave way to concern to expose the class basis of capitalist state intervention, and to demonstrate the incapacity of that state to fulfil the economic and social needs of the working class. Greater significance was attached to the role of the political process in relation to economic factors; new policies of class alliance in an anti-monopoly programme were elaborated to include, not only the industrial working class, but also the peasantry and broad sections of the middle class; new dimensions were added to analysis of the role of the modern capitalist state, which implied new roles for communist parties in Western European politics; in addition, there was a greater admission of the need to co-ordinate policies in Western Europe as a means of countervailing the trend to multinational capital.

Partly, this change was rooted in the political disasters of the 1930s, which orthodox doctrines on the inevitable collapse of capitalism had done much to foster. It is now widely acknowledged that the concept of hegemony, which the Italian communists acquired from Antonio Gramsci, and its related strategy for a politics of 'consensus', was a reaction to the failure of classic Leninist policies for seizure of power and 'smashing' the state apparatus through the establishment of dictatorship of the proletariat. Basically, Gramsci, in his *Prison Notebooks*, argued that the conditions for Leninist strategy had applied in Russia, where the Tsarist state had frustrated even a bourgeois political revolution. But in the more mature Western democracies, where the bourgeois revolution, in some cases centuries old, had delivered meaningful reforms to the working class, the viability of the capitalist state was based less on repression than on consent within civil society, however frustrated the expectations which it provoked. This consent had to be won by communist building of a hegemonic dominance, in the sense of a widely based support for the transformation of capitalism. The impact of these ideas on PCI thinking in the immediate post-war period was notable: the potential of Keynesian policies was clear to a party already open to new ideas on the role of the state in capitalist society.

In France, the commitment to classic Leninism was longer standing and deeper rooted. Between the wars, the French Communist Party had offered only passive support to Léon Blum's Popular Front government rather than jointly agreeing a 'Programme for Government' of the kind which emerged in 1972. In the immediate post-war period, their brief participation in a coalition government partly reflected the popular base which they had built in the Resistance with conservative nationalists, and partly Moscow's unwillingness to destabilize the spheres of influence for East and West which had been established at Yalta. It was only in the early 1960s that the PCF felt it had to recognize the implications of the phoenix-like French post-war recovery and admit that the state, through planning, public spending and public enterprise, had been able to influence the economy. Yet even here, especially in the stress on the links between state capitalist intervention and monopoly capital, there were echoes of classic Leninism.[2] In both political ideas and strategy for political action, the PCF lacked a Gramsci to wean them from the ghetto of old assumptions and old roles. Their emergence from such a ghetto during the period of the 'Common Programme of the Left' was to be partial and uncertain.

In Spain, the communist party's evolution was fashioned by its prolonged struggle in clandestinity against Franco's fascism. Until the early 1960s, its leadership had faithfully followed the orthodoxies of capitalism's inevitable collapse, and gravely underestimated the strength of the Franco régime. The culmination of this faith had come in 1959, when Franco had been forced to impose an austerity policy by the Western Powers, but took the precaution of voting additional funds for the police forces. The communists' call to a general strike failed utterly in that collaboration with other opposition parties proved fruitless, the workers refused to follow, and prominent members of the party in Spain were captured. Soon after, the Franco régime improved its relations with General de Gaulle and imported the techniques of planning whereby a strengthened civil service and state apparatus in France had been able to proceed with technocratic intervention to reconstruct French capital and establish 'national champions' among leading enterprises under its sponsorship.[3] Reluctantly at first, Santiago Carrillo – the PCE secretary-general – came round to accepting some of the party's internal discussions on the Franco régime as a 'Prussian state', powerfully intervening in the minutiae of the country's economic development.

By the mid 1960s, the major communist parties in Western Europe were faced with governments claiming to be converted to direction of economic forces, committed to some form of public intervention in the economy and claiming success in raising the standard of living for large sectors of the population. The thesis which the parties evolved to explain their new circumstances, and to serve as a guide for action, received its first formulation in 1964, in the form of the Italian communist leader, Togliatti's, Yalta memorandum. This was amplified at a joint meeting of the Western communist parties at Choisy-le-Roi in France, in 1966, and came to be known as the 'state monopoly capitalism' thesis.[4] Over simplified, it holds that the trend to monopoly, publicized by Lenin, and developed by Hilferding and Bukharin, had resulted in the establishment of an economic system dominated by large-scale monopolistic enterprise rather than the smaller-scale capitalism publicized in the predominantly liberal capitalist ideology of the 1960s. Banking cartels and corporations cohabit incestuously with public authorities to accelerate the rate of accumulation, in the name of national legitimacy or of free trade. In fact, the appeal to the authority of second-generation Marxists hides more than the habitual justification by communist parties of new theses in the name of old ones. All shifted Lenin's emphasis from international struggle between imperialist states to competitive struggle between multinational companies. In particular, they stressed the changed scope and scale of state intervention in capitalism, with the implicit admission that state subsidy and public purchasing, analysed by Bukharin in his *Imperialism and World Economy*,[5] could now achieve extensive real gains both for capital and for the working class. Their differences were also crucially reflected in political strategy: while Lenin saw state intervention mainly as a futile attempt to offset the impending crisis of capitalism for a while, and state capitalism as the ante-chamber to a socialist transformation of a capitalist society, the state monopoly capitalism thesis, as endorsed by the main communist parties in the mid 1960s, admitted the adaptive capacity of the modern capitalist state, and its relative ability to postpone and frustrate the transformation of capitalism through placation of broad sections of the working class.

Equally significant was the concern of different communist parties to stress the specificity of national conditions and to differentiate themselves from Moscow. French communist thinking, for example, bears the stamp of the still, as yet, un-rehabilitated Bukharin as well as of Lenin. For instance, while Lenin denied the feasibility of successful capitalism within the boundaries of the nation state, Bukharin addressed himself to the state's intervention through public purchasing and profit subsidy to assist and promote the expansion of monopoly capitalist trusts – a trend observed by many commentators of French industrial policy in the 1960s.[6] Similarly, the Spanish experience of extensive control over large sectors of the economy by a national banking cartel could draw on Hilferding's thesis on the interpenetration and dominance of German industrial and finance capital in the early twentieth century: Spanish capitalism hardly answered to the characteristics of an aggressive foreign expansion as described by Lenin in his famous pamphlet, *Imperialism, the Highest Stage of Capitalism*.[7]

Furthermore, Italy's communists are a case apart. Since the mid 1950s,[8] the PCI has given no priority to the extension of public enterprise, while admitting that circumstances may force it to bring sections of the private sector which are in profits crisis into public ownership. This reflected, no doubt, the considerable size and range of the existing sector in industry, banking and insurance in Italy. But it also bears implications for the role envisaged by the PCI for a 'mixed' economy. In practice there has, for a long time, been little to distinguish the PCI's position on the scale of public ownership from leading opinion and policy formers in either the Italian Socialist Party or the Christian Democratic Party. The contrast with Stalinist collectivization of all industry and finance, with the bulk of agriculture, is very clear.

These differences on national economic proposals are repeated in policies towards the European Economic Community (EEC). Broadly speaking, the PCI recognized in the 1960s that the economic consequences of Italian membership of the EEC had not been entirely negative. While Italy suffered a major balance-of-payments deficit within five years of joining the EEC, it recovered quickly enough – partly through a combination of Keynesian demand management and sustained foreign demand aided by a disguised devaluation. Moreover, especially under advocacy and pressure from the Amendola group within the party, and in view of the limited success of centre-left policies for national planning in the late 1960s, the view gained ground in the PCI that effective countervailance of monopoly and multinational capital would be reinforced by joint international action at Brussels.[9] This was apart from the fact that, at the political level, the PCI was concerned, even before the overthrow of Allende in Chile, with the question of legitimizing and ensuring its maintenance of office against both a neo-fascist reaction in Italy and foreign intervention from abroad. Thus, while not uncritical of the EEC or its major policies – including the Common

Agricultural Policy, which it wants to see revised – the PCI by the 1970s had come to endorse positively the proposals for a federal or supranational EEC.

Similarly, the PCE has adopted a critical but positive attitude towards European integration. Their position reflects three main elements in their general economic, political and social analysis: (a) what they call 'the necessity for a coordination of the struggle of classes in capitalist Europe' (rather than 'class struggle'); (b) the need to reduce and countervail the power of monopolies; and (c) the defence and extension of freedoms through a democratic 'transformation' of the EEC.[10] The parallels with the PCI in relation to the fear of a return to fascism or crypto-fascism, while not explicit, are none the less clear.

By contrast, the PCF continued to maintain that the EEC was essentially the instrument of monopoly and multinational capital, and resisted socialist pressures for endorsement of a so-called 'positive' attitude towards the community. Basically, the PCF is more nationalist in its approach to the EEC and community institutions, and insisted in the 'Common Programme' – signed with the socialists and left radicals in 1972 – that any action at community level by a government of the Left should be 'based on the nation state'. Various factors underlay the difference of position, and not least the *étatiste* tradition in France. But there is little doubt also that the formulated PCF analysis of state monopoly capitalism played a related part: capitalist state intervention in post-war France had been much more extensive in industry, finance and other sectors of economic activity than elsewhere in the EEC, and *its* transformation was the priority for the PCF in economic policy. Besides which, de Gaulle had shown from his gelding of majority voting in the Council of Ministers at Luxemburg in January 1966 that the community's pretensions to state power were veiled mainly by the fig-leaf of a Common Agricultural Policy absorbing up to four fifths of its budget, whose terms and conditions had substantially been imposed by France herself.

The PCF and the 'Common Programme'

The 'Common Programme of the Left', signed with much panache in June 1972, opens with those economic issues that were to underlie the later tensions between the communists, socialist and left radicals that came into the open in September 1977: wages, purchasing power, working conditions and employment.[11] This is followed by a lengthy section on Welfare State measures for a society which is notably privatized.[12] While these may look straightforward enough, they later became crucial in the question of what a government dominated by the socialists would do on the wage and employment front if gaining office in 'full crisis' in 1978. In other words, would it expand public spending, public enterprise and planning in such a way as to attempt to break through the crisis through reflation, or react defensively with attempts at a wages freeze, and public spending restraint, of a kind whose incidence would have to be borne mainly by the natural constituents of the PCF – the industrial working class?

The second main part of the programme is also concerned with economic issues: this time explicitly, under the title 'Democratizing the Economy, Extending the Public Sector and the Planning Process'.[13] It was in this area that differences between the communists and socialists were greatest. First, there was the interpretation to be placed on 'democratization' of the economy: with the PCF defending its concept of 'democratic centralism' and explicitly disagreeing with the socialists' conception of self-management or *autogestion*.

In addition, there was the question of extending the public sector. In the initial negotiations leading to the 'Common Programme', the PCF came with a shopping list of twenty-five companies to be brought into public ownership. It compromised initially with a list of less than half that number to be nationalized outright, or brought into the public sector through a controlling majority shareholding.[14] But this list came in addition to agreement in the programme that other broad areas of the economy would also be brought into public ownership, including all of the armaments industry, the aeronautics and space industry, nuclear power, pharmaceuticals, mineral resources, air and sea transport, water supply and distribution, the finance of tele-communications and motorway concessions. This was apart from nationalization of the whole banking sector, including the mer-chant and investment banks – the *banques d'affaires* – plus hire-purchase and credit institutions, and the large private insurance companies (excepting those which were genuinely cooperatives or mutual insurance societies). Compensation was included at the request of the left radicals, and a commitment made to 'an equitable solution', with special measures for 'an essential dis-tinction . . . between small and medium shareholders living from their own savings, and large shareholders'.[15]

By contrast to the Italian communist programme, this extended public sector was to play a key part in the national and regional planning objectives of the programme of the French Left. These were to be defined 'democratically' in the sense of winning parliamentary approval, and, as far as possible, to include workers' organizations within public or private firms, and also regional and local consumers' organizations. The plan was to be imperative for the public sector, but would respect management's autonomy.[16] The plan also would determine the larger investments in the private sector, and their means of finance. The public sector would be one of the three strategic features of democratic planning, jointly with the intervention of workers in decision-making 'at all levels', and the democratic use of credit, taxation and budgetary policy. In regional development, criteria would be established for the location of large firms, both public and private. Also, a major drive would be launched for the improvement of transport and telecommunications facilities (brought more directly into public ownership through the programme).

These main dimensions to the role of public enterprise in a planning framework parallel some of those already attempted by state capitalist policies in other EEC countries, or envisaged on a lesser scale by the 1966 Nora Committee for the public sector in France, which was favourably impressed, as others have been, by the model of the IRI state holding company in Italy, and led to a similar holding – the Industrial Development Institute (IDI) – for France.[17] One of the main contrasts with Nora was the downgrading of the role of the IDI (Institut pour le Développement Industriel), which was to be brought into a new National Investment Bank. But the general parallel between the new roles anticipated for public enterprise in the 'Programme of the Left' and state capitalist policies elsewhere was, while hardly explicit, none the less marked.

The parallel between state capitalism and aspects of the 'Common Programme' had its critics from within the communist party. Étienne Balibar, already notable for his attack on the abandonment of the concept of the dictatorship of the proletariat,[18] voiced his criticism of the alleged compromise with state capitalism in no uncertain terms in the period following the rupture of the Left and the run-up to the elections of March 1978. Put simply, state capitalism as commonly used *qua* concept means state intervention in an unreconstructed class framework to promote the further expansion of capital and capitalist relations of production, i.e. capitalist ownership and control. Balibar criticized the thesis of state monopoly capitalism which had emerged in the PCF from the early 1960s by arguing that it lacked a real appreciation of state power in a capitalist society. In other words, while assuming that the state could help and abet capital through intervention, it also assumed that the state could intervene in wider issues of social justice which capital itself neglected. Thus, Balibar maintained, the state monopoly capitalism thesis gave the state in capitalist society an independent or autonomous role of 'observer' of the two main social classes in society, neglecting the essential defence of capitalist class interests which it represented. It thereby gave the false impression to the working class that the state apparatus could be 'taken over' and used in its interests without a fundamental change in class relations.[19]

Balibar's criticisms could be regarded as representative of criticism of the PCF for involvement in the 'Common Programme' and a 'revisionist' strategy from its 'fundamental' left or ultra-left. The same issues are reflected in the extent to which the PCF resisted the principle of *autogestion* (self-management/ workers' control) as part of the 'Common Programme' package. *Autogestion* had been brought on the mainstream agenda of the French Left in the late 1960s by the impact of Trotskyite demands for direct democracy and workers' control in the period following May 1968, plus an independent push from the CERES group on the left of the French Socialist Party (PS), with echoes in the formerly predominantly Catholic trades union, the CFDT. Unsurprisingly, this appeared a very unholy alliance to many in the communist party. Besides, in the hands of most of its exponents in the socialist party, *autogestion* represented a key analytical and practical means of overcoming the statism and bureaucratic central control of the Soviet system. The implications of the Yugoslav system of self-management, and its challenge to the Soviet orthodoxies, were not lost on the exponents of *autogestion* on the French Left.[20]

Analytically, it might well have been thought that the principles of *autogestion* would appeal to those who, like Balibar, criticized the PCF for failure to take sufficient account of the class relations in society, or the social relations of production. After all, one of its essential points lay in the fact that while class domination in a capitalist society is a matter of both ownership *and* control of the means of production, the Soviet Union had got only to the half-way house of changing private to state ownership without socializing the control of the means of production through entrusting it to working people themselves – through those representative institutions which they chose to evolve and manage. But for militants in the PCF to accept either this principle, or the example of Yugoslav practice, meant an admission that the soviets of the USSR were not real or effective workers' councils, and that the 'democratic centralism' voiced since Lenin was not truly democratic. It was very much in this context that several fundamentalist contributions were collated in a largely anonymous volume of essays published in 1974 under the very explicit title, *Les Marxistes Contre l'Autogestion* (*Marxists Against Self-management*), and with the stated aim of 'combating the intoxication with self-management'.[21]

In fact – as already noted – the PCF, in the initial 'Common Programme' in 1972, agreed to differ with the socialists and the left radicals on the principle of extending self-management to the public sector. In itself this illustrated a certain unwillingness to ratify the divorce from Leninism or the Soviet model, and celebrate the wedding with the PSF in fact rather than form. Bigamy, if not indubitable, none the less was in question. The degree of difference between the CFDT and the PCF also showed itself in a series of acrimonious exchanges following the breakdown of the meetings to arrange the revision of the 'Common Programme' in 1977.[22]

The key phrase masking the ambiguity and difference of opinion between the communists and socialists, and embodied in the programme, read that 'on the basis of a large public and nationalized sector, the government will favour, in law and in reality, the development of democratic forms of management'.[23] The contrast with the explicit willingness of the Italian and Spanish communists to endorse both the spirit and letter of forms of industrial democracy is very clear. Hesitation on *autogestion* was very much the Achilles' heel of the French Communist Party in its efforts to convince a wider electorate that some citizens are not more equal than others. The party's lip-service to the concept during the 1978 're-negotiation' of the 'Common Programme' was too sudden and too late to carry much conviction.

Whatever the politics behind the breakdown in the September 1977 negotiations to revise the 'Common Programme', two issues were fundamental: (a) whether the subsidiaries with less than 100 per cent holdings of the firms listed for nationalization in the text of the 'Common Programme' were implied by the term 'group' and should be included with their parent companies; (b) whether a government of the Left would propose the nationalization of any particular company in the event of a majority of its workforce expressing their wish that it should be taken into the public sector. In the debate, then, between the representatives of the three parties, and in the subsequent debate in public meetings and in the press, other issues were to be added. They included: (c) the question whether compensation was to be paid for nationaliz-

ation of the companies specified in the 'Common Programme'
and (d) the overall cost of the programme itself in economic
terms.

On the related questions of whether the subsidiaries of listed
firms for nationalization were to be included in the extension of
public ownership, the nature of compensation and the cost of the
programme overall, it is possible to give the PCF a good deal of
benefit in the overall doubt.[24] It is not at all clear how meaningful
an extension of the public sector would have been, had subsidiaries
with 51 per cent or more holdings by the specific companies not
been included. Most big businesses are themselves composed of
subsidiaries with varying shares of percentage control. Without
much doubt, Georges Marchais and the PCF leadership might
have considered that the raising of the question itself raised the
commitment of the socialist party to a major change in the balance
of power through public ownership. If this was not in question,
the background position of the CFDT and some of the *auto-
gestionnaires* probably was: many of them argued that ownership
was irrelevant to self-management and workers' control – in
other words, they saw the key to socialism in a change in the social
relations of production and control, rather than in ownership as
a necessary condition for such control.[25] On the other hand,
before the 'rupture' of the Alliance of the Left in May 1977,
Georges Marchais had made public that he looked to an extension of the public sector on a major scale, and the clause of the
'Common Programme' giving workers the right to request
public ownership as essential to such a working programme.[26]

Similarly, the issue of whether and how to compensate for the
extension of the public sector had been raised before the breakdown of renegotiation of the 'Common Programme'. François
Mitterrand and Jacques Attali – one of his principal economic
advisers – had proposed in April 1977 that the privately held
shares in those enterprises to be nationalized should not be transferred to public ownership and control, but issued 'as new shares,
with an indexed income, freely exchangeable on the financial
market. The stock market would determine their value in terms
of their rate of return [which would be related to] the effectiveness

of the strategy and policy of the enterprises.' This would mean the realization of 'a system of finance which achieved the key objective for the least cost [to the government]: i.e. taking power in these firms without damaging the finance of shareholders'.[27]

Again, while the proposal no doubt had some economic merit on its side, in terms of reducing the sums which a government of the Left would need to shift to shareholders in order to gain control, it was not exactly what the PCF had in mind in agreeing to the 'Common Programme' in 1972. Once again, the PS was taking a position which implicitly assumed that the question of control, or the social relations of production, predominated over the question of ownership as a precondition of such control. As is indicated later, such a position in the PS was in some respects little different from that of the PCI, which argued with increased force in the early 1970s that it had no concern to extend the size of the public sector in Italy, rather than to ensure its democratization in a planning framework. But, in fact, the public sector was different in size in France and Italy, and if Georges Marchais and the PCF leadership had ceded the issue, jointly with the question of what subsidiaries should be brought into public ownership, they would at best have been moving on to even less familiar ideological ground, and at worst have confirmed the assumptions of those critics of the state monopoly capitalism thesis such as Balibar that they believed in an autonomously powerful state.[28]

The further issue of the cost of the 'Common Programme' was linked with this question of how many firms were to be brought into the public sector and with what compensation. It also concerned the scale and extent of feasible extension of public works and social expenditure during a period in the later 1970s when the French economy would be facing not only considerable hostility from international capital and its institutions, but also a world market in recession, with the twist of high oil-import prices in a country lacking virtually any large-scale deposits of indigenous fuel. Yet again, as far back as 1973, Georges Marchais had presented his general observations on the potential cost of the programme in a different manner from François Mitterrand.

In 1975, he had consciously abandoned the question of figuring the cost of the programme as such and stressed its importance as a series of 'objectives for struggle' in his party. In essence, the PCF saw the potential of the programme as a process which would achieve primary political aims, to which economic costs would be secondary. In a more banal sense, the differences between the PCF and the PSF on the question of the cost of the programme related to the envisaged real scale of change.[29]

With hindsight, the alliance of the Left can be seen as uneasy and fragile. The whole relationship between the communists and socialists represented an on-going polemic about the nature of transition to socialism itself. Not least, the PCF feared that Mitterrand and much of the PS were a potentially social democratic party, forced by circumstance to ally with themselves. They partly saw Mitterrand as a Schmidt *à la tricolore*. They also were basically apprehensive that the socialists in office might well offer them ministries of second- or third-rank importance, and demand in return a pact for wage restraint which could compromise the base of the party in the industrial working class.

Final judgements are both arbitrary and premature. In the context of Eurocommunist economics as a whole, it none the less should become clear that differences between parties such as the PCF and the PCI depend partly on ideological inheritance, partly on national factors, and very much on the specific political dialectics between themselves and the other main parties or forces on the Left. The political economy of the French Communist Party was French before it became half-heartedly European. Moreover, the reversion of the PCF into a posture of independence from the socialists does not mean a return to the barrenness and sterility of the 1950s or a blatant footing of the Moscow line.

If the communists have helped put public ownership on to the agenda of French politics, even the differences of opinion between themselves and the socialists have opened a debate within the party on the case for self-management and workers' control. Jointly with the rejection of the concept of the dictatorship of the proletariat, the formal commitment to 'democratization of the economy' may well prove irreversible. If the road from Moscow has proved both harder and longer for the PCF than for the PCI, the issues of political and industrial democracy appear to have been stamped firmly on its fabric.

The PCI: hegemony in question

Granted the ferment which accompanied the shaping of the 'Common Programme of the Left' in France in the late 1960s and early 1970s, it is notable that in Italy the PCI did not publish a medium-term programme until 1977. In part, this reflected its much more pragmatic approach to economic policy. Its policies on key questions such as the role of public enterprise and development of the South were not formulated behind closed doors 'at the top' in terms of past ideological orthodoxies, and then transmitted to cadres below. The party's research bureau, CESPE (Centre for Studies on Political Economy), sponsored wide-ranging debates on general economic issues, with a broad-based political composition, including socialist economists and politicians whose discussions were then published in full.[30] The process was notably open and transparent. It illustrated both the Gramscian strategy of seeking to build a consensus support wider than the party itself and paralleled the political tactic of inviting 'independent' economists – such as the Keynesian Luigi Spaventa – to stand with communist support for parliamentary elections.

The programme when published was some 120 pages in length, and designed for mass readership.[31] Its opening sentence argued that 'the need to shape a project for the transformation of Italian society stems from the fact of contradictions and disproportions blocking a new development of the country and threatening democratic institutions'. 'Contradictions' and 'disproportions' could be considered orthodox enough Marxist terminology, but certainly were relevant to the crisis of stagnant investment, spare capacity, under-consumption, rampant inflation and chronic regional imbalance in the country as a whole. The Gramscian element in the strategy of the programme was implicit rather than explicit. It argued that the fundamental objective of an expansion and reconversion of the productive base of the economy itself implied a profound change in the social relations of production, reducing vast areas of privilege and parasitic labour. But it stressed that 'such an objective can only be realized through consensus and thus by new ideals and aims, with development at the same time of economic reforms and of intellectual and moral reforms of society'.[32]

Reform of the 'social relations of production' was conceived in terms of extension not only of 'workers' participation and control within enterprise but also the establishment of democratic control over the economic policy of the country as a whole, with decentralization and increased accountability within a 'plural democratic and political' structure.[33] In both respects, the argument is notably different from the Soviet model. There is no reference to 'soviets' as such, nor an attempt to maintain that the aims of soviets are direct democracy and workers' control. The mechanisms of direct democracy within enterprise are not spelled out, but the statement of the programme includes the term 'control' rather than the weaker 'participation' alone. 'Democratic centralism' of the kind which in practice has masked undemocratic centralization of both economic and political control in the Soviet Union, is contradicted implicitly by the commitment to decentralization of decision-making in a democratized economy policy.

The case for economic planning in the programme is related both to the weakness of the market mechanism in ensuring a 'spontaneous' adjustment of factors of production, and to its failure to ensure the new economic needs 'which are being expressed both by the democratic growth of society and by the changes which have occurred in the international division of labour'. In other words, the case on the failure of the market is not simply a matter of lost consumer sovereignty, but of its inability to ensure the legitimate economic and social aspirations of working people. This is partly through oligarchic decision-making in monopoly enterprise and through the erosion of the effectiveness of national trade unions in an era of multinational capital. However, the planning mechanisms recommended do not envisage the suppression of the market on Soviet lines. The programme specifies that planning, through the selection of priorities and the establishment of balance, should ensure 'an increased capacity for innovation and competitiveness in the Italian economy . . . and especially guarantee the development of small firms and cooperatives'.[34]

The programme stresses that the role of planning is central to aspirations for a change in Italian society: 'In practice it is only on the basis of democratic planning that it will be possible positively to resolve the contradictions . . . between the claims of various social strata and the demands for a restoration of the economic and financial situation, with a recovery of productive investment.' There are three key conditions: (a) the planning of public expenditure, (b) the restraint of inflation and (c) the creation of employment, focused on the problem region of the South. The main aim is employment creation, which will need not just macroeconomic planning but direct intervention at the level of the firm and industry. On the other hand, the programme specifies that discretionary fiscal subsidies and intervention in favour of particular firms has been abused under the clientelism of previous governments. The discretion should be aimed mainly at the fiscal base of different social groups and a fairer incidence of taxation, to cover more expenditure through tax and avoid an inflationary expansion of the economy.[35]

The regional focus of planning, according to the programme, should be linked to a reform of local finance (where a plethora of special agencies for regional development has led to conflicting spheres of responsibility and influence, without an effective channelling of resources). In general, the programme argues that state intervention agencies (*enti di gestione*) should be reformed 'with provision for the break-up of such agencies and the passing of their respective functions to the regions and local authorities'.[36] Again there is a clear enough contrast with the centralization of the Soviet model. Rather than tightening central state control, the PCI commits itself through the programme to what in practice amounts to the regional devolution of decision-making. Thus the policy reflects national circumstances and specific political experience. It is an extrapolation from the success of the PCI in regional government in areas such as Emilia-Romagna. Bologna rather than Moscow is the model.

While the programme argues that state *intervention agencies* in general should be broken up and regrouped, it does not specify the same for the state *holding companies* which play so important a part in the contemporary Italian economy. The previous party proposals to regroup the state holdings in single-industry or sector groups, subject directly to ministerial control rather than with para-statal status, no longer rank a mention. This is very much consistent with the major CESPE debate on the role of public enterprise, and an implicit admission that there are some advantages from a flexible multi-sectoral means of public-enterprise intervention.[37] Also, in striking contrast with the whole PCF polemic on the extension of public enterprise in the debate on the 'Common Programme' in France, there is no reference to the need to extend the existing public sector through ownership.

However, the programme gives considerable weight to the question of who should *control* state-owned enterprise. In other words, it by no means assumes that the transfer of ownership of the means of production to the state will thereby assure control and effective accountability, and insists that mechanisms must be established for ensuring 'transparency' in the operation of public enterprise. It also specifies that the personnel of state and parastatal organizations should be more mobile both between industries and regions of the country.[38] The attitudes and the commitments reflect the specific features of the role of state enterprise in Italy, with the establishment of some scarcely accountable super-groups in which the state has either outright or major participation, operating in practice as 'states within the state'. The most notorious was ENI under Mattei. While this criticism was qualified by recognition of his considerable state entrepreneurship, the secrecy of groups such as ENI and Montedison – in particular – had become notorious.

While such specific factors were important, it none the less is

clear that the acceptance of the general operating framework of
state holding companies, and emphasis on the question of their
control, contrasts once more with older Soviet-based orthodoxies.
There is no assumption that the class basis of society as such is
transformed through a change in ownership from private hands
to the state. In other words, if class in capitalist society is based
upon ownership and control of the means of production, distribution and exchange, the PCI has learned the lesson that state
ownership alone, without democratization and accountability in
control, changes only the form rather than substance of capitalist
relations of production – i.e. the class relations between capital
and labour. This, of course, is also an important element in the
state monopoly capitalism thesis as developed by the French
communists. But with the greater emphasis on industrial democracy and workers' control *within* enterprise, and the admission
that changes in ownership mean only a change from a capitalist to
a state capitalist mode of production and control, the PCI is as
much expressing its own experience in the specific Italian case as
any general formulation about the new forms of state monopoly
capitalism.

Neither this factor, nor the lack of commitment to major
extension of public ownership, implies a half-heartedness in the
PCI about the role of public enterprise itself in economic planning.
The programme both stresses that new planning must be planning for change in the economy and society, and that the state
holding companies will have 'a determinant role in the realization
of the new industrial policy and the sectoral programmes needed
by the country'.[39] It also underlines that the state sector not only
should spearhead the recovery of investment in industry, but also
concern itself more with medium- and small-sized enterprise and
agriculture. This reflects less the lack of special state holding companies for small- and medium-sized enterprise – of which there
are several – than two further factors: (a) the realization that
large-scale job creation will depend on more extensive intervention at the level of the small firm, and (b) the neo-Gramscian
importance of gaining and maintaining the support of broad
sections of the self-employed petty bourgeoisie, as well as that of
workers in non-unionized small and medium enterprise.

Thus there is no priority for bigness as such in the PCI state enterprise policy. More significantly, the programme specifies that state enterprise should be expected to intervene 'especially in those investment projects where risk is particularly high or the rate of return particularly delayed' as well as where external economies or indirect benefits to the economy are concerned. Such a case for intervention differs little from the rationale for extended state enterprise made by probably the foremost economist in public service in post-war Italy – Pasquale Saraceno. Saraceno has been a committed planner and advocate of public enterprise in the Italian economy, basically drafting both the ten years 'Vanoni Programme' of 1955 and writing the key report which preceded the introduction of five-year planning in the mid and late 1960s.[40] But he also was a committed Christian democrat.

Put simply, one could say that the parallel or overlap between the arguments of the PCI and Saraceno illustrates the arbitrariness of left-right political divisions in contemporary Italy.[41] Certainly, some Catholics who in other countries might find themselves in social democratic or socialist parties have been found to be active Christian democratic proponents of major state intervention in the economy. Also, while the PCI is committed to a 'profound change in the use of resources' in the economy, and by this declares itself to mean a change in the social relations of production between capital and labour, there is little evidence that a Christian democrat exponent of major state intervention and planning such as Saraceno means the same.[42] However, it is easy enough to understand why – seen from the ultra-Left in the Manifesto and Proletarian Unity groups – the PCI's strategy for public enterprise and planning looks reformist.

PCI activists at local and national level are sensitive to the charge of reformism. It is claimed not only by the ultra-Left, but also by socialists in Italy and abroad, that in practice there is little to distinguish their Gramscian strategy of establishing consensus support from social democratic policies for governing by, and as far as one can gain consent for, specific policies. The British Labour Party and the French socialists – despite the differences between the PCF and the PS on nationalization of subsidiaries –

are committed to a greater extension of public ownership than the PCI. In addition, both the French 'Common Programme of the Left' and the British Labour Party's programmes of 1973 and 1976 are more explicit on the manner in which they envisage harnessing the power of big business through planning than is the PCI programme of 1977. Besides, there is the question of a possible wages and prices policy during a crisis period in which the communist party in Italy might participate in or form a government. The question clearly is posed whether a historic communist party, which has hitherto been polarized from socialists and social democrats, would not find that the moderate character of its economic strategy reduced it to trying to resolve the economic crisis in Italy through classic social democratic policies of wage restraint and incentives to private capital.

One thing is clear enough: the cold warriors and the ultra-Left cannot both be right in their reading of PCI economic policy and its implications for the political process. If Kissinger and his acolytes are correct in arguing that the leopard has not changed its Muscovite spots, then the apparent parallel between neo-Gramscian hegemony and social democratic consensus cannot be correct. Inversely, to the extent that the PCI strategy for building consensus for democratic economic policy is realized, the Kissinger doctrine falls. The old-style determinism, which he discerns, would be discredited.

In fact there are strong grounds for claiming that the neo-Gramscian and consensus approach of the PCI is already a historic strategy rather than a short-term political tactic. But also the PCI has reason to claim that it is not social democratic in the sense of aiming to fulfil the better management of capitalism than the capitalists can manage themselves – through wage restraint and keeping the trade unions 'in line'. The two issues can be considered briefly, but in more detail.

For instance, in the immediate post-war period, the PCI adopted a reconstruction programme which was predominantly Keynesian in character – stressing the necessity of sustained demand and public expenditure to ensure that any temporary recovery was not followed shortly thereafter by a recession destabilizing the democratic process – as had happened in Italy following the First World War.[43] But this also was accompanied in the post-war decade by a criticism of Keynesianism in direct enough terms – not least the fact that demand management and public expenditure alone did not change the social relations of production – between capital and labour as classes, and between management and workers within enterprise. By the Eighth Congress of the party in the year of the invasion of Hungary – 1956 – these state capitalist implications of Keynesianism were being raised in the wider non-Keynesian context of state intervention in the structure of supply rather than demand. In other words, the Keynesianism itself of the party's post-war reconstruction programme was critical and qualified.

On the other hand, its evolution of an analysis of post-war state capitalism in Italy by implication criticized and qualified classic Leninism. The issues have been made explicit by a leading PCI ideologue, Luciano Barca, who has emphasized the importance of the Tenth Party Congress in representing 'an advance in principle on the problems of state capitalism'. He admits that some people have seen this as a somewhat uncritical adoption of the arguments of Lenin on state capitalism as the ante-chamber of socialism. However, he points out that Lenin himself saw state capitalism not only as the ante-chamber or precursor of socialism, but also as the 'highest stage' of monopoly capitalism. Barca argues that by the time of the Eighth Party Congress in 1956, it was explicitly admitted that while 'the arrival of forms of state capitalism can open the road to socialism, wherever it is accompanied by a democratic political struggle . . . there is a danger that nationalization, rather than destroying the power of the monopolies, will only create a new form of backward and reactionary capitalism'.[44] In other words, the determinism assumed by Kissinger, whereby the PCI would assume that economic events led relentlessly to the advance to socialism, is contradicted by the admission that state capitalism may arrest the progress of society towards a socialist mode of production. Moreover, this happens in the mid 1950s rather than the mid 1970s. It is long-term and basic analysis rather than a short-term and cosmetic tactic.

It also implies a major ideological and political campaign to reveal the limits of state capitalism rather than a sudden attempt at the seizure of power.

This also is implied by the relations of the PCI with trade unionism in the post-war period. The so-called Italian economic miracle brought real wage gains to the Italian working class of a kind which it had never before experienced. According to PCI spokesmen themselves, it was not until 1962–6, with the first real check to the sustained expansion of real incomes and the first signs of real faltering in capital accumulation, that the PCI's political leadership could make much impact on a unionized labour force for whom an instrumental attitude to work and the role of take-home pay were predominant. Even then, in the mid 1960s, when there was an advance beyond mere concern with wage bargaining for broad sections of the organized working class, this was for a while focused on demands for sustained capital accumulation rather than qualitative demands for transformation of the system.[45]

The change came substantially with the second major crisis of the post-war period, in 1968 and 1969, when the leading three unions in industry united in a campaign which went beyond the traditional wage bargain. Even then, with the three-month engineering strike of the 'hot autumn' of 1969, residual expectations that managerial capitalism could 'deliver the goods' in terms of constantly increasing real wages exerted a considerable ratchet effect in the now institutionally unified trade-union base. It was only with the patent incidence of crisis on a major scale with the world recession following 1973–4 that broad sections of the Italian working class lost their confidence in the capacity of capitalism to maintain the income increases to which they had become accustomed, and widely admitted – with varying degrees of consciousness – the limits of state capitalism itself.[46]

In effect, it took twenty years from the evolution of the state capitalism thesis in the PCI for the party's natural constituents to accept the new party line. Thus, as in France, the road was hard and long. The difference lay (a) in dominant consensus support which the PCI had managed to secure for itself among the working class by that date, and (b) in the difference which an explicit ideological case for consensus-building – through Gramsci – made in its more full-hearted attitude towards an alliance of the working class and peasantry with the middle and petty bourgeoisie. If the socialists in France had been coalition partners of the Gaullists, it is possible that the PCF now would be in a similar position in France to that which the PCI has secured in Italy – by keeping its hands clean during a discrediting of 'centre-left' coalition government in the 1960s and early 1970s. Politically, the PCI let the PSI make the mistake of entering coalition government without a broadly based class support.

In itself, this says little or nothing about the feasibility of the PCI avoiding 'mistakes', if it forms a government, through seeking to resolve the crisis of Italian capitalism in the short term through restraining wages, and thereby losing its basic support as a party of and for change. It is arguable that, even during the medium term, any government of the Left in Italy would have to call for wage restraint in its struggle to combat inflation and balance-of-payments deficits. The alternatives are either a total siege economy of the kind which the PCI has rejected – not least because of its commitment to continued membership of the EEC – for mainly political reasons; or a combination of progressive taxation on wealth and income with price controls, reflation and import substitution. The PCI has committed itself in the 1977 programme to both a revision of the EEC's common agricultural policy, and a strategy of import substitution and self-sufficiency in agricultural products. If achieved, this could have a very considerable impact on the balance of payments: the most notable item in the payments deficit of 1963 – the first since the early 1950s – was beef. It also might achieve considerable import savings through the development of a nuclear-power programme – again specified as a priority objective in the 1977 programme.[47]

On the other hand, agricultural production is slow and difficult. Nuclear-power programmes are notorious for consuming more in investment and research than virtually any other form of project, with negligible commercial pay-off and substantial environmental hazards. If the PCI in government is to avoid wage restraint

234 The New Communist Economics

while restructuring investment and productivity, it will need to
cope with the problem of inflation and related balance-of-payments deficits at source.[48] It is the same problem as has confronted
the French Left and caused such basic underlying tensions in the
on-going differences over the 'Common Programme'. With a
key difference: in France the P C F thinks that the PS will try to
impose wage restraint to resolve the crisis. In Italy, the only party
capable of delivering a degree of negotiated wage restraint is the
PCI.[49]

It is in this perspective that the differences between social democratic consensus-building, in the sense of gaining majority support on the basis of the lowest common denominator agreeable
to different groups and classes, differs from the Gramscian concept
of *hegemonic* consensus. The differences become important in
distinguishing strategies for reform of capitalist society from a
strategy for its transformation. At the risk of oversimplification,
and with allowance for the fact that Gramsci himself is not wholly
consistent on the relations between the state and civil society, they
can be highlighted as follows.[50]

According to Gramsci, civil society is 'that ensemble of organ-
isms commonly called private', while political society is the
public realm including that of the state. Both are part of the
social and political 'super-structure' of capitalism. But the role
and activities of groups and classes within this superstructure is
not simply a reflex or servicing of the needs of the forces of production in the economic base or 'sub-structure' of the system. Nor
is the role of the state apparatus itself of necessity predominantly
repressive. In practice, 'the supremacy of a social group mani-
fests itself in two ways: as "domination" and as "intellectual and
moral leadership"'. Moreover, dominance and leadership are
not simply a matter of the exercise of state power: 'A social
group can, and indeed must, already exercise "leadership" before
winning governmental power . . . it subsequently becomes dominant when it exercises power, but even if it holds it in its grasp, it
must continue to "lead" as well.'[51]

Essentially, reformism is only the parliamentary expression of
intellectual, moral and political *hegemony*. Power stems from a

hegemonic position in civil society rather than occupying office. Gramsci stresses that 'undoubtedly the fact of hegemony presupposes that account be taken of the interests and tendencies of the groups over which hegemony is to be exercised, and that a certain *compromise equilibrium* should be formed'. However, such a compromise 'cannot touch the essential; for though hegemony is ethical-political, it must also be *economic* [and] must necessarily be based on the function exercised by the leading group in the decisive nucleus of economic activity'. Reformism excludes 'the transformation of the subordinate group into the dominant one, either because the problem [of hegemony] is not considered – Fabianism, De Man, and an important part of the Labour Party – or because it is posed in an inappropriate and ineffective form – social democratic tendencies in general – or because of a belief in the possibility of leaping from class society directly into a society of perfect equality . . .'[52]

If this leaves open the question whether the PCI has, through the historic compromise, in fact 'touched the essential' and compromised excessively on economic policy, it none the less illustrates the kind of framework within which the party perceives its own economic programme. It has opted clearly for the general Gramscian strategy of building up a hegemonic *position* of intellectual, ethical and political leadership, in contrast with the Leninist strategy of *manoeuvre* and seizure of state power through a vanguard movement which may or may not have the widespread support of different classes and strata in society. It could perhaps be commented that strategies of position which neglect manoeuvre and decisive leadership at particular junctures are as unsound as manoeuvres which are not backed by any established position. Gramsci himself commented that it is possible to achieve a dominant position without effective leadership, and that in such a position the domination 'will be exercised by a part of the social group over the entire group, and not by the latter over other forces in society in order to give power to the group [and] radicalize it'.[53] The dominance of Italian politics today when, at the time of writing, Italy is governed through the grace, favour and abstention of the PCI, may be a case in point.

The PCE: peninsular political economy

In the so-called Eurocommunist league, the PCE is a newcomer. Also, its electoral strength is a fraction that of the Italian and French parties: roughly a tenth of the total vote, against nearly two fifths for the PCI and over a fifth for the PCF. But neither its late arrival (or recent emergence from clandestinity), nor its relatively smaller political weight has prevented its imposing its mark on the Eurocommunist debate in a decisive manner. This is most notable in the extent to which Santiago Carrillo has made explicit key themes which have either been understated or until recently unstated by the PCI and PCF – most notably the rejection of Leninist policies for the 'smashing' of the state apparatus, related to abandonment (with the other Western European parties) of the concept of dictatorship of the proletariat.[54]

Carrillo has had his own problems in these respects within the PCE. He is under considerable criticism from both former members of the party who basically claim that he remains an unreconstructed Stalinist, such as Jorge Semprun, and others such as Enrique Lister who maintain that he has converted the PCE into a social democratic party.[55] Again, as with the debate on the PCI, both sides cannot be right, and in practice the real situation may well lie between the two. Certainly Carrillo has done more than any other communist leader in Western Europe to dissociate himself from both Stalinism and the contemporary régime in the Soviet Union. The exchange in which he stated that Spain had not abandoned one 'holy office of the inquisition' to submit itself to another – in the form of the Moscow line – was both more acerbic and more revealing of real difference than many Delphic utterances on relations with the USSR and the Soviet model emanating, for instance, from the PCF.

The character of the economic policies of the PCE can be evaluated both from the 1975 manifesto programme of the party, and from the rationale for them available in the arguments of Carrillo himself and the leading economist in the PCE – the exceptionally prolific Ramón Tamames, a member of both the central and executive committees of the Spanish party.[56] One of the striking features of both the 1975 programme and the work of Carrillo and Tamames lies in the explicit use to which they put the thesis of state monopoly capitalism, and the relation which they make between the case for a democratic political programme and the change in the economic role of the modern capitalist state.

Thus Carrillo argues that the achievement of a socialism which maintains, enriches and gives new economic and social dimensions to democratic political freedoms and human rights cannot be achieved simply by abandoning the concept of dictatorship of the proletariat, but needs a global analysis of developed capitalist society and its world context; of the consequences of progress in the means of production and the new social structures which it has promoted. In particular, it demands study and analysis of the modern capitalist state as it now is, rather than as it was analysed by past masters of Marxist theory. He argues that such analysis of the state and its contemporary economic and class role demonstrates why the PCE considers that its role can be transformed through democratic change rather than 'without the need to destroy it root and branch, by force'.[57]

In making the case, he specifies that effective democratic socialism will depend on the transformation of the state apparatus which, in a capitalist society, remains the instrument of class domination. He also argues that the state is not autonomous between classes, despite the fact that – within certain limits – it can exercise a relative autonomy for some period of time. However, he maintains that with the transformation of the forces of production in modern capitalism, and the trend to monopoly, a change has occurred within the social relations of production, or the class basis of the modern capitalist state. This is itself related to the internationalization and regionalization of capital on a global scale, which poses problems of imbalance, disproportion and maladjustment for the nation state relative to forces which lie substantially outside its control. The two factors, as stressed in the programme of 1975, result in a changed relationship between the state, the capitalist class and the international capitalist economy.[58]

Thus, in a section entitled 'State Monopoly Capitalism', the

1975 programme claims that under the dominion of monopoly capital, the power of the modern capitalist state has been considerably modified. Previously, and especially during the time when it was a revolutionary force, the bourgeoisie could present its own advance in power as an advance of all the citizens of a particular country. It was in this sense that the key bourgeois revolution in France of 1789 actually inscribed its advance as one of 'liberty and fraternity'. But, today, the increased domination of both national economies and the international capitalist system by a few monopolistic and multinational companies has undermined the pretension of the state to represent and protect either the general economic interests of citizens, or the bourgeois class as a whole. The state has become the instrument of the interests of the grande bourgeoisie and big business *versus* the interests of the numerical bulk of the middle class and the interests of medium and small enterprise – which are being crushed by the increased power of the new monopolies.[59] Hence the line 'give back power to parliament'.

Moreover, the 1975 programme claims that Spanish monopoly capital is dominated in particular by finance capital and banking. It illustrates this by arguing that, while no Spanish-owned industrial enterprise is represented among the 200 largest world corporations, Spain includes three of the fifty largest banks in the world. Also, these banks on average have been registering profit levels double those, for instance, in France. Analytically, it could be commented that this amounts to very much the situation of 'finance capital' analysed by Hilferding in Germany before the First World War. But the 1975 programme stresses the class alliance represented by the dominance of finance capital, between the classic aristocracy and the grande bourgeoisie. It ascribes this situation to the late modernization of the industrial economy of Spain, and its dependence on the financial power of national banks during nearly forty years of fascist rule.[60] A similar class alliance and domination between neo-feudal, aristocratic landowning families and the banking sector in fact was paralleled in Portugal during the same period.

The class implications of such an analysis are clear enough. Essentially, the PCE is arguing that both the working class of industrial and agricultural workers, and the petty bourgeoisie and middle class as a whole, are exploited by an alliance between the grande bourgeoisie and aristocracy. Therefore a programme for the transformation of the role and use of economic power in Spain should be based on a middle- and working-class alliance of forces against this aristocratic-bourgeois alliance. But such a 'therefore' has crucial implications in interpreting the general programme of the PCE. It indicates that the case for a broadly based class alliance is not simply a hangover from 'popular front' policies of the 1930s, or an electoral tactic during the thaw of fascism and the approach to working democratic institutions. The new political programme of the PCE is essentially *based on* its economic analysis of the new class structure in modern Spain. This is itself reflected in its own characterization of the aristo-cratic-grande bourgeoisie alliance as a 'capitalist oligarchy', and its specific case for democratization of the state apparatus which such an oligarchy at present largely commands.[61]

Similarly, the basic economic and social analysis of the PCE *implies* its specific economic policies. These lay heavy emphasis on the nationalization of banking and insurance, with monopoly industrial enterprise and extensive fiscal reform as the basis for providing education and health at all levels as a public service. This 'anti-monopolist' strategy, based on assumption of the feasibility of a class alliance between the working class and the mainstream middle class, is paralleled by an 'anti-latifundist' strategy for agriculture, with proposals for reform of the large neo-feudal landholdings which have inhibited the development of modern agriculture in Spain. The proposals for both industrial democracy and democratic management of agriculture through the extension of producer and distribution cooperatives, relate essentially to this broader class basis for democratization.[62]

A contrast can be drawn with Italy and the PCI programme of 1977. For one thing, the state sector in Italian industry is con-siderably more extensive than in Spain, with a plurality of state holding companies on a major scale (IRI, ENI, EFIM and the state holding in Montedison) as against only one large state holding company in Spain – the National Industrial Institute (INI). Also, in Italy, three of the largest banks in the country, the so-called banks of 'national interest', are already part of the public sector through controlling shareholdings. But a contrast also can be drawn with the nationalization demands of the PCF in France. Put simply, it can be argued with some credibility that the PCF case for public ownership of the means of production, distribution and exchange is much more classically Leninist in character than in either PCI or PCE policy. Similarly, the hesitation of the PCF in endorsing industrial democracy and workers' control (rather than a form of words on democratic management of the public sector) illustrates the extent to which its policies reflect an implicit assumption that changes in ownership of the means of production will thereby bring about changes in the social relations of production, provided a 'democratic centralist' exercise of state power is in the interests of the working class as a whole.

It is plausible that the position of the French Communist Party reflects the extent to which the French socialists have pre-empted a strategy of a broader-based class alliance over the last ten years. The PSF originally negotiated the 'Common Programme of the Left' under pressure from the CERES group on its own left wing, but Mitterrand has consistently bid for support from the middle and centre of the political spectrum. The very fear in the PCF that, once in office, Mitterrand would do his utmost to assert the moderation of the PSF, if not transform it into a tricolour SPD, very probably has helped to polarize the political-economic programmes of the two main parties of the French Left, and inhibit a more explicitly Gramscian strategy of consensus-building by the PCF.

The PCE in Spain has been under no such inhibitions in the 1970s, either with respect to the use of Gramsci, or to an explicit distancing from the Leninist model. Thus Carrillo is quite explicit on the importance of Gramsci in emphasizing that the modern capitalist state serves and protects the interests of a capitalist class not simply through the repressive power of the police, army and judiciary – which, he adds, is much less in some states than others – but also through the hold of a dominant ideological consensus: i.e. the extent to which the perceptions, presumptions and prejudices of working people serve to support a system which exploits them economically, while gaining their passive support through the assumption that there is no alternative to such a form of economy and society. Similarly, Carrillo not only has been foremost among the Eurocommunist leaders in criticism of the Soviet model, but also has categorized Lenin as himself a revisionist *vis-à-vis* Marx's original writings on the state and economic power.[63] In France, one scarcely finds such a pretension, while in Italy it is the prerogative of ideologues or functionaries who are not of primary rank within the party.[64] Besides which, the Spanish Communist Party has accepted the principle of wage controls as part of an inter-party programme of national reconstruction, without participation in government. While Henry Kissinger in exile may regard this as the tactics of shock-troops precursing Soviet invasion, others might well regard it as the rearguard of *révolution manquée*, at least on the lines of 1917. It appears that only Cunhal, in the isolation of the Portuguese party, still believes in the spirit of Petrograd and all power to the soviets.

Notes and references

1. I am very much indebted to David Bell, of Sussex University, for discussion, comment and some material used in this chapter. Naturally enough, he is absolved of responsibility for its content.

2. The fullest statement of PCF views on this theory is to be found in Traité Marxiste d'Économie Politique, *Le Capitalisme monopoliste d'état*, 2 vols., Paris, 1971.

3. See, *inter alia*, Raymond Vernon (ed.), *Big Business and the State*, London, 1974, Chapter 1.

4. See Barnado Valli, *Gli EuroComunisti*, Milan, 1976.

5. Nikolai Bukharin, *Imperialism and World Economy* (with an introduction by V. I. Lenin), London, 1972.

6. Andrew Shonfield, *Modern Capitalism*, London and Oxford, 1965.

7. V. I. Lenin, *Imperialism, the Highest State of Capitalism: Selected Works*, vol. 1, Part 2, Moscow, 1952.

8. See further, Luciano Barca, Franco Botta and Alberto Zevi, *I Communistie l'Economia Italiana 1944–1974*, De Donato, 1975, Chapter 1.

9. For background on the PCI position, see further, *I Communisti italiani e l'Europa*, Atti del Convegno promosso dal CESPE e dai gruppi parlamentari del PCI, Rome, 23–5 November 1971, published in *Quaderni di Politica ed Economia*, No. 3, 1972.

10. Segunda Conferencia Nacional del Partido Comunista de España, *Manifesto Program del Partido Comunista de España*, Paris, 1975, pp. 102–3.

11. Parti Communiste et Parti Socialiste, *Programme Commun de Gouvernement*, Paris, 1972, Chapter 1.

12. ibid., pp. 53–102.

13. ibid., pp. 105–39. Part 2 of the programme covers not only democratization of enterprise and national planning, plus extension of the public sector, but also regional and agricultural policy; trade; small and medium enterprise; budgetary, fiscal and financial policy; and price controls.

14. The list included Dassault, Roussel-Uclaf, Rhône Poulenc, Pechiney-Ugine-Kuhlmann, Saint-Gobain-Pont à Mousson, ITT France, Thomson-Brandt, Honeywell-Bull, Compagnie Générale d'Électricité, Usinor-Vallourec, Wendel Sidelor, Schneider, Compagnie Française des Pétroles-CFR-Total.

15. *Programme Commun de Gouvernement*, Part 2.

16. 'Le Plan s'imposera au secteur public dans le respect de l'autonomie de gestion des entreprises, dont il favorisera la coordination' – ibid., p. 118.

17. A parallel noted by Paul Fabra in 'Les nationalisations aujourd'hui et demain', in *Le Monde*, 2 July 1977.

18. Étienne Balibar, *La Dictature du prolétariat*, published in English translation as *Dictatorship of the Proletariat*, London, 1976.

19. See further, Thierry Pfister, 'M. Balibar critique la théorie du capitalisme monopoliste d'État développée par le PCF', *Le Monde*, 12 January 1978.

20. For the pseudonymous Daniel Chauvey, in *Autogestion*, Paris, 1970, autogestion meant 'the intersection of planning and the market – under

workers' control', while democratic socialism itself was equated with 'information plus self-management'.

21. *Les Marxistes contre l'Autogestion: recueil d'analyses, d'articles et des documents écrits de 1962 à 1974 pour combattre l'intoxication auto-gestionnaire*, Selio, 1977.

22. See *inter alia*, 'La CFDT précise ses priorités pour 1978: Donner des réels pouvoirs aux travailleurs', *Le Monde*, 14 June 1977; and 'M. Maire (CFDT) continue de critiquer la stratégie communiste', *Le Monde*, 11 October 1977.

23. *Programme Commun de Gouvernement*, p. 105.

24. See further Raymond Barrillon, 'L'Irréparable? Le Second Échec du "Sommet" de la Gauche', and Gilbert Matthieu, 'Le Vrai Dossier économique des nationalisations', *Le Monde*, 24 September 1977.

25. With qualifications, this was very much the position of Michel Rocard.

26. Thierry Pfister, 'Pour M. Marchais, l'actualisation du Programme Commun suppose aussi l'extension des nationalisations', *Le Monde*, 20 May 1977.

27. Philippe Labarde and François Renard, 'Que nationaliser, et comment?', *Le Monde*, 16 April 1977.

28. cf. Thierry Pfister in *Le Monde*, 23 January 1978.

29. Gilbert Matthieu and Thierry Pfister, 'Le Chiffrage du PC – L'Embarras du PS', *Le Monde*, 12 May 1977; and Raymond Barrillon, 'Le PS n'accepte pas le "Chiffrage" du PC', *Le Monde*, 14 May 1977.

30. *PCI Proposta di Progetto a Medio Termine*, Rome, July 1977.

31. See, *inter alia*, *I Comunisti italiani e l'Europa*; CESPE, *Imprese Pubbliche e Programmazione Democratica*, published in *Quaderni di Politica ed Economia*, Nos. 7 and 8, 1973; and *Il Mezzogiorno nella Crisi Italiana*, published in *Quaderni di Politica ed Economia*, No. 4, 1975.

32. *PCI Proposta di Progetto . . .*, p. 25.

33. ibid., pp. 38–48.

34. ibid., pp. 52–3.

35. ibid., pp. 47–58.

36. ibid., p. 61.

37. CESPE, *Imprese Pubbliche* . . .

38. *PCI Proposta di Progetto* . . ., p. 61.

39. ibid., P. 72.

40. See further, Stuart Holland (ed.), *The State as Entrepreneur*, London, 1972, Chapter 1.

41. Luciano Barca, a leading economic spokesman of the PCI, pays specific credit to Christian democrat economists such as Saraceno, and socialists such as Paolo Sylos-Labini in widening the terms of reference of debate on the Italian economy; cf. Barca, Botta and Zevi, *I Comunisti e l'Economia Italiana*, p. 29.

42. *PCI Proposta di Progetto* . . ., p. 22.

43. The programme was forwarded by the PCI-dominated union, CGIL, on which Napoleone Colajanni (later vice-president of the senate) has commented that this was 'substantially a Keynesian plan, based on the attainment of global employment'. See further CESPE, *Imprese Pubbliche* . . ., p. 131.

44. Barca, Botta and Zevi, *I Comunisti e l'Economia Italiana*, pp. 25–6.

45. See further, D. Grisoni and H. Portelli, *Luttes ouvrières en Italie de 1960 à 1976*, Paris, 1976; and Lucio Libertini and Bruno Trentin, *L'Industria Italiana alla Svolta*, 1975.

46. Barca, Botta and Zevi, *I Comunisti e l'Economia Italiana*, p. 31.

47. *PCI Proposta di Progetto* . . ., pp. 67 and 71.

48. It is of some interest that Eugenio Peggio, head of CESPE, is on record as endorsing the analysis of inflation made by the EEC Maldague group in 1976, which argued that inflationary pressures under monopoly conditions were increased by deflation, which raised fixed costs, and therefore concluded that only a combination of reflation with price controls could cope with the current inflationary problem. See further, EEC Commission, *Report on Inflation*, 1976 (cyclostyled).

49. The vocabulary of an 'active manpower policy' and labour redistribution is nominally shared by the PCI with the German SPD – however different its implications for the two parties. See further, *PCI Proposta di Progetto*. . ., p. 74.

50. See especially, Perry Anderson, 'The Antimonies of Antonio Gramsci', in *New Left Review*, No. 100, 1975–6.

51. *Selections from the Prison Notebooks of Antonio Gramsci*, edited and translated by Quintin Hoare and Geoffrey Nowell Smith, London, 1971, pp. 12 and 57–8.

52. ibid., pp. 160–61 (our emphases).

53. ibid., p. 106.

54. Santiago Carrillo, *'Eurocomunismo' y Estado, Barcelona*, 1977, Chapter 6 (English translation: *'Eurocommunism' and the State*, 1977.)

55. See, *inter alia*, Jorge Semprun, 'Tribuna Libre', *El Pais*, 8 January 1978 and Enrique Lister, 'El PCE se ha convertido en un partido de corte social-democrata', *El Pais*, 7 January 1978; also Enrique Lister, 'Semprun y Azcarate hacen trampa', *Diario 16*, 10 January 1978.

56. *Manifesto Programma del PEC*; and Ramón Tamames, *Una Nueva Politica Economica para España*, 1968; and *Adonde Vas España?*, 1975.

57. Carrillo, *'Eurocomunismo' y Estado*, p. 17.

58. ibid., pp. 18–20 and 59.

59. *Manifesto Programma del PCE*, pp. 113–14.

60. ibid., pp. 104–7.

61. ibid., p. 104.

62. ibid., pp. 118–21.

63. Carrillo, *'Eurocomunismo' y Estado*, p. 26.

64. Notably Franco Rodano, *Sulla Politica del Comunisti*, Turin, 1975, pp. 57–9.

Part Three

8. The Challenge to Soviet Leadership: Effects in Eastern Europe

Archie Brown and George Schöpflin

One of the grander simplifications to be found in Soviet political literature is the view that there is essentially world-wide competition between only two social systems and two ideologies. As a corollary of this belief, the idea that there can be more than one kind of 'socialism' or different types of 'communism' is rejected. In matters of detail, account can and should be taken within the various communist states of the specific national characteristics of countries, but the political and ideological essence of the systems should be common to all.

For some years a distinction (though one which is now beginning to wear thin) has been made in the Soviet Union between different roads to socialism and different forms of socialism. The idea of 'different roads' has been generally accepted. The Soviet path of seizure of power by a well-organized revolutionary group which did not command majority support among the anti-Tsarist forces in the Russia of 1917[1] and the Czechoslovak road whereby the Communist Party of Czechoslovakia became the largest single party within the Czechoslovak National Assembly in free elections in 1946 and assumed full power in a bloodless *coup* in February 1948 have both been accorded legitimacy by Soviet theorists. When, however, twenty years after the February events of 1948 Czechoslovak communists attempted to institutionalize fundamental reforms of the system and to create a 'pluralistic socialism' or (in Dubček's popular phrase) 'socialism with a human face', they were countered not only by Soviet tanks but, at an ideological level, by the response that while there may indeed be different *roads* to socialism, *there is only one socialism*.

Though in the realm of political action things have to be

handled somewhat differently, an exact parallel exists between the Soviet ideological response to the Czechoslovak developments of 1968 and their ideological criticism of Eurocommunism. The Soviet weekly, *New Times*, in its lengthy and highly critical review of Santiago Carrillo's book, '*Eurocommunism' and the State*, laid stress on the point that the very concept of 'Eurocommunism' was erroneous because it seemed to refer not to

some specific features of the strategy of the communist parties of some countries, but some sort of specific brand of communism . . . Yet [the review continued] *there is only one communism* [our italics] – if we speak of true, scientific communism – namely, that whose foundations were laid by Marx, Engels and Lenin, and whose principles are adhered to by the present-day communist movement.[2]

Eurocommunism and the Soviet Union

The one scientific socialism or communism, according to this view, is that practised in the Soviet Union and by its more reliable East European allies. The most essential features of this system (an assessment based not only upon observation of the workings of the system but on the stress laid upon these features by official Soviet spokesmen) are the following: (a) the leading role of the party (to which is linked the leading role of the working class); (b) democratic centralism within the party; (c) political censorship and implacable opposition to 'pluralism' within the mass media, the arts and culture as well as in political life; and (d) proletarian internationalism.

Each of these features calls for brief interpretation. The 'leading role of the party' connotes the hegemonic power of the communist party *vis-à-vis* all other institutions and groups within the society. In practice, the 'leading role of the working class' (which in the immediate post-revolutionary period is known as the 'dictatorship of the proletariat') is subsumed in the concept of the 'leading role of the party', for since the communist party is composed of the most politically advanced members of the working class and represents the interests of the entire working class (even if not all of them realize it), there can be no conflict between the party's leading role and the dominance of the working class. The orthodox communist view of this relationship has been particularly clearly expressed by a member of the central committee of the Communist Party of Czechoslovakia and present chairman of the Chamber of Nationalities of the Federal Assembly of Czechoslovakia, Dalibor Hanes, writing in *World Marxist Review*:

Every ruling class delegates direction of the state to its political vanguard, which knows its interests and is able consistently to uphold them. This applies to the working class too. Marxist-Leninists frankly admit this historical reality. They do not have to conceal it, for the communist party's aims and efforts fully coincide with the interests of the working class and the working people generally.[3]

'Democratic centralism' has, throughout the Soviet period, been regarded as the guiding principle of party life, and in the 1977 Soviet Constitution the applicability of the doctrine has been extended so that it now officially becomes the organizational basis of the entire Soviet state.[4] In party parlance, a distinction is made between 'democratic centralism' and 'bureaucratic centralism'. The former concept, unlike the latter, connotes, in principle at least, a willingness on the part of higher party organs to listen to views emanating from below. But, in practice, the doctrine has been most frequently applied to reinforce the overwhelmingly hierarchical nature of the party and the power of the full-time professional party apparatus. It has been used to sustain strict party discipline and to prevent both frank criticism on major party issues and attempts from below to exercise control, or even real influence, over leading party officials. Democratic centralism is described by a recent Soviet author as 'centralism of a new type, a principle qualitatively distinguishing a party of communists from bourgeois and reformist political parties'.[5]

The importance attached by Soviet leaders even in the post-Stalin period, during which the stringency of censorship has been somewhat relaxed, to the necessity of political censorship has never been in doubt. It is one of the points of principle which divides Soviet communists from Eurocommunists of the Carrillo type, just as it was a major issue dividing the Soviet Communist Party from reformist Czech communists in 1968. (One of the most pressing demands made by Soviet leaders in their successive meetings with the leadership of the Communist Party of Czechoslovakia was for the restoration of a strict censorship, a demand which was only partially acceded to in the first six months after August 1968, but systematically achieved after Husák succeeded Dubček as party leader in April 1969.) Though there are at present very substantial differences of degree in the way in which censorship operates within the various communist states, Czechoslovakia remains the only communist country to have abolished completely (for those few brief months in 1968) the institution of censorship.[6]

Soviet insistence on the inviolability of 'proletarian internationalism' is even more central to the debate with the Eurocommunists. In his speech to the Conference of European Communist and Workers' Parties held in Berlin at the end of June and beginning of July 1976, Leonid Brezhnev defended the concept of proletarian internationalism against those who had suggested it was outmoded. He told the delegates that it did not imply the creation of an organizational centre, but implied rather the solidarity of the working class and of communists of all countries in the struggle for their common goals.[7] The nub of the argument, however, is over whether the Soviet Union has a right to define the goals and whether the Eurocommunists are in fact pursuing the 'common goal' of building socialism on the Soviet model. The latter, at any rate, seemed to entertain doubts about the validity of Brezhnev's argument, for the combined opposition of West European Communists and of the Yugoslav delegation (led by Tito) resulted in the exclusion of any reference to 'proletarian internationalism' in the final document released at the end of the conference.[8] 'Proletarian internationalism' has in fact become the not-so-esoteric euphemism for acceptance of Soviet guidance in all matters of political importance (and rejection of all criticism of the Soviet Union), and so, behind the argument over jargon, lie vital issues of political goals and political independence.

The degree of deviation of the various communist parties which may qualify for the description 'Eurocommunist' may perhaps best be measured in terms of their attitudes to and practices in respect of these four features of orthodox Soviet communism. It is the Soviet fear that the contemporary attitudes and actions of parties such as the Spanish and Italian ones may, by the time they obtain office, have become firmly entrenched habits – and a condition of their popular support – which has led to a blurring of their distinction between *different roads* to socialism (permissible) and *different models* of socialism (impermissible). Such questions as whether the profession of Eurocommunist principles represents short-term tactics or long-term strategy, expediency or principle, a commitment which will prove to be binding or one which may be easily cast aside by West European communist parties need not detain us in the present context. The important point is that the Soviet Union *perceives* Eurocommunism as a threat – above all, in terms of its attractiveness to large sectors of the population of East Europe.

A Eurocommunist party in power practising what it currently preaches would be an even greater potential attraction as a model for East Europeans, and a correspondingly greater threat to the dominant position of the Soviet Union in East Europe, than any communist party in opposition can possibly be – and this has led to a Soviet ambivalence about the desirability of Eurocommunist parties coming to power. Basically, however, the Soviet approach has been to combine arguments with, and attempts to undermine the position of, those within West European communist parties who criticize the Soviet Union (and such essential features of the Soviet political system and ideology as those outlined above) with continuing dialogue and 'fraternal relations' with the parties.

The Soviet leaders recognize that it is not in their interest to break with a strong, though unorthodox, Western communist party before it comes to power, for then the Soviet Union would be unable to share in the credit and enhanced international prestige which would accompany such success and, more important, would lose the opportunity of influencing decisively further developments within that state. Any premature break, moreover, would be likely to lead to the further disintegration of the international communist movement, and so, while the Soviet leaders will not avoid it at *all* costs, they will go to very great lengths to prevent it.[9]

As things are, if Soviet spokesmen do not succeed in persuading the Eurocommunists of the error of their ways before the latter obtain power, they may reasonably hope that a Western communist party in power would be driven into dependence upon them. There are various ways in which this could happen. Domestic political opposition to the communists in power might rapidly become so strong – and possibly violent – that it would provoke, or at least provide an excuse for, harsh repressive measures and so strengthen the hand of the hard-liners within the party. A sudden loss of foreign capital – a spontaneous withdrawal by foreign investors whether or not reinforced by economic sanctions from Western governments of the kind which Kissinger apparently favoured – could also drive a communist party in power into economic dependence upon the Soviet Union.

Factors such as these reinforce the Soviet leadership's belief in the virtue of patience, even while they step up the ideological offensive against West European 'revisionists' and 'opportunists', and in East Europe attempt to strengthen the ideological-cultural as well as the economic and political links between the Soviet Union and the other members of Comecon and the Warsaw Pact. The recent intertwining of the issues of roads to socialism and models of socialism (which is to be found, for instance, in the writings of Konstantin Zarodov[10] and Yuri Krasin,[11] and, at a more exalted party level, of Boris Ponomarev[12] and Mikhail Zimyanin[13]) has, as we suggested earlier, significantly modified a distinction which had apparently become well-established in the post-Stalin years. An attempt is being made to show that the question of roads to socialism is bound up with the ultimate outcome of the revolutionary process. The form of struggle adopted, it is argued, will determine whether 'real socialism' (i.e. socialism on the Soviet model) will be achieved, or whether it will degenerate into an opportunistic social democracy or even (as in Chile) a victory for the forces of outright reaction.

The example of Chile has figured prominently in the arguments.

The journal, *World Marxist Review* (published in Prague, but generally reflecting the Soviet view), printed in five successive issues in 1977 a series of articles entitled 'Lessons of Chile', lessons which were clearly intended to contribute to the education of West European as well as Latin American communists, dealing, as they did, with 'that key question of all revolutions, the question of power, and more particularly, how to defend and maintain power'.[14] Explicitly criticizing the shortcomings of the Allende government and implicitly attacking the Eurocommunist legitimation of party competition, the series concludes that 'one of the absolute conditions for defending revolutionary gains' is that *'democracy must serve the people and not allow freedom of action for the counter-revolutionary forces'*.[15] The paramount importance of 'the leading role of the working class' (which in this context, as in others, is a euphemism for the dominant position within the political movement of the communist party) is emphasized, and it is underlined that 'the need for a broad front cannot be replaced by a "pluralistic" approach that forfeits or weakens the leading role of the working class'.[16]

The year of the sixtieth anniversary of the foundation of the Soviet state and of the October Revolution was also used to reemphasize the continuing international relevance of Lenin's strategy and tactics. This, for example, was the main theme of the address by Mikhail Zimyanin, the secretary of the central committee responsible for culture and ideology, on the occasion of the 107th anniversary of Lenin's birth (22 April 1977). Zimyanin declared:

The principal features of the October Revolution and the building of a new society in the Soviet Union have proved their value as general laws of the struggle of the working class for power and for the construction of socialism and communism. The revolutionary practice of many nations, who have set out on the path of socialist creation, has refuted the allegations of bourgeois ideologists and revisionists concerning the 'national particularity' of the Soviet experience and their fabrications about Leninism as a 'purely Russian' phenomenon.[17]

The celebration of the actual anniversary of the Bolshevik Revolution in Moscow later in the year provided an even better occasion for emphasizing the lasting relevance of the Soviet example. (A few foreign delegates were bold enough to stress the distinctiveness of their 'na ional roads' and for travelling too far in that direction Santiago Carrillo was refused permission to deliver the speech he had prepared, and submitted for translation, though a number of leaders of smaller communist parties were called to the rostrum.)[18]

In the major anniversary speech, the general secretary of the Soviet Communist Party, Leonid Brezhnev, referred openly and critically to China, but not explicitly to West European communist parties. A number of his remarks, however, were clearly directed towards them. He recognized that the transition to socialism of other nations and countries with different levels of development and national traditions would bring a 'still greater variety of concrete forms of socialist construction'. However, 'general, fundamental and inalienable features of socialist revolution and socialist construction remain and preserve their force'. As in the past, so in the present, he argued, the question of power was paramount. The choice was between the power of the working class (united with all working people) and the power of the bourgeoisie. There was no third way. The transition to socialism, moreover, could only take place if the working class and its allies seized real political power and used it for the liquidation of the socio-economic dominance of capitalist and other exploiters. The victory of socialism was possible 'if the working class and its communist vanguard' were able to inspire and unite the working masses in the struggle for 'the transformation on socialist principles of the economy and of all social relations'. But socialism would become firmly established only if the power of the working people was able to defend the revolution from the attacks of the class enemy, for such attacks, Brezhnev added, were inevitable.[19]

Though there are no doubt differences of opinion among the Soviet leaders on the best tactics for dealing with the Eurocommunists, their deep-rooted opposition in principle to any form of pluralistic socialism or competitive party politics is not in doubt. Brezhnev's sixtieth anniversary address is merely the most recent and authoritative confirmation of that fact. Before turning to a consideration of the impact of Eurocommunism in Eastern Europe – and it is its potential impact there which is the major Soviet cause for concern – brief notice should also be taken of some unofficial Soviet reactions.

Among those within the Soviet Union who are critical of the *status quo*, there would appear to be comparatively weak support for the domestic application of Eurocommunist ideas (in comparison, for instance, with the greater numerical strength of Russian nationalist and 'westernizing' liberal dissent), but it is not to be discounted totally. Communists (and expelled communists) among the non-Russian nationalities, dissatisfied with the degree of national autonomy which they possess within their union republics, have felt the attraction of the Eurocommunist emphasis on national independence. Thus, for example, in the summer of 1971 a group of Latvian communists wrote to the leaderships of a number of West European communist parties, drawing attention to what they called 'the eradication of everything national' in Latvia.

Among Russians, the views closest to those of Berlinguer or Carrillo are held within the group whose most prominent spokesman is Roy Medvedev. Those whom Medvedev calls the 'party democrats' profess loyalty to Marxism-Leninism, but seek, in Medvedev's words, 'a more extensive and consistent democratization of our party and public life' which would include 'greater freedom of speech, freedom of the press, freedom of assembly and organization; and freedom for science, scholarship, and the arts ...'[20] Medvedev himself also wishes, for example, to see 'an element of contest' in elections to Soviets, and argues that 'the rights and responsibilities of the Union Republics ought to be increased to make democratic principles effective for the national minorities, both large and small'.[21]

After discussing these and other beliefs which he shares with the 'party democrats', Medvedev adds: 'One is bound to note a striking resemblance between this trend in our party and certain currents in the world communist movement – for example, in the Italian, Spanish, Australian and certain other parties.'[22] While the growth within the Soviet Communist Party of views which have something in common with those of Eurocommunism cannot be ruled out, it must be noted that Medvedev regards this tendency within the party as weaker than the predominant conservative tendency, and weaker, too, than the tendency towards neo-Stalinism. The ideological offensive against all forms of revisionism, and against the notion of 'Eurocommunism' explicitly, also means that any Soviet communist advocating even a cautious move in the direction of a socialist pluralism runs the serious risk of expulsion from the party. (Roy Medvedev himself was expelled from the party in 1969.)

Since Eastern Europe rather than the territory of the USSR provides more fertile soil for the growth of Eurocommunist ideas, it is to a consideration of its impact there that we must now turn.[23]

Eurocommunism and Eastern Europe

The primary impact of Eurocommunism on Eastern Europe is to be detected in a changed atmosphere rather than in actual changes of policy or political action. This applies equally to the official and to the unofficial response to the Eurocommunist challenge. The East European parties had to make their assessments in the light of their own relations with the Soviet Union and with their domestic populations. Thus, Yugoslavia and Romania responded positively to Eurocommunism because they saw it as an instrument for strengthening their independence *vis-à-vis* Moscow. The Czechoslovak party, on the other hand, reacted extremely negatively because, quite correctly, it saw Eurocommunism as a challenge, both direct and indirect, to such legitimacy as it might possess, in view of the part which the invasion of Czechoslovakia still plays in Eurocommunist thinking. Other East European parties – the East German and the Bulgarian – lined up with the Soviet party for reasons of loyalty and dislike of the ideological implications of Eurocommunism. The Hungarian and Polish parties initially adopted intermediate positions of neutrality and even sympathy towards Eurocommunism. However, it is clear that they came under great pressure from the Soviet Union, and in the face of it there was growing evidence in the second half of 1977 of a retreat from their earlier positions. The Albanians, for their part, found no difficulty in dismissing Eurocommunism as a revisionist heresy.

The emergent opposition in Eastern Europe also responded to Eurocommunism, though, not surprisingly, in rather a different fashion from the party leaderships. Two aspects of the impact of Eurocommunism on the East European opposition are worth stressing. First, there has been the specific assistance rendered by Western parties – appeals, denunciations, intercessions – in individual cases of repression. The condemnation of the East Germans' expatriation of Wolf Biermann, writer and performer of dissident satirical ballads, was a good illustration of this, as was the support for the Charter 77 initiative in Czechoslovakia. Such moves by Eurocommunist parties help to sustain the morale of the opposition in East Europe. The second aspect is linked with the first. Eurocommunism has been perceived and used by the opposition as support for its own legitimacy – not necessarily the principal instrument sustaining that legitimacy, but a valuable one nevertheless, in as much as reference to democratic principles or legality (and the infringement of these in East Europe) by a Western communist party cannot be shrugged off so easily by the ruling parties as criticism in terms of 'bourgeois' democratic principles. Thus, East Europeans in conflict with their governments have felt able to quote the views and protests of Italian or French party members precisely because these were communist statements and could hardly fail to be recognized as such. It is this status of Eurocommunist doctrines which made it imperative for the Soviet Communist Party to challenge their right to speak in the name of the international communist movement and thus attempt to curb their persuasiveness. It is this which helps to explain the denunciation of Santiago Carrillo's '*Eurocommunism' and the State* in such far-reaching terms in the summer of 1977. (One paradox, however, deserves mention – the ambiguous position of dissidents in pro-Eurocommunist states, i.e. in Yugoslavia and Romania. The existence of persecuted dissent in these two countries was certainly embarrassing both for the Eurocommunists, who placed great emphasis on civil rights in East Europe, and for the Yugoslav and Romanian authorities, whose repression of civil rights activists, on a lesser scale in Yugoslavia and much more extensively in Romania, brought their Eurocommunist credentials into question.)

The lack of direct influence of Eurocommunism on policies pursued in Eastern Europe does not mean that it did not play a significant off-stage role in East European politics in the mid 1970s. For the ruling parties, Eurocommunism represents a dangerous corpus of ideas which has had to be fought, since potentially these ideas could undermine not only the partial legitimacy which the régimes have attained, but might even lead in time to major changes which could no longer be controlled from above. Eurocommunism, by making concepts such as competitive party systems, alternative governments, elections and freedom of criticism (concepts which are either totally rejected or accepted in a purely formal or façade manner in the Soviet Union) respectable in 'communist' terms, has provided important ideological support for the emergent opposition. The legitimacy conferred by Eurocommunism, which could be 'viewed as a viable within-system alternative to the Soviet model',[24] potentially reinforced a pre-existing set of aspirations for developing a communist model free of the limitations imposed by the Soviet experience.[25]

The political and ideological support of West European communist parties is thus particularly important in a tactical sense. The political cultures of the East European societies differ from that of the Soviet Union (and from each other), and in virtually all of the countries of East Europe there exists a body of locally developed Marxist ideas which – in a favourable situation – could be combined with Eurocommunism to produce nationally distinctive political models which would owe little to either a Eurocommunist example or a Soviet example and more to their own distinctive traditions. The reform movement in Czechoslovak communism in the 1960s, culminating in the radical political reorientation which took place in the first eight months of 1968, is the most striking illustration of this.

That movement was, however, exceptional in post-war East Europe. In general, East Europeans are only too well aware of geo-political constraints upon their freedom of action and there is a long-standing tradition of looking to international developments to create a situation where domestic change may become possible. The communist period has provided its own precedents for this – Soviet de-Stalinization (and, most notably, Khrushchev's 1956 'secret speech' which had a tremendous impact) and the Sino-Soviet rift – and in pre-Communist times there tended to be a strong reliance on the West (most notably, for the establishment of independent nation states after 1918).

Czechoslovakia, Bulgaria and the GDR

The Communist Party of Czechoslovakia fell most clearly into the category of a party which was in no fit state to tolerate Eurocommunism. Its legitimacy was exceptionally weak in that the great majority of people in Czechoslovakia had continued to withhold acceptance of the results of the invasion of 1968 and had retreated into their private lives and a temporary apoliticality. The party itself was divided and suffered from low morale. A majority even of those members who remained in the party in the mid 1970s had supported the Action Programme of 1968, now condemned as revisionist (though all the most active party reformers had been removed from membership in 1970). Within the party leadership, two conflicting tendencies could be discerned. There were the conservatives, among them the party leader, Gustáv Husák, who were prepared to make some cautious concessions to such former party members as were no longer taking part in any kind of oppositional or quasi-oppositional political activity, and might be considered possible candidates for a return to party and public life. But there was a stronger tendency represented by hard-line leaders for whom even mild concessions were anathema, and these latter leaders were powerful enough to prevent the implementation of any concessions that were actually offered. Both groups continued to be aware of their weakness in the country, of their dependence upon Soviet backing and, indeed, of their dependence upon one another. They were aware of the obvious danger of a process of political movement in Czechoslovakia getting out of control and going far beyond personnel changes in the leadership.

Thus, the Czechoslovak party lined up unambiguously with the Soviet Communist Party and gave it maximum support in the struggle against Eurocommunism in various international forums. Indeed, at times the Czechoslovak spokesmen, and most notably Vasil Bil'ak, one of Husák's rivals within the praesidium and the secretary responsible for inter-party relations, seemed to be taking a harder line than the Soviet Communist Party itself. To some extent, this may have been an internationally coordinated policy conducted for tactical reasons, in as much as statements from Prague could be more easily overlooked, and if necessary disavowed, than pronouncements from Moscow. Nevertheless, the Czechoslovak ultra-hard line had its authentic domestic roots in the vulnerable position of the contemporary leadership of that country.

The gist of the Czechoslovak line was unconditional loyalty to the Soviet Union and denunciation of any and all who challenged this in any way. It was the Czechoslovak press which floated ideas like 'the creation of a single socialist people' and issued accusations that the West European communists were allowing themselves to be manipulated by imperialism (an argument deployed by a praesidium member, Josef Kempný, on 14 March 1976 at Ostrava).[26] The coverage of the June 1976 Berlin summit was heavily selective and strongly critical of Eurocommunist positions. Following that summit, the Czechoslovak party emerged as the most forthright and fundamentalist defender of proletarian internationalism. Declaration after declaration insisted that total support for the Soviet Union was the only possible yardstick of communist orthodoxy, and that such support was the most basic duty of every communist. Carrillo's '*Eurocommunism' and the State* was condemned as a 'cuckoo's egg' in the socialist movement, and Bil'ak launched some of the most violent polemics heard in the debate. In June 1977, he not only argued that Eurocommunism was a product of imperialism, but he went on to say that 'the term, "Eurocommunism", belongs among those which no true communist professes . . . its content is tantamount to treason'.[27] On 11 August 1977, his sixtieth birthday, Bil'ak was awarded the Order of Lenin, a signal honour which indicated that he continued to enjoy the confidence of Moscow, and perhaps that, in his outspokenness, he was fulfilling a task allotted to him by the Soviet leadership.

The Bulgarians took an equally hard line against Eurocommunism. Loyalty to the Soviet Union has played a key role, for the Bulgarian party has aligned itself closely with Moscow for reasons of history as much as for the political and economic support which it receives from the Soviet Union. Thus, when the Bulgarian party leader, Todor Zhivkov, launched his attack on Eurocommunism at the end of 1976, this was correctly interpreted as expressing the Soviet view. Zhivkov argued that Eurocommunism was a bourgeois invention, 'inspired by anti-Sovietism',[28] which was directed against proletarian internationalism and was dangerous. Making very little effort to disguise the real nature of his target, Zhivkov defined Eurocommunist ideology as an attempt to reject the revolutionary experience of the Soviet Union and to substitute 'national peculiarities for those general laws and universally valid aspects of revolutionary experience' whose worth had been demonstrated by those countries which had achieved socialism. The concept of 'Eurocommunism' betrayed the desire of reactionaries 'to raise a wall between the brother parties of the socialist community and those of the West European capitalist countries . . .'[29]

Zhivkov's somewhat turgid attack on Eurocommunism was immediately recognized for what it was: the opening of a Soviet counter-offensive after the East Berlin summit and the relative truce that had ensued. *L'Unità* stated that Zhivkov's article had seriously distorted the position of the West European communist parties. It was especially grave that he had attempted to present every autonomous critical trend as anti-Soviet. The Bulgarian central committee secretary in charge of ideology, Alexander Lilov, returned to Zhivkov's theme once or twice, but thereafter the Bulgarians said little more on Eurocommunism. They lined up with the Soviet Communist Party in the summer of 1977 on the sensitive subject of Carrillo's book and attacked Carrillo for having tried to interfere in the internal affairs of Communist countries by putting forward his own model of socialism.

The position of the GDR on Eurocommunism has also been strongly pro-Soviet, but it has been argued with greater politeness and, unlike the Czechs, the East Germans have not broken off contacts with the Eurocommunists. Evidently, they felt confident enough of their position to engage in a direct debate with the Italians in particular. *Neues Deutschland* was the only East European party daily to carry a full text of the communiqué issued after the Madrid summit, and, as hosts, the East Germans had already published a full account of the proceedings of the East Berlin summit. They avoided polemics, but stated their position firmly. Thus, for example, Paul Verner (speaking at the *World Marxist Review* conference in Prague in June 1977) made it clear that the East Germans accepted the contention that there were universally applicable laws governing socialist revolutions – namely, those which had been successfully applied in the Bolshevik Revolution.[30] At the same time, the East Germans did not indulge in the kind of gratuitous acrimony favoured by the Czechs. Indeed, there is some evidence that some high-ranking SED members accepted Eurocommunism on its ideological merits and wished to take part in serious debate with the Eurocommunists.[31]

Hungary and Poland

Somewhere between the firm loyalists and the autonomists were the two East European parties which evidently sympathized with aspects of Eurocommunism, but for a variety of reasons could not afford to flout the Soviet Union on this (or any other comparable) issue. For a brief period – the first half of 1977 – the Hungarians actually appeared to be out on a limb of their own. János Kádár, the Hungarian party leader, expressly contradicted

Zhivkov when he stated that he did not share the view that Euro-communism was a form of anti-Sovietism.[32] He returned to this theme in an article in *World Marxist Review* which used the classic technique of comment by omission.[33] Although Kádár accepted that there were objective laws governing socialism, he emphasized that national peculiarities also had to be taken into account and he carefully avoided condemning Eurocommunism. Subsequently, Hungarian spokesmen hardened their line some-what, but it is clear that at least a section of the Hungarian party sympathizes with the Eurocommunist tendency within the inter-national communist movement and is reluctant to be drawn into hostilities. Links between the Hungarians and the Italian party, for example, are of very long standing, and the Hungarians are most unwilling to sacrifice these good relations.

A similar attitude is to be found in Poland where the party, for the most part, has been equally adept at keeping out of the debate. Thus the Polish press published the minimum necessary to avoid causing offence in Moscow, but otherwise has pursued a kind of neutrality. In the debate over Carrillo, for instance, *Trybuna ludu* reprinted the *New Times* attack on '*Eurocommunism' and the State* but its own comments were more moderate.[34] The party monthly, *Nowe drogi*, observed that, in any given country, the local communists knew best how to conduct their own affairs, but it added that solidarity remained an important factor and was a feature absent from Carrillo's book.[35] The Yugoslav agency, Tanjug, noted that the Poles had sought to stay out of the debate and had commented only 'in a very modest fashion', giving the topic limited publicity. Differences among communists were accepted as normal, as something originating in objective con-ditions, and not so important as they were deemed to be by the Soviet leadership.[36]

Romania and Yugoslavia

The Romanian Communist Party and the Yugoslav League of Communists have usually been lumped together as the autonomist, pro-Eurocommunist parties in Eastern Europe. This is correct only at one level, for both Romania and Yugoslavia have sought to use Eurocommunism for their own ends, and these ends differ from one another. What has linked them has been the determination of the party leaderships, in which they have enjoyed wide popular backing, to maintain domestic control over their policies and to sustain their efforts to preserve autonomy *vis-à-vis* the Soviet Union. In their domestic policies, however, there is little trace of Eurocommunism to be found in Yugoslavia, and none at all in Romania. Yugoslavia pursues moderated authoritarian policies – moderated by enormous local and regional variations, by self-management and by the emergence of a measure of political tolerance over the last thirty years. Romania, by contrast, is a strictly authoritarian state, in which almost all political initiative derives from the top and where autonomous political action is quickly suppressed, whether by police intervention or by resort to the well-tried techniques of cooptation. As a general rule, both Romania and Yugoslavia support Eurocommunism for reasons of foreign policy; they reject any suggestion that the political concepts of Eurocommunism which relate to domestic politics – civil rights, free elections, competitive party systems – might be applicable to them.

Within this general framework, it must in fairness be added that both the Yugoslav and the Romanian parties have made significant contributions to the emergence of the Eurocommunist phenomenon within the international communist movement. The antecedents of this can be traced back to their reaction to the Soviet invasion of Czechoslovakia – which they condemned – and, indeed, to earlier moves. Where their support of the Eurocommunists was of particular value was in the jockeying for power over the preparations for the East Berlin summit. The Yugoslavs emerged as one of the strongest proponents of the right of each party to decide its strategy and ideology, and the prestige which President Tito brought to this argument was of unquestionable significance. Indeed, in East Berlin itself much of the attention was actually focused on the meeting between Tito and Brezhnev, as symbolizing the abandonment of Soviet claims to hegemony in inter-party relations. (The significance of the meeting was, indeed, largely symbolic.) Equally, the Romanians served the Eurocommunist cause by their repeated reiteration of the right to autonomy of each communist party.

The Romanian argument has scarcely varied over the years. It was first enunciated in 1964 and, with a few variations in tone, has amounted to the insistence on the right of each party to elaborate its own policies as it saw fit. In this context, there could be no single world centre of communism, 'no single recipe . . . compulsory model . . . or immutable pattern that should be recommended or imposed on other countries or peoples'.[37]

The Romanians had no intention of following the Eurocommunists' advice on the treatment of dissidents. The *Scînteia* article cited above made this clear when it noted that, in Eastern Europe, communists came to power in circumstances very different from those prevailing 'in countries characterized by an advanced level of social and economic development', and therefore, it argued, the political rights espoused by the Eurocommunists were not applicable to Romanian conditions. The existence of different points of view among communists should not, it was maintained, become a matter of dispute, but should be discussed 'in a spirit of mutual esteem and regard without labelling parties, pronouncing anathemas and allocating blame'.[38] The gist of the position of the Romanian party leadership is that their primary concern is with their country's relations with the Soviet Union, and if it can use aspects of the Eurocommunist doctrine to shore up its autonomy, it will do so. But, that apart, the Romanians have reserved the right to follow their own road to neo-Stalinism.

The Yugoslav position on Eurocommunism has been a more complex one, and Yugoslav spokesmen have evidently given greater thought to the doctrines of Eurocommunism than have their Romanian counterparts. In an important statement in the spring of 1977, the late Edward Kardelj, whose declarations on ideology had the highest status, accepted that Eurocommunism was a most important development: 'I would say, almost a turning-point in the history of the Communist movement.'[39] It is of interest, however, that just as the Romanians put their own gloss on Eurocommunism, so did Kardelj, for he saw it first and foremost as a movement directed against power blocs; in other words, as a support for Yugoslavia's non-alignment. Kardelj's general assessment of Eurocommunism was positive. He saw it as helping to destroy the dogmas which had shackled communism and as a political phenomenon which would make for major change in Western Europe. Another leading Yugoslav, Stane Dolanc, was similarly well disposed towards Eurocommunism. He saw its main importance as lying in its negation of a single world centre of communism and added that it had 'emerged in the struggle for independence, integrity, and one's own way in the construction of new and better socialist relationships in individual countries'.[40]

Eurocommunism and the Opposition

The emergence and continued activity of overt opposition movements in Eastern Europe – in Poland and Czechoslovakia above all – were unquestionably assisted by the existence of an alternative set of communist ideas in Western Europe. But this assistance, by definition, could only be partial. It is a basic rule of contemporary inter-party relations, and this was strongly emphasized at East Berlin, that mutual criticism and polemics relating to the internal affairs of a fraternal party should be avoided as far as possible. This rule, breached often enough in individual cases, has been of two-fold significance. On the one hand, it has been a useful safeguard for the Eurocommunists against interference from the Soviet Communist Party and its supporters; but on the other, it has been an obstacle against thoroughgoing and far-reaching critiques of politics and society in Eastern Europe on the part of the Eurocommunists. Non-intervention is a two-way street. In spite of occasional statements to the effect that a Marxist analysis of the situation in East Europe would be valuable, the Eurocommunists have been inhibited from going too far in their critiques.

It is clear to both sides that if such analyses were made and incorporated into Eurocommunist doctrine, there would be a danger of an unbridgeable gap appearing between Soviet-type communism and Eurocommunism. There would also be a severe risk of splits within the Eurocommunist parties, for they all harbour strong minorities of uncritically pro-Soviet militants. The nearest that any Eurocommunist has come to making a far-reaching analysis was Carrillo in his much-attacked '*Euro-communism' and the State*, where he discussed in some detail what he saw as distortions imposed on Marxism in the Soviet Union.

From the standpoint of the East European opposition, such Eurocommunist support as existed was useful, though what was happening within each individual East European country was clearly much more important. The various oppositions have had to take account of local conditions, pressures and counter-pressures. The way the Polish opposition movement, in which a wide range of non-communists were involved, grew entirely from Polish roots, illustrates this point clearly. Nevertheless, even the *ad hoc* support of Eurocommunist spokesmen and publications was welcome and probably not uninfluential on occasion.

The Biermann affair in the GDR showed how this could work. Following Biermann's expatriation, there was a significant wave of protests among East German intellectuals, the first such expression of widespread intellectual dissent since 1957. The party leadership were able to damp down this dissent fairly rapidly and prevent it from developing into the kind of organized opposition which has grown up in Poland. While it is evident that domestic reasons persuaded the East German authorities to move against their dissidents with circumspection, it is highly likely that the criticism by the Eurocommunists, which must have been rather unexpected, was also a factor inducing them to act with some moderation. Both the French and the Spanish parties reacted quickly to Biermann's expatriation, but, interestingly, the Italian party, which has continued to nurture its connections with the SED, took several days to comment. Not long afterwards, the Italian ideologist, Lucio Lombardo Radice, undertook a study tour of the GDR, in the course of which he had a meeting with the dissident Robert Havemann as well as with East German party officials. The PCI was clearly anxious to keep channels of communication open and to avoid polemics.

For those former members of the communist party in Czecho-slovakia who still attempt to maintain some form of struggle, or at least protest, against the Husák régime, interventions on their side by the Eurocommunists are always welcome. The wave of such protests following on the repression by the Czechoslovak authorities of the signatories of Charter 77 had, however, only a limited impact. Charter 77 itself was very much a product of Czechoslovak conditions and the 1968 and post-1968 experience, though the Helsinki Agreement, the June 1976 Berlin meeting of European communist parties and, to a lesser extent, the example of the Polish opposition were also influences. The references to Czechoslovakia in the speeches of Berlinguer (at, for example, the 1976 Berlin summit) and Carrillo are simply not reported by the Czechoslovak mass media, and relations between the Czechoslo-vak party leadership and the Eurocommunists are acrimonious. Members of the Czechoslovak socialist opposition still, however, feel it worth while to seek the support of the latter, and in March 1977 a group of eleven formerly senior party members appealed to West European communists to take all practical steps possible to alleviate the situation in Czechoslovakia. This appeal was issued not long after the Madrid meeting of Eurocommunist leaders (if, stretching a point, Marchais can be so described) at which the three foremost West European party heads avoided making any mention of support for civil rights in Eastern Europe.

The 'single instance' approach to support for members of socialist oppositions in Eastern Europe has been shown to be of limited effectiveness. While it may have been partially helpful in the Biermann case, it appeared to exercise little influence on the course of events in Poland (the unrest in Radom and elsewhere) after the food price rises of June 1976. The Polish opposition activist, Jacek Kuroń, sent an appeal to Berlinguer shortly after the arrests of workers began, asking the PCI leader to intercede on their behalf with the Polish government. The Italian Communist Party did so. In a message to the Polish party, it expressed concern about the trials of workers and called for moderation and clemency. This was probably the bluntest message sent by a Eurocommunist party to a ruling party in support of oppositional activists. Its results were negligible. Privately, Berlinguer's message was dismissed by Polish communists as 'monstrous arrogance'; publicly, nothing was done. The subsequent release of the imprisoned workers was largely a consequence of the sustained pressure on the Polish authorities by the domestic opposition.

It is also by no means clear that significant changes could be brought about in Eastern Europe either by fundamental critiques or by constant intercessions on the part of the Eurocommunists. First, certain geo-political realities (and notably the power of the Soviet Union) remain facts of life. Secondly, fundamental critiques of what the Soviet leaders and their most loyal East European allies call 'real socialism' could split Eurocommunist parties. And thirdly, constant intercessions might become progressively less effective (in comparison with rationed responses).

None the less, the more thoughtful Eurocommunists still appear to feel the need for a Eurocommunist Marxist analysis of political and social conditions in contemporary East Europe. Frane Barbieri, for example, the Yugoslav-Italian journalist who is among those who have claimed to have invented the term 'Eurocommunism', made this point expressly in an interview in *Deutschland-Archiv* in the spring of 1977.[41] Another Yugoslav, Milovan Djilas, has attributed considerable importance to the rise of Eurocommunism while accepting that it has had few results for Yugoslavia except in the sphere of Soviet-Yugoslav relations. In Djilas's words:

They [the Eurocommunist parties] are new and Yugoslavia is no model for them. Nor do I believe that these parties can exercise a decisive influence and thereby so change conditions in Yugoslavia that some kind of multi-party system could come about. Yet, for all that, Euro-communism has a positive impact not just on Yugoslavia but on the rest of Eastern Europe as well, in the sense that the hard-line ideology will weaken and that caution will be used in cultural matters.[42]

Djilas's conclusion, in other words, is that the forces favouring a greater pluralism and a greater tolerance in Eastern Europe are somewhat strengthened by Eurocommunism, but that the Eurocommunists are unlikely to be harbingers of dramatic change. The strength of the Soviet reaction to Eurocommunism is indicative of Soviet fears that the dangers (from the standpoint of the present party leadership in the USSR) may be rather greater than that. The greatest danger of all for the Moscow leadership is of Eurocommunist ideas spreading through East European communist *parties* and being popular not merely with their socialist *oppositions*. It was precisely the growth of heterodox ideas within the Communist Party of Czechoslovakia in the 1960s (albeit, in that case, an indigenous movement) which presented the CPSU with its greatest political challenge since 1956, and the fear was and is that the ideas of the Czech forerunners of the Eurocommunists, and now of the Eurocommunists themselves, might find support in the ranks of a number of East European communist parties and undermine the position of their conservative leaders. That was the fear in 1968 not only of Brezhnev and his Soviet colleagues, but also of Ulbricht and Gomułka. It is the fear today not only of the Soviet politburo, but also of Husák and Honecker. What the future holds for the relationship of East and West European communism remains to be seen, but up to the present Djilas's rather cautious expectations of the impact of Eurocommunism on Eastern Europe have been largely borne out.

Notes and references

1. When elections to a Constituent Assembly in Russia produced an anti-Bolshevik majority, with the Socialist Revolutionaries emerging as

the largest single party, the Bolsheviks simply resorted to armed force and promptly closed down the assembly when it was convened in January 1918. The Soviet view remains that to put too much stress on mere arithmetical majorities is to fall into the trap of 'parliamentary cretinism'. What is required is a 'dialectical understanding of a majority', a point elaborated in a recent article by Yu. A. Krasin in *Kommunist*, No. 10, July 1977, pp. 33–44 ('Problema bol'shinstva v sotsialisticheskoy revolyutsii'). See also the book by the same author: *Revolyutsiey ustrashennye: Kriticheskiy ocherk burzhyaznykh kontseptsiy sotsial'noy revolyutsii*, Moscow, 1975.

2. 'Contrary to the Interests of Peace and Socialism in Europe: Concerning the book "*Eurocommunism" and the State* by Santiago Carrillo, General Secretary of the Communist Party of Spain', *New Times*, No. 26, June 1977 (pp, 9–13), p. 10.

3. Dalibor Hanes, 'Democracy in the Service of Peace and Man', *World Marxist Review*, vol. 19, No. 4, April 1976 (pp. 17–20), p. 20.

4. Article 3 of the new Soviet Constitution (adopted by the Supreme Soviet of the USSR in October 1977) reads: 'The organization and work of the Soviet state is constructed in accordance with the principle of democratic centralism: the election of all organs of state power from the bottom to the top, their accountability to the people, and the obligatoriness of decisions of higher organs for lower organs. Democratic centralism combines single leadership with local initiative and creative activity, and with the responsibility of every state organ and official for the work on hand' (*Pravda*, 8 October 1977, p. 3).

5. Yu. G. Turishchev, *KPSS – zhivoy, razvivayushchiysya politicheskiy organizm*, Moscow, 1975, p. 120.

6. Revealing accounts of the Soviet censorship are to be found in Martin Dewhirst and Robert Farrell (eds.), *The Soviet Censorship*, Metuchen, N.J., 1973; and in Roy A. Medvedev, *On Socialist Democracy*, London, 1975, Chapter IX, 'Freedom of Speech and the Press', pp. 164–209. The major scholarly work on Czechoslovakia 1968 is by H. Gordon Skilling, *Czechoslovakia's Interrupted Revolution*, Princeton, N.J., 1976. For a very interesting account of the censorship in Poland, based on the official instructions given to the censors, see two recent articles by Leo Labedz, 'The Finely-tuned Machinery That Selects What Poles May Read', *The Times*, 26 September 1977; and 'How the Blue Pencil Can Be Blunted', *The Times*, 27 September 1977.

7. *Pravda*, 30 June 1976, p. 2.

8. For the full text of the final document which emerged from the Berlin Conference ('For Peace, Security, Cooperation and Social Progress in Europe'), see *Pravda*, 1 July 1976, pp. 1–2.

9. A 'break' would, in effect, mean a 'split', for in every case it is predictable that a new pro-Soviet communist party would be founded. Though its size would vary from country to country, within every communist party there are people for whom the slogan, 'With the Soviet Union for all time', is their conditioned response to all political developments.

10. See especially his article, 'Leninskaya strategiya i taktika revolyutsionnoy bor'by', *Pravda*, 6 August 1975, pp. 2–3.

11. See the references in n. 1 above.

12. See, for example, his speech, 'Leninizm – revolyutsionnoe znamya nashey epokhi', *Pravda*, 23 April 1977, p. 1.

13. See, for example, his recent articles, 'Communist Solidarity is the True Road for Peace and Socialism', *World Marxist Review*, vol. 20, No. 7, July 1977, pp. 10–20; and 'On the Theoretical Work of the CPSU in the 60 Years since the October Revolution', *World Marxist Review*, vol. 20, No. 9, September 1977, pp. 6–18 (esp. pp. 13–15).

14. Pedro Rodriguez, 'Defending the People's Power. Lessons of Chile. Article 5', *World Marxist Review*, vol. 20, No. 6, June 1977, p. 47. (The author belongs to the leadership of the Chilean Communist Party.)

15. ibid., p. 55. (The italics are in the original.)

16. ibid.

17. M. V. Zimyanin, 'Leninizm – revolyutsionnoe znamya nashey epokhi', *Pravda*, 23 April 1977, p. 1. Earlier in his speech he stated unambiguously: 'Leninism is the Marxism of the contemporary epoch, the theory and method of revolutionary transformation of the world proved by life!'

18. See report, and also leading article, *The Times*, 4 November 1977.

19. L. I. Brezhnev, 'Velikiy oktyabr' i progress chelovechestva', *Pravda*, 3 November 1977, p. 3.

20. Medvedev, *On Socialist Democracy*, p. 56.

21. ibid., p. 57.

22. ibid., p. 58.

23. For further discussion of the impact of Eurocommunism on the Soviet Union and Eastern Europe, see the contributions of John C. Campbell, William E. Griffith, Robert Legvold and Rudolf L. Tökés in their major contribution to the literature on Eurocommunism: Rudolf L. Tökés (ed., for the Council on Foreign Relations), *Eurocommunism and Détente*, New York, 1978.

24. Charles Gati, 'The "Europeanization" of Communism?', *Foreign Affairs*, vol. 55, No. 33, April 1977, p. 547.

25. For discussion and analysis of the values and beliefs and political knowledge and expectations to be found in a number of East European societies, as well as in the Soviet Union, see Archie Brown and Jack Gray (eds.), *Political Culture and Political Change in Communist States*, London and New York, 1977.

26. *Nová svoboda*, 18 March 1976.

27. In his speech to the Congress of Czechoslovak Journalists, reported by Prague Radio and ČTK (Czechoslovak Press Agency), 17 June 1977.

28. Todor Zhivkov, 'Year of Peace, Year of Struggle', *World Marxist Review*, vol. 19, No. 12, December 1976, p. 3.

29. ibid.

30. ADN (East German Newsagency), 29 June 1977.

31. High-ranking West European communists have confirmed this in private conversation.

32. At a press conference during a visit to Vienna, as reported by Western newspapers, e.g. *Frankfurter Allgemeine Zeitung*, 8 December 1976; in its report of the press conference, the Hungarian Newsagency MTI obscured what Kádár had actually said by switching at this point of its version into indirect speech. See *Népszabadság*, 8 December 1976.

33. J. Kádár, 'Some Lessons of Socialist Construction in Hungary', *World Marxist Review*, vol. 20, No. 1, January 1977, pp. 4–11.

34. 23 June 1977.

35. August 1977.

36. In a commentary with a Warsaw dateline from the Tanjug agency, 18 July 1977.

37. *Scînteia*, 5 July 1977.

38. ibid.

39. In the Sarajevo theoretical monthly *Dijalog*, reported by *Borba*, 19 March 1977. Kardelj performed something of a tactical retreat in a subsequent interview which he gave to the Italian communist weekly, *Rinascità*, 9 September 1977. In this interview he stressed the anti-capitalist nature of Eurocommunism, rather than its role in inter-party relations as a counterweight to Moscow. He did, however, condemn 'dogmatic Stalinism' and the negative influence of Marxist thought in socialist countries on the development of Marxism in the international workers' movement in general.

40. *Komunist* (Belgrade), 6 June 1977.

41. Manfred Steinkühler, 'Ursprung und Konzept des Eurokommunismus – Gespräch mit Frane Barbieri', *Deutschland-Archiv*, vol. 10, No. 4, April 1977, pp. 347–50.

42. *Frankfurter Allgemeine Zeitung*, 3 March 1977.

Editors note:
This article was completed in late 1977 and does not therefore deal with developments since that date.

9. The US Response

Godfrey Hodgson

What is the United States' attitude to Eurocommunism? The question is important for Europeans, because the United States has it in its power profoundly to affect the evolution and the prospects of the European Left; perhaps even the ability to decide whether the Left can ever win and exercise power. And it is important for Americans, because what is now happening on the European Left, particularly in France, Italy, Spain and Portugal, could bring to an end the difficult but on balance extremely advantageous relationship which has subsisted between the United States and Western Europe since the Truman/Marshall/Acheson commitments of 1947.

In one sense, the question is not hard to answer. Americans have no sympathy for communism of any variety. Whatever the nuances of policy or of its formulation – and there have been important changes of nuance, as we shall see – the United States has not, under the Carter administration, changed its basic position. It does not like communism. It does not welcome any advance towards power on the part of any communist party, in Western Europe or anywhere else.

Both the administration and informed American opinion generally remain profoundly sceptical – far more sceptical, on the whole, than most moderate conservative opinion in Europe – about the extent to which the Western European communist parties have changed, or can change. And even if it has to be conceded that some change has occurred and that more is to be expected in the future, Washington can foresee only trouble and danger from any increased participation by those parties in government.

As one would expect, there is rather more debate and division in the wider foreign policy community than in the administration itself. Among that community of specialists in foundations, universities and the press (and also in certain enclaves within the administration, such as the State Department's policy planning staff, for example), it is possible to encounter an awareness that there is both a formidable demand and also a demonstrable need for fundamental political and institutional change in Western Europe: it would not be hard to find people in those circles who would agree, for example, that some modification of the rigidity of the French state and of the French educational system, or of the clientelistic character of Italian Christian democracy and much publicly owned industry in Italy, or the reform of the Spanish constitution are both desirable in themselves and compatible with America's long-term interests. But, almost without exception, even this 'liberal' community resists the argument that communist participation will be needed to carry such transformation through.

Washington, and the US foreign policy community generally, still hankers for the Centre-Left. In France, as soon as the difficulties of the Union de la Gauche became apparent in September 1977, the administration's preference was for a centre-left solution – either Mitterrand–Giscard or Mitterrand–Barre – whose viability, even if the left had won, it certainly exaggerated. In Italy, it is not hard to recognize that the Centre-Left is not a plausible scenario for the time being. Washington is therefore banking on the Christian democrats' being able to transform themselves and devour the communists before the latter can win any solid gains in either power or legitimacy from their present ambiguous association with the Andreotti government.

Outside the comparatively narrow circles of professional foreign-policy specialists, the lack of sympathy for Eurocommunism and for the European socialist Left as a whole is even more resounding. For the present, to be sure, the issue is not, as they say in Washington, 'on the front burner'. To the extent that events do compel the administration to focus on the possibility of a substantial shift to the left in France, Italy or Spain, however, new forces will come into the equation. They will make the administration more, not less, resistant to the Eurocommunists' claims to legitimacy. For in Congress, in the media generally across the country, and in those circles that respond to the claim of 'national security', there is little sympathy for socialism either as an ideal or an economic strategy, and no sympathy whatever for communism of any description.

That is not to imply that the United States as a whole remains frozen in primitive, visceral anti-communist attitudes of the Manichean variety which flourished thirty years ago. McCarthyism was essentially an episode in US domestic politics, fuelled in the last analysis more by fears of communist influence inside the United States than by cool appreciation of the real danger from Soviet power.

With insignificant exceptions, all Americans – those who have studied the matter closely, and those who have scarcely given it a moment's thought, the Liberals as much as the Right – all instinctively share the same wish. They would prefer that there were no possibility of communists acquiring power in Western Europe. The question is not, as one US official after another told me in private conversation, 'whether we want to see communists in power in Europe. The question is, how do you keep them out?'

The preference, then, is clear enough. But the reality is that, both in France and in Italy, the communist parties have staked their claims to a share in government with the approval of millions of citizens; a fifth of the French, say, and a third of the Italians. It is when one turns to examine precisely what the US has done, is doing and plans to do when confronted with the complex realities of European politics that the picture becomes infinitely more confused. Or, to put the same thought in a different way, American opinion about the doctrines and organization of the Western communist parties is of less interest than the concrete question: how will the US actually react in the event of communists 'coming to power' in Western Europe?

But what does 'coming to power' mean? A brief sortie into the conceptual fog is unavoidable.

There is at the moment, and there has been throughout the whole period of the discussion which began in earnest after the near-success of the Left's candidate in the French presidential elections of 1974, no likelihood whatsoever that any communist party itself, alone or as a majority party, would form a government in any Western European country.

In Portugal, there *was* a danger that a military government of the Jacobin Left might come to power and take the country in the direction both of alignment with Soviet foreign policy and of far-reaching and possibly dictatorial domestic revolution. That danger has been removed for the foreseeable future, and the Portuguese Communist Party seems unlikely to play any major role.

In Spain, the communist party, though ideologically as bold as any in Europe, polled under 10 per cent of the vote in the June 1977 parliamentary elections. Though it improved that percentage slightly in the 1979 local elections, it certainly does not, as yet, aspire to more than a minority role in a coalition of the Left.

In France, *if* the Union de la Gauche had won the legislative elections in March 1978, the communists would have formed part of the governing coalition, and there would have been several communist ministers. That opportunity passed. The communist leadership, confronted with the prospect of playing second fiddle to a victorious and governing socialist party, preferred to retreat to winter quarters in order to protect its traditional working-class base from socialist competition. Whatever the reason for the PCF's decision to break up the Union of the Left, the situation today is as it was before: there is no possibility of the PCF 'winning power' in France, even if the fortunes of the Left improve and if its unity is restored. The PCF may conceivably share power. It can never win power.

In Italy the situation is more complex. Before the 1976 elections the PCI had begun already to enter what the Italians call 'the area of power'. Either alone, or in alliance with other parties, the communists now govern several important regions and cities, and real power is being devolved to the regions. Because of their general weight and especially because of their power in the unions, no economic policy could hope to lead Italy out of economic crisis without communist cooperation. After the 1976 election, the communists demanded to be consulted on other key issues as well including foreign policy, police and public order, education, and appointments to nationalized industries. The result was the 'programmatic accord', whereby the communists were to be consulted on a wide range of policy in return for allowing the Andreotti government to exist by agreeing to abstain in parliament.

At the end of 1977, when rank-and-file party members made plain their feeling that the party and its supporters were getting too little out of the deal, the communists unleashed a political crisis and brought the government down. The upshot of a prolonged political tussle was that the communists made another subtle but real advance into the 'area of power', by becoming voting, rather than abstaining, members of the coalition behind the new government. The Moro kidnapping and the subsequent local elections in the spring of 1978 seem to have marked a halt in the communists' advance. The subsequent fall of the Andreotti government was an opportunity the communists were unable to seize, and there is evidence of uncertainty and division in the party's ranks. Yet the communists' position of power in Italian life, at the centre and even more in the regions, is massively strong. Even so, there is no question of the communists forming a government. Since Enrico Berlinguer's celebrated 'reflection' on the events in Chile at the end of 1973, they have set their face firmly against even trying to win power by winning an electoral majority, either on their own or as partners in a popular front.

The question, then, 'What will the United States do if the communists get into power in Western Europe' always grossly over-simplified the range of situations which the United States might be faced with. Specialists in the State Department, CIA, White House staff, of course, were perfectly aware of this. Yet, for both the Ford and Carter administrations, concerned as they must be with political reactions both in Washington and in Europe, when the question had to be answered, it took this generic, over-simplified form.

In retrospect, it seems odd that the question did not arise sooner. Since 1972, after all, there was at least a theoretical possibility of communists entering government in France, and after François Mitterrand's surprisingly strong showing in the 1974 presidential election, the possibility was more than theoretical.

282 The US Response

Yet it was not until the spring of 1975 that the State Department began to be actively concerned with the Eurocommunists, and then in the context of Italy.

As Washington saw it, the issue was forced by the Italian communists themselves. The PCI was then engaged in a diplomatic campaign to win acceptance in Germany, Britain and Scandinavia and in Brussels. Two things forced the Americans to react. One was the application for visas to visit the United States on behalf of prominent members of the PCI leadership. The second was that, as it seemed to the Americans, the PCI 'surfaced' the long-standing middle-level contacts between themselves and the US embassy in Rome. At first, the US reaction was – revealingly enough – that the Italian communists were acting as cat's-paws for the Soviet Union. On second thoughts, Washington concluded that the PCI was trying to suggest that, if it did come closer to power, Washington would not object. At that time, responsible officials in Washington recollect, the Christian democrats in Rome were 'beseeching' Washington to 'say it isn't so'. Washington's concern was to take this plank out of the PCI's platform for the 1975 regional and municipal elections. 'Italy was the catalyst,' one official involved at the time reminisced to me. 'There was leftist turmoil everywhere in Southern Europe. We were afraid of a left-right split in Spain. Portugal was a concern. But France wasn't up on the screen yet.'

Since the question first arose in the context of Italy, in any case, successive formal statements of US policy towards the hypothetical advent of communists to government in Western Europe have been remarkably consistent through two administrations. It will be as well to look more closely, to see whether the consistency of these formal statements hid important nuances of intention. But first it will be worth briefly cataloguing some of the more important of those statements.

1. On 6 November 1975, Henry Kissinger (then, of course, already Secretary of State) was asked by Congressman Lester Wolff in the course of hearings held by the International Relations Committee of the House of Representatives what steps could be taken in view of 'the move towards the extreme Left in Italy?'

He replied that the government was 'of course disturbed by the dramatic gains made by the communist party' in the June 1975 Italian regional and local elections.

Basically [he said] the United States cannot determine the domestic structure of Italy ... the future of Italy is not an American foreign-policy problem. Having said this, however, the United States hopes very much that the Christian democratic party will revitalize itself ... [to] prevent the entry into government of the Communist Party of Italy, since the impact on NATO ... would be very severe.

2. Henry Kissinger achieved an even more concise formulation when he was asked by a journalist in Copenhagen on 20 January 1976 whether he would leave it to each NATO country whether or not to allow communists in its government:

The domestic evolution of European countries has to be for each European country to determine. On the other hand, when we are asked for our opinion, we give our views, and we will not falsify our views. Our view is that participation of communist parties in European governments will have consequences for NATO, will have consequences for international policies in general. Having said that, I agree that it is up to each government to decide for itself how to proceed.

3. Less than a fortnight later, on 2 February, Kissinger was asked about the European communists at a 'Blue Ribbon panel' in Los Angeles. Did he believe that there had been a fundamental change in the nature of the West European communists? This was the first time he had spoken publicly on the *nature* of Euro-communism. He had this to say:

Whether the communist parties have changed or not is something that no one can really know at this moment, because at this moment pru-dence coincides with the policy they are adopting. It is in their interest to claim that they have changed. I personally find it hard to believe that communist parties, which after all distinguish themselves from the other socialist parties because they insisted that a minority had to seize power and advance the course of history – that those parties have suddenly become democratic socialists or have used the democratic process in coming to power, which will permit the democratic process to reverse the course of history.

One can think of few other American statesmen who would even attempt to explain Lenin's theory of the vanguard party to a business audience in Los Angeles. But one can't help feeling that the Secretary of State failed to deploy his usual instinct to see things pragmatically.

4. On 11 March, the Secretary of State essayed a broader answer. The US attitude towards Eurocommunism, he told the Boston World Affairs Council, must be seen in the context of the ideals it shared with 'our closest allies, the great industrial democracies', namely, a 'deep-seated belief in freedom and in the hope of a better future for all mankind'.

Our ties with the great industrial democracies are not alliances of convenience but a union of principle in defence of values and a way of life.

It is in this context that we must be concerned about the possibility of communist parties coming to power – or sharing in power – in NATO countries.

Ultimately the decision must of course be made by the voters of the countries concerned. But no one should expect that this question is not of concern to this government.

Whether or not some of the communist parties in Western Europe are, in fact, independent of Moscow cannot be determined when their electoral self-interest so overwhelmingly coincides with their claims. Their internal procedures – their Leninist principles and dogmas – remain the antithesis of democratic parties. And were they to gain power they would do so after having advocated for decades programmes and values detrimental to our traditional ties.

By that record they would inevitably give low priority to security and Western defence efforts ... They would be tempted to orient their economies to a much greater extent towards the East ... steer their countries' policies toward the position of the non-aligned. The political solidarity and collective defence of the West – and thus NATO – would be inevitably weakened . . . The commitment of the American people to maintain the balance of power in Europe – justified though it might be on pragmatic, geopolitical grounds – would lack the moral base on which it has stood for thirty years.

5. Already in the spring of 1976 the presidential election monopolized attention in Washington. Western Europe in general, and Eurocommunism in particular, dropped out of sight as far as the warring candidates were concerned. There were no votes there. Just once the issue of Eurocommunism was squarely joined between the two candidates, in the second of their televised debates in San Francisco on 8 October 1976:

PRESIDENT FORD: Mr Carter has indicated he would look with sympathy to a communist government in NATO.

GOVERNOR CARTER (interrupting): Mr Ford unfortunately just made a statement that's not true. I have never advocated a communist government for Italy. That would obviously be a ridiculous thing for anyone to do who wanted to be president of this country.

6. Though Eurocommunism and the proper US response to it had a far lower priority for the incoming Carter administration than a number of other foreign policy issues (the Middle East, SALT, 'human rights', Southern Africa, for example), by April it was felt that the time had come to state the administration's policy on this subject. Hodding Carter III (no relation), the Assistant Secretary of State for Public Affairs, made the following statement in the course of a routine briefing of correspondents assigned to cover the State Department:

We believe that the position of a communist party in a particular country is a matter to be decided by the people and government of the country concerned. We do not propose to involve ourselves in the processes by which they reach their decisions on it. This does not mean that our attitude is one of indifference. We attach great importance to our ability to work with the countries of Western Europe on matters of vital interest. Our ability to do so could be impaired if these governments came to be dominated by political parties whose particular traditions, values and practices are alien to the fundamental democratic principles and common interests on which our relations with Western Europe are based.

It will be seen that the Carter administration's policy followed very closely the dualistic formula laid down by Henry Kissinger: *on the one hand* we do not interfere . . .; *on the other hand,* we cannot remain indifferent. It also went – as Kissinger had done in Los Angeles and more formally in Boston – one step beyond that: without going so far as to state in so many words that specific communist parties were incompatible with 'the fundamental democratic principles . . . on which our relations with Western Europe are based', it left the very strong inference that the administration needed to be convinced that this was not the case.

The matter was not to be left there, however. For one thing the State Department correspondents did not convey in the stories they wrote precisely the impression the administration sought to leave. And secondly, Henry Kissinger further clouded that impression. At Georgetown University he weighed in with almost the only serious criticism of the Carter foreign policy since he left office.

The decision was taken that the President himself must remove the doubts raised by Henry Kissinger's speech. On 25 April, he received four European journalists in the Oval office. Vittorio Zucconi, the correspondent of *La Stampa,* duly asked him how he would react to 'the growth of the Marxist Left' in Italy and France, and to 'the possibility of coalition governments in a NATO country with a role for communists in it'.

The President answered carefully and at some length:

I think the first premise on which we function is that the European citizens are perfectly capable of making their own decisions about political matters through the free election process.

Within my own memory, this is the first time that all the NATO countries have been democracies. And I think this is a very good evolution that we have already witnessed.

Secondly, we prefer that the governments involved continue to be democratic and that no totalitarian elements become either influential or dominant. And I would hope that the democratic parties would prevail during the coming years in the struggle for political authority.

I believe the best way we can prevent the enhancement of Communist political strength in Europe is to show that democratically controlled governments can function effectively and openly and with humaneness and a genuine and continuing comprehension of what people need and expect from government.

To the extent that we fail as democracies, as democratic leaders, to live up to the ideals that exemplify our own commitments, to that extent we open the opportunity for communist parties to be more successful.

So, to summarize, I think each country has to make its own decisions in the electoral process. I am pleased at the enhanced degree of commitment to the democratic governments. We certainly prefer that the democratic parties prevail in the future. And we can encourage that process, not by interfering in electoral procedures within countries themselves, but making the system work ourselves.

At the level of formal pronouncements, then, successive US spokesmen for two administrations have stressed the same two points over and over again. *On the one hand*, the United States does not, and will not, interfere in the internal policies of European allies; *on the other hand*, the United States cannot remain indifferent to any advance of communism in European governments.

At one level, this almost monotonous series of consistent, restrained and faintly sibylline pronouncements can be taken as evidence of the growing subtlety and professionalism of US diplomacy as compared with what might have been expected thirty years ago. Aware of the complexity of the interests involved, and aware, too, of the 'Michelson–Morley effect', whereby any US pronouncement might affect the outcome of the situation, US diplomacy kept its head. But the dualistic refrain was not merely a clever use of lawyer-like language. It also reflected a genuine and intractable dilemma for US policy.

'Policy' can be used to refer to the *statements* a government makes about its attitudes and intentions. It can also mean the general line of a government's *actions* in furtherance of its goals. And, in fact, the smooth continuity of Washington's statements about Eurocommunism conceals three distinguishable phases not so much in the evolution of US policy as in Washington's actions.

Henry Kissinger might choose to stress that the United States would abstain from interfering in European domestic politics. Yet – though this is a cloudy area screened by secrecy and mutual paranoia – there is good reason to believe that, as long as he was able to do so, Henry Kissinger did in fact interfere in Italian politics.

The evidence is necessarily both fragmentary and disputed. But first of all – and especially during the period 1969–71, when Graham Martin was the US ambassador in Rome – the embassy and the CIA station there went well beyond the mere maintenance of contacts for information-gathering purposes in its dealings with the extreme, neo-fascist Right in Italy.

The tangled thickets of the *trami neri* should be parted with caution. But it must be remembered that high officers of the Italian secret services (called first SIFAR and later SID) have been implicated in a whole series of violent intrigues explicable only in terms of a 'strategy of tension' intended to keep the centre of gravity of Italian politics from drifting to the Left, and even in a whole series of (admittedly ludicrous) attempted *coups d'état* such as those of General de Lorenzo in 1964 and Prince Juan Valerio Borghese in 1970. Many of these officers, such as General Micelli, later tried for his alleged part in the Piazza Fontana bombing in Milan in December 1970, have avowed links with the Movimento Sociale Italiano, as the neo-fascist party is called. Micelli and de Lorenzo both sat in parliament as neo-fascist deputies. And these high-ranking Italian intelligence officers, with their penchant for covert action intended either to strengthen the Right or to discredit the Left, were undoubtedly in close contact with their US opposite numbers in the Rome CIA station. General de Lorenzo, for example, is a close personal friend of General Vernon Walters, subsequently deputy director of the CIA during the Nixon administration. The Italian secret services are believed to have received heavy subsidies from Washington during Graham Martin's time at the Rome embassy. In any event, it is in the last degree unlikely that they would have engaged in these various covert right-wing actions if the word from Washington had been that such actions would be unwelcome there.

Bearing in mind that the communist party's change of tactics and its adoption of the 'historic compromise' were so specifically affected by the Chilean experience, I once asked a leading member of the PCI's *direzione* whether the party was afraid of US clandestine activities *à la chilienne* in the future. (I was referring to those disclosed, for example, in the Church Committee's reports.) His reaction was interesting: he took it for granted, he said, that US clandestine activities aimed at putting the PCI in a bad light had already taken place. But he brushed the matter aside. The PCI was too massive a presence in Italian life, he said, to be vulnerable to such pressures.

In any case, US interference in Italian politics under Kissinger was not limited to these more or less melodramatic activities of the CIA and its Italian 'correspondents'. In 1974, for example, Irving Brown, known to have acted as a CIA agent in France and Italy during the late 1940s, visited Italy, on his own admission, to try to wean two of Italy's trade-union federations away from the third, the CGIL, which is dominated by the communists. Brown, who is the AFL-CIO's representative in Europe, played a key role in setting up anti-communist unions in Europe during the post-war period, and also in encouraging the split in the Italian Socialist Party which led to the creation of the Italian Social Democratic Party. In 1974, Brown admitted that money would be available for unions which opposed the 'historic compromise' from the Italian-American Labor Council, a body which has connections with the US intelligence community going back to the days of the OSS before the end of the Second World War. Brown also made no bones about the fact that he had met Senator Amintore Fanfani, the chieftain of the right wing of the Christian democrats, in an effort to stiffen Fanfani's resistance to the 'historic compromise'. (In 1971, there were reports in the Italian press that Fanfani was offered a $1 million fund by Ambassador Graham Martin: the story was, naturally, denied.) In July 1974, Brown also saw Mario Tanassi, president of the social democratic party, reportedly to persuade him to bring down the centre-left coalition government in order to prompt early elections and so delay the arrival of the communists in the 'area of power'. Whether as a result of Brown's persuasions or not, Tanassi did, in fact, shortly after meeting Brown, announce that both the then government and the centre-left formula as a whole were finished.

In October 1974, a new controversy erupted when a left-wing Christian democrat, Carlo Donat-Cattin, accused the US ambassador, John Volpe, of urging on him the formation of a new centre government to carry through early elections with the same objective. The embassy explained lamely that Donat-Cattin had 'misunderstood' Volpe.

None of these cases, perhaps, can be proven beyond all doubt. Taken together, though, with many similar episodes, they do suggest that, up to and even after the fall of Richard Nixon, the US government, led by Henry Kissinger, did indeed interfere systematically, though by no means always effectively, in Italian politics.

As late as the beginning of 1976, interference on a somewhat massive scale was apparently still contemplated. In January 1976, Representative Leo Ryan, a Democratic congressman from California, revealed that the previous month the CIA director, William Colby, had told the House International Relations Committee that he planned to spend $6 million in secret funds to influence the imminent Italian parliamentary elections. It appears that this money was to be diverted from other covert expenditure planned in Italy. Colby seemed indirectly to confirm this when he commented: 'We have not spent a nickel in Italy in the past few months. I am not at liberty to discuss details.'

This first phase of policy, then, from the early days of the Nixon administration until the beginning of President Ford's last year in office, represented the continuation of the long-standing US policy of intervening, secretly and not so secretly, in Italian politics with the strategic purpose of keeping the communists out of power.

There was, perhaps, one difference about the Kissinger years.

US policy in Europe has, of course, been unwaveringly anti-communist since the 1940s. But, in general, it has showed little sympathy for the extreme Right. Both at the level of announced policy and at the level of covert action, US aid has always tended to go to governments and political parties of the moderate Right and, more particularly, of the moderate Left. If there has been a constant preference, it has been for the Centre-Left. There is the intriguing suggestion, therefore, that in this respect Henry Kissinger may have departed from a classic orientation of US policy, in that he seems to have encouraged the extreme Right. It is, of course, impossible to be sure how much of the support that was given to the various pieces on the Italian chessboard was given with Dr Kissinger's knowledge and approval. No doubt this is one of the matters on which he will enlighten us in his memoirs.

The period of roughly a year leading up to the 1976 presidential election marks, in any case, a second, transitional phase in the development of US policy towards Eurocommunism in the country – Italy – where it was first perceived as being 'up on the screen'.

From the beginning of 1976, Henry Kissinger himself became an issue in the election campaign. Both Ronald Reagan, challenging President Ford from the Right within the Republican party, and a substantial section of the Democratic party, including former Defense Secretary James R. Schlesinger, Senator Henry 'Scoop' Jackson and others, criticized the policy of détente with which Kissinger's reputation was inseparably identified. The Secretary of State sent trusted emissaries out around the country to find what 'opinion formers' thought about him and his policies in places like Milwaukee and Minneapolis. The verdict was that the leaders of Middle America found his policies, at best, incomprehensible, and, where they understood them, morally shocking. Kissinger seemed (probably wrongly) to be becoming a serious electoral liability to President Ford. He had good reason to keep a low profile.

At the same time Jimmy Carter was consciously campaigning against him. Carter recognized, and no doubt also shared, a new mood in America. There was growing pressure for change in foreign policy; a growing wave of criticism of 'covert activities'; a demand that US actions be more visibly in consonance with the country's traditional values. In all of this there was a new impatience with US commitments around the world.

Carter was influenced by this mood, and did his best to feed it. Early in 1976, too, he urgently needed to acquire the reputation of a candidate whose grasp of foreign policy would make him look credibly 'presidential'. As a short cut to achieving that reputation, he reached out and corralled into his team the only people who could instantly confer authority on his foreign policy. Some, like Zbigniew Brzezinski, had been in contact with Carter for some time. Others, like Cyrus Vance, were new recruits. All shared one characteristic: they were the liberal Democratic 'government in exile': members, that is, of what is known as the 'foreign policy establishment' in New York, Washington and the great eastern graduate schools. Most had served the Kennedy and Johnson administrations, and had drifted into an unhappy exile from power under Nixon. They had been predominantly – if sometimes tardily – critical of the Vietnam War. They had no reason to like, and in some individual cases they actively hated, Henry Kissinger. They needed to choose a foreign-policy stance which, while reassuring to the electorate and in no danger of being outflanked on the Right, could be clearly distinguished from Kissinger's. In the post-convention stages of the campaign, with all Democrats now rallied round candidate Carter, this orientation was reinforced ay a superficially contrary group. Carter began to listen to a more conservative group of experts, Schlesinger and retired Admiral Elmo Zumwalt among them.

The net outcome was a rather neat inversion. Where Kissinger had striven, above all, for better relations with the Soviet Union, for detente, but had reacted with suspicion and severity to other, peripheral movements towards the Left around the world (Chile, but also Cambodia, Bangladesh, Cyprus among others), now Carter and his advisers proposed exactly the opposite course. They began to attack Kissinger (and President Ford) for being at one and the same time too paranoid and too interventionist with regard to left-wing movements on the geo-political periphery, and too friendly with Leonid Brezhnev and the historical bastion of communist power.

This evolution of the presidential campaign goes some way to explain a new, more defensive tone in which the Secretary of State began (as in his Boston speech) to articulate an essentially unchanged position. It also helps to explain another development. From the spring of 1976 on, the United States begins to do multi-laterally, in consort with its allies, what before it had done unilaterally and in secret.

In the course of 1975, Henry Kissinger had been compelled to recognize the greater effectiveness of Helmut Schmidt's multi-lateral approach to the problem of Portugal. Schmidt quietly organized an operation in which several West European socialist parties were involved, to bolster up Mário Soares and his Portu-guese Socialist Party as an alternative both to the communists and to the leftist elements in the armed forces. In the summer of 1976, this multilateral approach was applied to Italy.

A week after the 20 June elections in Italy, the seven principal Western industrial powers met in Puerto Rico for an economic summit. Italy, Canada and Japan were not invited to the crucial meeting on the Italian problem. The Christian democrats had emerged from the elections with a slim margin over the com-munists, and while Aldo Moro represented Italy in Puerto Rico, Giulio Andreotti, as prime minister designate, was already begin-ning consultations to establish on what terms a government could be formed. According to the 'indiscretions' of Helmut Schmidt later in Washington, the United States, West Germany, France and Britain agreed that the international credit which Italy needed should not be forthcoming if the communists entered government.

Schmidt's revelation provoked the predictable explosion of indignation from the left-wing press in Italy. The leak came at the very moment when Andreotti was at the most delicate stage of his negotiations with the political parties, including the communists. He had to establish on what terms they could be persuaded to support a minority Christian democratic government. Both the original decision to use the loans as a lever, and the secondary decision to leak it, were a calculated form of international pressure, exercised essentially by the United States and West Germany, acting in concert with the acquiescence of France and Britain. Ironically, it seems likely that both Moro and Andreotti, who a few months earlier were begging for this kind of help, had by now decided that there was no alternative to a deal with the communists.

The Puerto Rican story is well known. What is not widely known is that, three weeks after Puerto Rico – that is, at almost exactly the same moment when Schmidt was executing his leak in Washington – one of Henry Kissinger's most trusted subordinates set out on a secret mission to London, Paris and Bonn to coordinate secret multilateral actions to stiffen the Christian democrats' resolve to exclude the communists from government. As a result of this mission, a whole series of individuals, including representatives of the Catholic Church and the trade unions, made concerted private visits to Italy to talk to their opposite numbers there and persuade them to do what they could to exert pressure on Andreotti not to yield too much to the communists. Such contacts have continued. It seems likely, for example, that American and West German influence contributed to Andreotti's decision not to agree to the communists' demand to be consulted on foreign policy.

From the beginning of 1976, as we saw, Henry Kissinger's authority had been seriously weakened. He chose to continue on a multilateral basis, with the willing assistance of Helmut Schmidt, essentially the same policy of covert interference which he had pursued alone when he could. But, in November 1976, Henry Kissinger's opinions and statements ceased to define US policy. A third phase was about to begin. So much is clear. What is less clear is the substance of political intention behind a subtle change in the tonality of the political music.

As the foreign policy experts of the new administration gathered in Washington in January 1977, there was a general reaction against Henry Kissinger's policy. He had been too obsessed, they believed, with the central superpower relationship with the Soviet Union, and too ready to pay too high a price, in different currencies, for that relationship. Vance, Brzezinski and their colleagues wanted to set up a less lopsided network of relationships between the United States and the rest of the world. Due attention must be paid, they felt, not only to the unilateral relationship with the Soviet Union, but also to 'trilateral' relationships with Europe and Japan, especially in the economic field, and to 'north–south' relations with the developing countries.

Already France was 'coming up on the screen'. Two leading French socialists, Michel Rocard and Jean-Pierre Cot, visited the United States in January and saw Vance. The new Secretary of State expressed the administration's willingness to work with a government of the Left in France that included communists, but, he said, the administration had real doubts about the communists' ability to work with them. He made it plain that Washington continued to have real worries about the lack of internal democracy in the French party, about its apparent continuing allegiance to the Soviet Union and, especially, about its foreign policy, which seemed to the Americans to follow that of the Soviet Union faithfully on most issues in spite of the disagreement between the French and Soviet parties on the amount of independence the French party should have.

In February, Brzezinski's national security staff in the White House carried out a formal review of US policy towards Eurocommunism, the first since an inter-agency study commissioned by Kissinger in 1975. A policy document was written in the White House, with inputs from the other agencies (State, Pentagon, CIA and so forth) and with help from the American ambassadors designate, Arthur Hartman (Paris) and Richard Gardner (Rome).

A certain reaction against the Kissinger style was perceptible in this document. There was a softening of tone. The paper recognized that the United States, in Kissinger's time, had over-reacted to communist gains in Western Europe. It was argued that it would be very much in the US interest to improve the underlying economic situation in Western Europe. In Italy, moreover, the White House document recognized that the necessary economic and social reform would not be possible unless the Italian Christian Democratic Party first reformed itself.

On the central issue, however, there was little change. The

Carter administration was no more complacent about the prospect of communists entering power in Western European governments than its predecessor. 'Anybody who is in any doubt that we don't want to see the communists in power', one influential official told me privately, 'simply hasn't been listening.' (Some legitimate confusion was caused by a change in Washington's policy on the issuing of visas to West European communists. The administration considered this to be essentially a response to the Helsinki agreement on human rights, not a policy signal.)

Washington does now recognize, more clearly than in Kissinger's time, the need for fundamental change in Western Europe. It does not accept that the help of the communists is indispensable to carry out that change. It looks with general sympathy, tempered by some misgivings on matters of detail, on the French socialists. It lives in the (probably sanguine) hope that the younger generation of Christian democrats in Italy will be significantly different from their elders. It remains profoundly sceptical about the extent to which the communists have changed their spots.

Early in October 1977, Zbigniew Brzezinski expounded the administration's view very clearly in an interview with the English journalist Jonathan Power in the *International Herald Tribune*.

We do not wish the communist parties to come to power in Western Europe [Brzezinski began].

Secondly, we have confidence that the West European electorates will use their best judgement to preserve democratic systems and will therefore opt for democratic parties.

Thirdly, we have to deal with the world as it is.

Fourthly, the existence of Eurocommunist parties, as of themselves, does encourage change in the nature of communism, and it is unwise for the United States to engage in direct interference in domestic affairs of other countries of the sort that could make the Eurocommunist parties symbols of national independence.

Lastly, Eurocommunism is a highly differentiated phenomenon ... Some of these parties are still highly Stalinist, like the Portuguese. Some of them have begun de-Stalinization, but they've only begun it, like the French. Some of them are relatively de-Stalinized, but are still highly Leninist, like the Italian. Some have de-Stalinized themselves, and probably are already de-Leninized, such as the Spanish.

Power then asked him whether there would be any circumstances under which Brzezinski would use covert action against European communists in government.

> Well [Brzezinski replied], I'm not going to make a blanket promise...
> it depends a great deal on circumstances, the degree of legitimacy of
> the political change involved. But as a general principle I can state
> flatly that it is the principle of this administration ... not to interfere
> with democratic political processes.

The force of that guarantee is perhaps weakened a little by the fact that Brzezinski, in his earlier answer, quite clearly placed the communist parties in contradistinction to 'democratic parties'. And when Power pressed Brzezinski a second time for a definite pledge not to engage in covert action, he retreated behind a huffy little dust-storm:

> I think if somebody came to me and asked me to make a promise not
> to beat my wife, I would find that an offensive requirement, and I think
> if anybody came and asked this country to make that kind of promise,
> which is implied in your question, I would reply in similar fashion.

In spite of this equivocation (in view of the long record of US interference in Italy and elsewhere, it has to be classified as such) I believe that Brzezinski was accurately stating the Carter administration's policy. It has made a solemn commitment to abstain from interfering in the domestic politics of other countries. It is aware of the unpopularity of such activities in the United States. And it is also aware of its own limited power to affect the situation in Italy, and even more in France.

The Carter administration came to the conclusion that it would be more effective to help the communists' opponents than to try to obstruct the communists directly. Thus the Andreotti government in Italy was given discreet US help and encouragement in a number of ways. More specifically, the Carter administration made some effort to improve relations with the French President Giscard d'Estaing. His prime minister, Raymond Barre, was given red-carpet treatment when he visited Washington in the summer of 1977. And it was knowingly as part of Giscard's strategy for defeating the communists in the French legislative elections due in March 1978 that Jimmy Carter agreed to visit France during his whirlwind world tour at New Year 1978.

Moreover, while in Paris, Carter met François Mitterrand. The French socialist leader had tried in vain to arrange a meeting with Carter during the previous summer, before the break-up of the Union of the Left in September. Now Carter himself made the approach, and told Mitterrand, in words carefully leaked to the press, 'you have played a good and beneficial role in France'. In private, Carter stressed to Mitterrand his hope that, in the event of the Left winning, the communists would not enter the government.

In the meantime, Washington became even more seriously alarmed about the situation in Italy, where the Andreotti government seemed in danger of falling at any minute, and for a moment it seemed that communist entry into a coalition government might be imminent.

The US ambassador to Rome, Richard Gardner, was hastily summoned to Washington, where, on 12 January, the State Department issued its strongest statement so far on that eventuality.

There has been no change in the administration's attitude toward Western communist parties [it read] . . . Our position is clear: We do not favor [communist] participation [in West European governments] and would like to see communist influence in any Western European country reduced . . . The United States and Italy share profound democratic values and interests, and we do not believe that the communists share those values and interests.

The reaction in Europe was more than predictably outraged. The US statement was furiously denounced as 'interference' by both communists and socialists in Italy, naturally, but it was also denounced by such normally moderate newspapers as the *Guardian*, which called the statement 'dishonest' and commented that it was tantamount to saying that 'the rules of the democratic game are sacrosanct as long as the outcome suits the United States'. Even more sharply, *Le Monde* compared Carter's position to the Brezhnev doctrine of 'limited sovereignty'. The outcry in France spread across the whole political spectrum, with not only President Giscard and his prime minister, Barre, severely critical, but right-wingers like the former interior minister, Michel Poniatowski, and former foreign minister, Couve de Murville, agreeing that the statement implied a 'shocking' degree of American interference.

To sum up then: in Phase I Henry Kissinger said he would not interfere in Italy or elsewhere to keep the communists from power – while at the same time he was, in practice, interfering when he thought fit. In Phase II, Kissinger was no longer free to intervene unilaterally. But he joined in multilateral interference with the West Germans and other allies, while still proclaiming that he was not interfering at all. In Phase III, the Carter administration, while no keener than its predecessor on seeing the communists advance towards power, also says that it does not contemplate interference. In general, it probably means what it says. Only for a brief moment at the beginning of 1978 did it yield to those who thought there was a real danger of communist participation in government in both France and Italy, and to those in France and Italy who wanted an open American commitment against such a development. The moment passed. The Italian crisis was resolved. The Left failed to win the French elections. For the time being, with a sigh of relief, Washington can leave European politics to the Europeans.

In the long run, however, great powers' actions are perhaps determined less by their intentions than by their interests. What, then, is at stake for the United States if communist power and influence continue to grow in Western Europe? The answer can be attempted under four headings: (a) investments, (b) more general economic considerations, (c) defence and (d) broad political considerations.

The United States has substantial business interests in Italy. Some 700 US companies operate there, and direct investment is estimated at more than $2,000 million. None of this is immediately threatened by the PCI, which actively opposes further nationalizations. It considers the public sector in Italy to be big enough to allow effective management of the economy, and to be too big on other grounds. Nevertheless, with few if any exceptions, US businessmen and managers in Italy, with their Italian customers, partners, bankers and friends, are vehemently opposed to the PCI, and are not without a considerable capacity to lobby for their interests in Washington. Former secretary of the Treasury, John Connally, is associated with a group of American and Italo-American investors who have announced their intention both of buying major stakes in Italian industry (they have already bought one big company) and of doing what they can to lobby against the communists.

In France, the US business community is equally hostile to the communist party, and therefore to the prospect of a Left union government, but with the additional reason that the 'Common Programme of the Left' proposed to nationalize a substantial proportion of French large-scale industry. The nationalizations contemplated would have affected US interests little. ITT France would be nationalized, and so would substantial US holdings in Alsthom and in other companies on the list. But the US embassy in Paris was not worried by the prospect of powerful interests in the US lobbying, as they did in Chile, and on other occasions when private US holdings in Latin America have been threatened with expropriation. Provided that compensation was adequate and prompt, specific US interests in France were never thought likely to lead to serious tension between Washington and a French government of the Left.

More important and more immediate as a source of concern in the US would be the overall economic impact of Left governments in France or Italy. (Or for that matter in Spain, Portugal or Greece.)

In Italy, the communist party is wholly committed for the foreseeable future to a 'crisis-managing' economic policy. It is true that the party defends the *scala mobile*, the sliding scale which partially ties Italian workers' wages to the index of inflation. But, in general, it has taken a strong anti-inflationary stand. Over-all, not only is it *not* true that increased communist power would increase the dangers of economic confusion, as US experts see it: it is quite widely agreed in US business circles that there is no hope of improving the Italian economy without the active collaboration of the PCI and of the CGIL trade unions, which are largely run by communists. (US banks are very heavily committed in Italy. The Chase Manhattan and the First National City Bank of New York, second and third largest banks in the United States, each had well over $500 million out in loans to Italian public corporations, some of them of dubious solvency. It may be inferred that the Rockefeller interests, and New York banking circles generally, are rather less keen on using credit pressures on the Italian economy than they might otherwise have been.)

In France, United States experts were always divided about the long-term economic effect of a government of the Left. There were even some, particularly in the banking sector, who believed that the Left would be more likely than President Giscard to put an end to 'Gaullist' projects aimed at national independence in such fields as aviation and computer technology. Accordingly, under a government of the Left, France would become both a less troublesome competitor and a better market for US industry. But the majority view would be that such advantages would be cancelled out by the inevitably inflationary effect of the kind of redistributive policies which any government of the Left would presumably apply. Whatever judgement is made, in other words, about the long-term effect of the social, economic and industrial transformations which a government of the Left would be bound to attempt, there is striking unanimity among American observers that the short-term results of such transformations would be highly deleterious. For a transitional period, at least, United States observers assume that the victory of a government of the Left would be followed by steeper rates of inflation, poorer export performance, balance of payments difficulties, increased capital flight, a shortage of investment capital, and an urgent need, in consequence, for foreign financing. That would have to come from the EEC and the IMF. Reductively, that means that major transformations in France could come about only with the assent of West Germany and the United States – or so the Americans believe.

Bluntly, there are few in Washington who feel any great

inclination to help French society transform or modernize itself, let alone feel any sympathy for the ideals of French socialists or communists. Most of the United States foreign-policy community feels perfectly comfortable with Giscard. 'The problem,' one middle-level State Department official said to me with something close to a snarl, 'is less that we would be unreasonable than that others would expect us to pick up the tab for their little experiments.'

Even more visceral is Washington's concern for defence. Here, too, Italy and France present quite different problems. France has, since de Gaulle, been a member of the North Atlantic alliance without belonging to the North Atlantic Treaty Organization. Though NATO, therefore, does without French troops, NATO without a French government that was at least basically sympathetic would be strategically unviable. Even though (with an abruptness which cast doubt on its new-claimed 'pluralism') the French Communist Party has come out for the maintenance of the French independent nuclear *force de frappe*, the Pentagon hardly finds this reassuring. For one thing, the Kanapa report, in which the PCF defined its new strategic policy in May 1977, went out of its way to stress that the French forces ought to be aimed *tous azimuths* – 'in all directions'. Though this was true in de Gaulle's day, too, US military men fear that France's nuclear weapons could be targeted not against the Soviet Union but against West Germany or NATO targets in West Germany. More fundamentally still, the Pentagon fears that French communist influence in government would inevitably be exercised in the long run in favour of an increasingly neutralist French foreign policy.

In the case of Italy, specific NATO assets are at risk, and also US military assets. The headquarters of the NATO Southern Command are in Naples. Gaeta is an important base for the Sixth Fleet, which is increasingly short of bases now that Greek, Turkish and some Spanish ports are denied it. One ship-day out of every three in port is now spent by the Sixth Fleet in Italian ports. If the Sixth Fleet were to be forced out of Italy, it would have to fall back to Spain; if forced out of Spain, it would have to operate out of Norfolk, Virginia.

There are powerful US F-4 squadrons based in Vicenza and other bases in the Veneto, and nuclear-powered hunter-killer subs operate out of La Maddalena in northern Sardinia.

Italy's own contribution to NATO, US officials stress, is by no means purely nominal. Italian naval and air units are, in particular, essential to the defensive strategy of NATO's weakened southern flank.

Even more important than any of these specific forces or bases, or even than the communications networks that link them together, however, is the strategic geographical situation of the country, stretching from France to Greece right across the waist of the Mediterranean. NATO forces in Italy protect Western Europe's main oil-supply route. If NATO was thrown out of Italy, US defence planners in the Pentagon insist a trifle defensively, it would not necessarily mean that the US would have to leave the Mediterranean. But they acknowledge that the southern flank of NATO would be drastically weakened.

But would Italy be taken out of NATO on any realistic hypothesis about either the PCI's policy or its power? The party has defended Italian participation in NATO for some years now. Partly, no doubt, this is for domestic electoral and political reasons. Yet there are in Rome many who believe that the PCI's commitment to NATO is motivated by other calculations. The Italian communists are looking warily to what they call *il dopo Tito*: what happens after Tito dies? They do not think their hopes of an independent socialist Italy are favoured by the prospect of Warsaw Pact troops on Italy's north-east frontier.

The Pentagon does not dismiss arguments about the Italian communists' intentions so much as ignore them. It may be that these are quite unlike those of any other communists, they thus say in effect, but we cannot afford to wait and see or gamble on their good will. They see three separate dangers from the PCI's presence in government. First of all, even if the party does support Italy's membership in NATO, what level of specific commitment to NATO does it support? Secondly, Italian communists in power would raise all sorts of troubling minor problems, from security and secrecy (the Pentagon and NATO are specially worried because Italy is a member of NATO's inner Nuclear Planning Group) to the level of cooperation to be expected from local authorities round NATO bases. Or so the Pentagon assumes. Most seriously, US military planners simply cannot dismiss from their minds the possibility that, whatever they may say now, the Italian communists might at some future time leave NATO and throw NATO out.

Beyond and behind all these particular calculations of tangible national interest there lie even more decisively determining considerations for US policy: considerations of geopolitics, ideology and even national identity. At the risk of restating the obvious, let me try to sum up why no American administration can look without something close to horror on the prospect of communists in power in France or Italy.

Since 1917, and even more since 1941, the United States has been utterly committed to preventing the industrialized and democratic nations of Western Europe from falling into hands that were inimical either to American notions of democracy or to American economic interests. The two conceptions are so inextricably mingled that it is a waste of time to try to say which has primacy. China is lost. So is South-East Asia. Latin America may be slipping away. The US position in Europe guarantees America status as a world power. The United States has paid dear in blood and treasure to fulfil that commitment, which over the past thirty years has come to be identified with a commitment to save democracy in Europe *from communism*. If it should turn out that the workings of European democracy should result in the arrival of communists in power, then a theoretical dilemma would already be present. Which is the higher duty: to defend democracy in Europe, even if it means installing some version of communism there? Or to defend Europe from communism, even if that means limiting the freedom of European democracy?

American policymakers tend to be impatient of such theoretical questions. They are the products of a society in which socialism is exotic, and communism still generally regarded as the national enemy. It is as hard for them to draw subtle distinctions between one brand of communism and another as it is dangerous for them to be wrong in their analysis. They are aware that it may be in their long-term interest to allow the less successful nations of Southern and Western Europe, in the aftermath of the economic crisis of 1973, to undertake profound reforms. Such reforms, after all, would to some extent take the form of making those societies more like American society. Yet they find it virtually impossible to accept that the inner divisions of French, Italian or Spanish society could mean that in practice such changes can come about only with the help of the communist parties. They are not, as one State Department analyst put it to me, about to invite the American people to spend its money and send its boys overseas to defend one kind of communist against another.

So the theoretical dilemma does ultimately resolve into a dilemma of policy. If the march of the Western European communists towards 'winning power' does go on, then the United States could find itself confronted by an impossible choice: either to withdraw from Western Europe, or to intervene in such a way as to exclude the communists from power. Both alternatives are at the moment unthinkable. But – as I have argued – it is not likely that any communist party will form a government, or even play more than a minor role in government in any of the West European countries. What is certain is that the communist parties will continue to hold, as they have done since the Second World War, a formidable quantum of power in at least three countries, and they will have to be taken into account by whoever would either govern or transform those societies. The Carter administration, just as much as the Nixon and Ford administration under the influence of Henry Kissinger, persists in regarding the communist parties as outside the pale of democratic societies. Yet in those societies – in France, in Spain, above all in Italy – the communists are not regarded as outside the pale. They may be hated by some, suspected by many, resisted by the majority. They are not now anathemized. A gap has opened up between the realities of politics in these European countries and Washington's perception of those realities. For the time being, Washington can afford to heave a sigh of relief and interpret the hair's-breadth failure of the Left in the March 1978 elections in France, and the marginal reversal of the PCI's fortunes in Italy, as confirming that the danger of communism in Western Europe can be forgotten. Washington wishes that the communists would go away. But they won't. They will probably continue to evolve in ways which will make them more attractive to some democratic voters, and they will certainly continue to be a force to be reckoned with – not least by the Americans. No wonder one of the most thoughtful, of those responsible for policy towards Europe in the present administration said to me pensively that 'over the next ten years Western Europe will become our number one foreign-policy problem'.

10. The Vatican and Eurocommunism
Peter Nichols

From the Vatican's point of view, destiny's choice of Russia as the scene of the revolution, so remote from Rome's influence, meant that the decisive political event of the century was outside the Vatican's normal sphere of influence. Papal policy was prudent towards the new state. As late as 1923, the Vatican was able to establish a new diocese in Russia (at Vladivostok) and several more years were to pass before a final denunciation came of Soviet communism. A series of criticisms found their final outspoken condemnation in Pius XI's encyclical, *Divini redemptoris*, of March 1937, which is the great set-piece of modern papal denunciations: 'Communism is intrinsically wrong and no one who would save Christian civilization may collaborate with it in any field whatsoever.'

The *Communist Manifesto* and its insistence on Europe,[1] like the Vatican's attempt at maintaining relations with the revolutionaries – to the horror of Russian exiles – raise an issue which needs to be faced early. This is the facile view that Catholicism and communism are much the same in outlook and behaviour, except for differences in the all-embracing doctrines which they each impose on their followers.

This view leads mainly in two directions. Both are probably false. The first is that Catholicism and communism can never, by the natural order of things, ever agree because similar does not attract similar but rather rejects it. The second is that an instinctive similarity must surely mean that in the end the two sides will be able to come to an understanding because, essentially, they speak the same language of discipline and imposed authority. In this second process, Eurocommunism could be seen as having its part in bringing about understanding because it is a form of communism ostensibly devised for that area of the world where the Catholic Church feels more at home and has its seat, and has been devised by men who are supposed to be at home with the Catholic approach and explicitly aim at gaining the understanding of Catholics. Everybody knows that Berlinguer's wife is a practising Catholic, that his children take instruction from a Jesuit and that he can turn his hand to a letter addressed to a bishop as if to the manner born. The Church's vision of Europe, however, is such that a Berlinguer, or someone like him, could be welcomed if he should appear in Poland or in Hungary or in Czechoslovakia. But his presence in the West can only be regarded with suspicion or, at most, prudent attention.

1. The identity of Europe

This is not duplicity. It is an attitude involving two questions of identity. They are both fundamental to the Vatican's thinking on Eurocommunism. The first is Europe's own identity. Paul VI's outlook as he expressed it in his Strasbourg message[2] came close to seeing the Christian spirit and the true European spirit as one. This view has been described in the Italian press as 'Eurochristian'. It has been carried forward with great clarity by Cardinal Benelli who, before being appointed Archbishop of Florence, was undersecretary at the Vatican and the Pope's principal executive.

He does not always pick the best occasions on which to make his pronouncements. His most striking explanation of the Church's thinking on Europe came a matter of months after his appointment to Florence when he attended a two-day meeting on Christianity and Europe held in the Benedictine abbey of Ottobeuren in Bavaria in September 1977. Politically, the meeting was openly conservative. The outstanding politician present was Franz Josef Strauss, who naturally took the occasion to attack Eurocommunism. The cardinal appeared on the second day and spoke twice.

In a simple homily delivered in the course of a pontifical mass, he explained the natural, Christian sentiment within man for unity, and described the difficulties which worked against the achievement of this aim of human unity. Later on the same day he delivered a more detailed speech in which he enlarged on this Christian outlook on European unity with an account of how the Church saw the European character. He made no specific reference to Eurocommunism, though what he said quite obviously took, and was intended to be taking, this phenomenon into account.

He rejected the claims of economic and political structures as a basis for future unity. 'In my humble opinion, they will never be the main column supporting the edifice called Europe.' Economic values, he said, had been given precedence over spiritual and moral values. This could not be admitted in the light of Christianity, which saw things in exactly the reverse order. Christianity was an essential and determining factor in being European. Believers would accept this fact from the religious standpoint, whereas non-believers would regard it as simply a cultural factor. But no one could deny this reality, this deep and irreplaceable substratum of Europe's culture. The Christian inspiration had given to the people of Europe

the sense of their individual and collective existence; the deep and unconditional respect for the dignity of man; liberty as an irrenounceable condition for the full development of man; the idea of solidarity founded on justice; love and respect for others in a complementary sense; in a word, the harmony between the individual and the community, between God and man.

The cardinal went on:

I think that a Europe truly one will not be made, that the European ideal will not be sufficiently strong and decisive, to encourage individual states to give up part of their sovereignty if these values, anchored in the purest Christian tradition, do not find their place at the centre of the achievement of a new community which embraces the whole continent, historically and culturally forged on the basis of these very values.

His conclusion was clear:

Europe will find its soul again if Christians understand that it is up to them in the first place to give concrete form in the Europe of the future to the values of unity and brotherhood proclaimed by the Gospel.

The cardinal was announcing an active strategy by the Church aimed at reviving Europe's fortunes on the foundation of a spiritual revival. He was not only referring to the EEC, which the Vatican regards as insufficient both in moral and geographical terms. He was referring to the whole continent. Despite his avoidance of any specific reference to Eurocommunism, his speech was widely interpreted as the Church's more intransigent line of thinking on how to oppose the threat of Eurocommunist hegemony over the continent, even if there is something in his views both of de Gaulle's vision of Europe and Berlinguer's own statements on Europe's place as a third force.

This broad view of Europe's character as a whole continent and not just the Western part of it has probably been prompted by the appearance of Eurocommunism in the West. Berlinguer talks of Italian communism as something which has been evolved to meet the requirements of Western Europe. But the party makes no secret of Eurocommunism's usefulness in Eastern Europe's future development, and, directly or indirectly, it is surely this aspect of Eurocommunism which is potentially most interesting to an organization that bases its diplomacy and foreign relations on the overriding need for obtaining and maintaining the required degree of freedom for carrying out its spiritual functions, however broad they may at times seem to be. This is the fundamental consideration in the Vatican's political dealings. It was expressed with colour and accuracy in May 1929 by Pius XI: 'Where there is the question of saving souls, we feel the courage to treat with the Devil in person.'

The idea that Europe is in the Vatican's eyes the whole continent and not just the West is a constructive part of the Vatican's policies and not just a dream of past, and more comfortable, days. The Church has a 'Council of the Episcopal Conferences of Europe', presided over by Monsignor Etchegaray, the Archbishop of Marseilles and chairman of the French Episcopal Conference. The council's membership includes bishops from Eastern Europe. At their meeting in Rome in December 1977, bishops attended from East Germany, Poland and Hungary as well as from the West.

This council followed up the Pope's Strasbourg message by publishing a declaration entitled: 'In the Service of Europe'. It was signed by fifteen chairmen of European episcopal conferences. Monsignor Etchegaray introduced it by saying that Europe was 'opening a road towards the future, providing itself, step by step, with a new structure. The Church cannot remain indifferent to these efforts.' He went on to point out that the task facing them was to place the dynamism of the Christian faith at the service of the construction of Europe; 'of a wider Europe, over and above the two blocs'. One of the council's objectives is to bring together the episcopates of Eastern and Western Europe.

The European Community has the Vatican's approval, so far as it goes. So much was made clear by Monsignor Agostino Casaroli, the Vatican's leading policy-maker, in a lecture on Europe which he delivered at Linz University at the end of 1977. He made the point that the Holy See did not regard the EEC as an impediment to an eventual, broader unity in the future. He expressed the Vatican's great interest in the Helsinki Conference. It was the first concrete example, he said, of the unity of Europe 'from the Atlantic to the Urals'. The philosophy of Helsinki tended to overcome pragmatically Europe's ideological split. This philosophy, he pointed out, was intended not only to guarantee security but to indicate various fields of cooperation to break down the deep distrust between the two sides. He expressed himself as convinced of Europe's capacity for future progress. The necessary condition was that political tension be resolved, that ideological opposition lose the character of struggle and menace, that a meeting-ground be found of a practical kind and that common values be recognized in common.

2. The identity of the Church

The idea of a meeting-ground leads back naturally enough to Eurocommunism, and on to the second question of identity felt at the Vatican after that of Europe itself. This second issue is the

Christian identity and is one of the Vatican's most pressing considerations in devising its attitude to Eurocommunism.

This consideration is part of the traditional, and actual, duty felt by the Catholic Church to preserve the purity of the faith. The point even arises in the letter which Monsignor Luigi Bettazzi, the Bishop of Ivrea, wrote to Enrico Berlinguer in July 1977 (stimulating the still more famous reply). The bishop refers to the communist decision to allow a group of well-known Catholics to appear as candidates on the party's lists. The fact that this group of people accepted the communist offer brought an angry reaction from the Italian hierarchy and from the Pope himself. Monsignor Bettazzi comments:

> Among you there have always been some Christians, by origin and by the maintenance of a certain religious practice. But never had there been such sensational cases involving well-known Christians, publicly committed to remaining so. The reaction of the Catholic hierarchy is understandable, given its concern to avoid not only ideological confusion but, above all, upset in the 'Catholic world' in the face of such a new development, raising so many new problems.

The Vatican is well aware that the Church is under strong pressure from the Italian and Spanish communist parties to cooperate with them in a way that it has hitherto refused. Carrillo sees the Church as undergoing a crisis perhaps deeper than that of the Protestant Reformation. But the crisis of the Church, he writes, as an ideologically capitalist body, does not mean that the Christian faith is undergoing a crisis. In fact, the hierarchy has, he says, already placed a certain distance between itself and capitalism (without accepting Marxism), and the idea of the faith as a stimulus to human liberation suggests to him that a new revolutionary strategy should be adopted, aimed at adapting religious sentiments to social transformation.

It is only fair at this point to let Cardinal Benelli sum up the dangers and limitations of a dialogue such as Carrillo is proposing: fair, because one of the cardinal's replies to accusations of being reactionary is that he approved the Church's opposition to Franco's régime in the final period of the dictator's rule. In an address to the Austrian Society for Foreign Policy, which he gave in Vienna while still under-secretary at the Vatican, he summed up the Church's approach to the problem of dialogue with communists. He prefaced his conclusions with the assertion that Marxism, as a concept of men and of history, was 'in open conflict' with the principles of Christianity. His conclusions were:

If it is a matter of a true dialogue, that is an expression of the will for love in truth and of service, such a dialogue is always on the Church's side, towards all men, believers or atheists. If it is a matter of accepting Marxist theories or belonging to movements which draw their inspiration from atheistic Marxism, such conduct is *never* possible for a Christian. As to forms of collaboration, they are always dangerous and risky both for the faith itself of the Christians and for their liberty as citizens. Given that every *practice* is the expression of an idea, by admitting a collaboration on the practical plane does one not implicitly accept the ideology from which such practice is derived?

And his final conclusion is that 'Christianity and the Church cannot sacrifice their identity and their mission'.

3. Alliance for progress?

The Church suffers the embarrassment, however, and this is especially so in Italy, of seeing specifically Catholic parties who have not lived up to such ideals. And this, too, is a form of pressure on Catholics to look to the Left. The failure of Christian democracy to carry out the obligations which the confessional link entails has strengthened the claims of Eurocommunism in the eyes of the electorate. The Italian Communist Party has managed to appear the party of balanced social protest, and so has reinforced its ranks with protest voters, but to win sufficient weight to govern, it needs much more. Berlinguer has said that even 51 per cent of the vote would not be enough. Having about 34 per cent in hand, he must logically look elsewhere for support and does so towards the Catholic ranks.

Arguably, this search is a belated recognition by the Left of the usefulness of the Catholic activism generated by the Counter-Reformation. Thus Berlinguer's type of communism can look beguiling as a means of carrying through social reforms which are favoured by many Catholics intent on greater social justice.

The Declaration on Europe of the European Episcopal Conference contains this passage:

Social injustices must be eliminated. We must be ready to share the fate of others more than in the past. To act as Christians means to give up greediness and the thirst for power, place ourselves disinterestedly at the disposal of others without expecting recompense. To be Christian means to live in such a way that others can also live.

Cannot a Marxist feel the same and, combining resources with socially minded Catholics, have a better chance of achieving a better society? The Jesuits have attempted an answer as a consequence of a specific request from the Pope to the order as a whole to oppose the 'tremendous danger which threatens humanity, namely atheism'. The approach they have elaborated was summarized by Father Bartolomeo Sorge, editor of the Jesuit periodical, *Civiltà Cattolica*. He, too, seeks to place the problem in the widest possible frame. Mankind is at the end of an epoch. 'We are living through a cultural transition of hitherto unknown proportions.' The choices made today will bear on humanity's future for a long time to come. Only by showing that the Church is still the bearer of hope for men can the Church meet the fundamental challenges which the world places before it. He points out that the Christian hope is not based on a philosophy or an ideology, nor just on human forces or those of a social class. It is based on God. To leave aside this religious and transcendent dimension, or place it in the shadows in order to present it exclusively or prevalently as a promise of social and political liberation, is the equivalent, to use the incisive expression of St Paul, 'of watering the Word of God as innkeepers water the wine'. He goes on: 'In reality, we are not Christians because we hope for the end of the capitalist system of production or in the fall of totalitarian régimes in the East and in Latin America . . .'

He deals respectfully with Marxism, which 'certainly appears to many people the greatest hope that man ever conceived to free himself and redeem himself with his own strength alone'. Marxism has contributed, he says, to develop in the world a hope of liberation which is in itself fine and good and should not be disappointed.

The deadly error is in the method and the solutions which it proposes of which we are all aware; lacking an integral and transcendent vision of man and history, Marxism makes absolute realities which in fact are only partial, and thus inadequate intrinsically to realize the hope of a more just and fraternal world. Also *a posteriori*, the historical experience of all socialist régimes shows, without possibility of doubt, that in them men are not all equal as one had been given to hope: that not all enjoy equal rights and fundamental liberties of thought, of conscience, of speech, of association; that the domination of man over man not only has not disappeared but has reached the point of the construction of walls of separation and iron curtains, and of filling concentration camps and psychiatric hospitals.

4. The Italian dimension

In all these questions of European identity, of Christian identity and the stage reached in universal history, Eurocommunism's part is necessarily reduced to one element among many others. The suggestion was put forward at the International Synod – as an example of other elements to be taken into consideration – that Western apathy, agnosticism and even atheism are a more insidious danger to the faith of young people than Eastern Marxism. But the birthplace of Eurocommunism as a powerful political force is Italy, and this presence cannot be neatly fitted into a broader perspective because it concerns everyday affairs and the fact that the communists, with a third of the national vote, are the country's second largest political party.

The relationship between the Vatican and Italy is obviously different and closer than with any other country. The Vatican in its modern historical form is the creation of Italians who still dominate its administrative structure. The Pope includes among his titles that of Primate of Italy, and, of course, is Pope by virtue of being Bishop of Rome and not vice versa. Hence, the distinction cannot be completely made between the Catholic hierarchy in Italy and the Vatican because the latter, too, is directly concerned in Italian affairs. The communists are fully aware of the Church's influence and are by a long way less anti-clerical than most other lay parties.

They see some justification for demanding respect in the passage in John XXIII's first encyclical, *Pacem in terris*, in which he made the distinction between false philosophies and practice based on them. He said:

Again it is perfectly legitimate to make a clear distinction between a false philosophy of the nature, origin and purpose of men and the world, and an economic, social, cultural and political programme, even when such a programme draws its origin and inspiration from that philosophy ... Besides, who can deny the possible existence of good and commendable elements in these programmes, elements which indeed conform to the dictates of right reason and are expressions of man's lawful aspirations?

John himself was not, however, by any means inclined towards an impulsive cooperation with Marxism, despite the allegations of his critics. In the same encyclical he pointed out that such matters were for prudence to decide. And here he was deferring to one of the characteristic principles of the Vatican's policies on almost any subject. It is the principle still being followed in the Church's outlook on Eurocommunism – 'prudence, the queen of all the virtues which rule the life of men both as individuals and in society'. And he went on to remind Catholics of the obligation on them to follow the Church's teaching in this as in other respects:

For it must not be forgotten that the Church has the right and the duty not only to safeguard her teaching on faith and morals, but also to exercise her authority over her sons by intervening in their external affairs whenever a judgement has to be made concerning the practical application of that teaching.

Paul VI had recourse to this 'right and duty' in the 1976 general election in Italy. He made one of the weightiest interventions of post-war years against the communists.

What he said was certainly not the last word. The fact that Monsignor Casaroli took over the handling of Italian affairs at the Vatican after the departure of the more intransigent Benelli is an indication that such developments as may occur in communist thinking will be carefully watched and weighed. Theory aside, the Vatican has such practical matters as a revision of the Concordat and the application of the law making over social services to the regions to bear in mind. But prudence will not be discarded.

For the time being, the conclusion is that of Antonio Caruso, reviewing Carrillo's book '*Eurocommunism' and the State* in *Civiltà Cattolica*: 'without a radical transformation in relations with Marxist-Leninist ideology and with the Soviet Union, Eurocommunism remains a dream'.

Notes and references

1. The opening words of the Communist Manifesto are: 'A spectre is haunting Europe – the spectre of communism. All the powers of old Europe have entered into a holy alliance to exorcize this spectre.'

2. Message on the inauguration of the Palais de l'Europe in Strasbourg, 26 January 1977.

Editors' note: This chapter was completed shortly before the death of Pope Paul VI.

Editors' Conclusion

The flowers of Eurocommunism did not blossom in the spring of 1978 in the way that some observers expected or hoped. In France, the union of the Left did not come to power, and this fact appeared closely connected with a partial reversion by the leadership of the French Communist Party to the old methods and attitudes of Stalinism. In Italy, the communists, at the very moment of their formal accession to membership of the governing majority, found themselves caught between the hammer of pseudo-leftist terrorism and the anvil of conservative resentment. In an attempt to avoid any identification with the kidnappers of Aldo Moro, they found themselves obliged not only to oppose any hint of concessions by the state but also to indulge in public breast-beating about their own use of negative and extremist slogans against Christian democracy in the past, and to soft-pedal even the most mild and reformist of their own political demands. Yet all this was not enough, and in local elections held a few days after Moro's death, the PCI suffered a severe setback. The delicate *modus vivendi* achieved with the Christian democrats survived these shocks, but came under increasingly open attack from the socialists, who were now said to be lavishly financed by the West German SPD. They were able to force the early resignation of the Christian democrat President of the Republic, Leone, and to obtain the election of one of their own party to a post which would almost certainly have fallen to Aldo Moro had he been still alive. (Moro was the architect of the entente between communists and Christian democrats, and his election would have been seen as a further step towards the realization of Berlinguer's 'historic compromise'.)

Even in the Spanish Communist Party – now clearly the most

audacious in developing the specific themes of Eurocommunism and in courting the wrath of Moscow – strong resistance emerged to Santiago Carrillo's policies of abandoning the party's official commitment to Leninism and of collaborating with the monarchy and the bourgeois parties: though here admittedly the fact that this resistance could express itself in both speeches and votes at the party's congress can be taken as evidence that there is a genuine acceptance of intra-party democracy.

These very different upheavals within the three principal Euro-communist parties help to emphasize the point made by Giorgio Amendola in his recent interview with Henri Weber for the *New Left Review*.

The European communist parties have as many strategies as they need. The communist parties oppose the re-establishment of a single world centre for the communist movement in Moscow and they are not going to establish a single centre of 'Eurocommunism' in Rome, Paris or anywhere else.

This pluralist approach has reinforced the view of many non-communist politicians and intellectuals that there is actually no such thing as Eurocommunism. And several of the authors of this book – not only those concentrating on one or other of the national parties, but also Neil McInnes in his account of the origins of the phenomenon and Stuart Holland in his analysis of the communist parties' economic policies – have highlighted the strong differences between them, resulting from the different histories, economic conditions and social structures of the countries concerned.

This is perhaps the place to stress the similarities which none the less exist. All the parties known as 'Eurocommunist', while continuing to use the name 'communist' and to claim continuity with parties founded in the wake of the Russian Revolution as sections of the Communist International, none the less categorically reject both the model of the Russian Revolution and the international discipline which was the *raison d'être* of the Comintern. While for the most part accepting that Soviet society is in some sense 'socialist' (though Carrillo has questioned even this), they insist that the 'socialism' they wish to build in their own countries is completely different from what exists today in the Soviet Union and Eastern Europe, and they insist on the right of each communist party to work out its own policies in total independence from Moscow or any other capital with pretensions to a 'guiding role'.

This is what distinguishes the present, Eurocommunist phase in the history of the communist movement in Western Europe from that earlier phase which at first sight bears some resemblance to it, the period of 1944-7. At that time, communist parties in both Western and Eastern Europe proclaimed that they were following a peaceful road to socialism, different from the violent seizure of power by the Bolsheviks in 1917. But they continued to describe the society resulting from the Bolshevik Revolution in Russia as democratic and admirable. The difference was not in the objective but only in the path chosen to reach it. Today it is the validity of Soviet 'socialism' as a goal which is openly rejected. The Eurocommunists not only reject it as a model for their own countries, but also point out its inability to solve the problems of the countries where it is practised, and the injustices and hardships suffered by Russians and other East Europeans as a result. A recent and striking example is provided by the vigorous protests of all the Eurocommunist parties against the trials of Shcharansky and Ginzburg in July 1978, with French communist leaders even taking part in a mass demonstration on the issue in Paris. (Almost simultaneously, the PCI's intellectuals launched their campaign for the rehabilitation of Bukharin – a move of double-edged significance since it seemed to imply both a challenge to the Bolshevik legitimacy of the present Soviet leadership and a claim to a legitimate Bolshevik ancestry for Eurocommunism itself.) Such criticisms were unheard of in the communist parties of 1944-7, when there was never the slightest questioning in public of the leadership provided for progressive and democratic forces throughout the world by that supreme hero, *le génial Staline*.

The above remarks are valid for quite a number of communist parties in Europe (for instance, those of Scandinavia, Switzerland, Belgium, Great Britain) and some outside (notably those of Australia and Japan). None the less we have in this book concentrated mainly on three parties: those of Italy, France and Spain. Few would deny that these three countries taken together constitute the heartland of Eurocommunism. In other West European countries such as those mentioned above, the fact that communist parties adopt 'Eurocommunist' positions is of little consequence, since communist parties play only a marginal role in the political life of those countries. But in Italy, France and Spain, the communist parties enjoy a following, particularly among the organized working class, which obliges other parties to take account of them. In none of these countries can a left-wing (as opposed to 'centre-left') majority be imagined that would not include the communists: and in none of these countries can the government negotiate a 'social contract' or similar understanding with leaders of the main trade-union movements without finding itself face to face with leading members of the communist party.

There is, of course, one other European country of which these last remarks are true, namely Portugal. Objectively, therefore, it would seem that the conditions created in Portugal by the revolution of 1974 should have been favourable to the development of Eurocommunism. In fact, as Diana Smith's chapter shows, the leaders of the PCP had a different analysis of Portuguese society, based in part on different personal experience, and they chose a different road. That has been a source of acute embarrassment to the Eurocommunist parties, but it would have been worse if the PCP had succeeded in its attempt to seize power in Portugal by working through the armed forces and various 'mass organizations' in defiance of the wishes of the majority of the people as expressed in a general election. As it is, although Cunhal claims success in breaking the power of 'the monopolies' in Portugal, and apparently considers that Portuguese society has been successfully launched on some kind of transition to socialism, the general view is that the PCP has failed; and that failure can serve as a kind of cautionary tale, which Berlinguer and Carrillo can repeat to those wayward members of their own parties whom the

Chilean cautionary tale (so far away, after all – and so ambiguous – for were not the Chilean communists model democrats in their behaviour?) has not been enough to convince. It shows what happens in a capitalist 'Latin European' country if you try to apply the classic Leninist formula for seizing power.

But, at the same time, the Portuguese example should remind us that there is no automatic connection between the Eurocommunist discourse and the 'Latin' context in which it happens to have assumed its main importance. We tend to think of Eurocommunism as a 'Latin' phenomenon, but that is because the Italian, French and Spanish parties are strong: and the historical roots of their strength have to be sought far back in the period *before* they became recognizably Eurocommunist. One can certainly point to similarities in the history and culture of Italy, France and Spain which help to explain the emergence of strong communist parties in those countries, but those similarities do not explain the emergence of Eurocommunism as such. Rather should Eurocommunism be seen as the rational reaction of communist parties, whether strong or weak, to two conditions: (a) the lack of any revolutionary perspective in their own countries and (b) the gradual disintegration of Soviet hegemony within the world communist movement. The value of studying Eurocommunism in a 'Latin' context is simply that it is in those three countries (and perhaps eventually in Portugal as well) that the other political forces find themselves to some extent obliged to play the roles assigned to them in the Eurocommunist scenario.

What is that scenario? The difficulty is that no one seems to be sure. A number of scripts have been sketched out, some by the Eurocommunists themselves, others by people outside the communist parties whose own projects and ambitions depend on the communists behaving in a certain way. Thus Eurocommunism is not simply the creation of Berlinguer, Marchais and Carrillo. Among its inventors may be counted also François Mitterrand in France, Aldo Moro in Italy, Adolfo Suárez in Spain. Eurocommunism was not dreamed up by any visionary in a garret. There is no Eurocommunist bible defining the essential doctrine. Any such definition has to be arrived at inductively, by seeking a common theme in the various pronouncements and actions of different communist leaders over a period of time – leaders of already established parties acting and speaking under a wide variety of political pressures.

Of course, these leaders were communists long before they were Eurocommunists. Their long-term theoretical commitment is to the abolition of capitalism and of the exploitation of man by man, to the creation of a classless society in which the means of production, distribution and exchange will be owned in common. The same, it has been pointed out, is true of many – if not most – social democrats. What has traditionally distinguished social democrats from communists has been that the former were committed to bringing this about only when they had mobilized the explicit support of the majority of the population, whereas the latter believed they had the right and the duty to seize power and impose the change as a conscious minority, the 'vanguard of the working class'. If Eurocommunists have genuinely renounced this pretension, are they not now to all intents and purposes social democrats? Should the great splits of 1919–21 in the social democratic parties of Western Europe not now be healed, and communists and socialists rejoin each other in a united and powerful labour movement?

Logically, no doubt they should, and it is possible that over the next generation that will indeed be the result. But the mutual hostility and suspicions accumulated during half a century of bitter rivalry make it unlikely to happen quickly. Few communists would accept that the only difference between themselves and social democrats was that just referred to. To them the social democrats have traditionally been 'the last support of dying capitalism . . . the watchdogs of capitalism that bark furiously at anyone who approaches their master's lair . . . the last bourgeois barricade that the working class in revolt must storm in order to triumph . . . more despicable even than the kings of the stock market and the sharks of capital'. Today, it is true, such terms are no longer used by communists about socialists in Western Europe, but by the new far Left about the Eurocommunists themselves. Yet their very anxiety to refute these accusations makes Eurocommunists reluctant to identify completely with social democrats, whom they still regard as lacking that serious dedication to the radical transformation of society and ultimate abolition of capitalism that they claim for themselves.

On the socialist side, there is an equal reluctance, or at least hesitation, to take at face value the Eurocommunists' protestations of conversion to democracy. Such suspicions are sharpened, in a manner which is less paradoxical than it may appear, by the Eurocommunists' flirtations with other parties to the right of the socialists. To the latter it often seems that the Eurocommunists are not seriously addressing themselves to the task of building an alliance capable of winning majority support for socialist transformation. Such an alliance should surely offer itself as a clear and preferable alternative to the existing capitalist order and the parties identified with it: whereas – in Italy and Spain at least – the communist parties have been more preoccupied with getting themselves accepted as legitimate participants in conventional politics, even as partners, by the capitalists themselves and the other political and social forces associated with the existing order, both nationally and internationally (the Catholic Church, the armed forces, the United States, the governments of other West European countries, and in Spain the monarchy). In France, by contrast, the PCF did seem to have dedicated itself wholeheartedly over a long period to the construction of a left-wing alternative, undeterred even by the catastrophe which overtook the Chilean Unidad Popular. But France's socialists were to receive a rude jolt when the PCF chose, on the brink of what seemed almost certain victory, to subject the alliance to a profound and apparently gratuitous crisis. The conclusion generally drawn, at least within the French Socialist Party, was that for the PCF's leaders it was more important to dominate the Left than to defeat the Right.

An essential part of Eurocommunism is acceptance of the idea of alternation in power – the idea that government and opposition can change places as the result of an election. Yet, though they accept it in theory, the Eurocommunist parties still do not seem convinced that things will happen like that in practice. Whether or not they themselves are sincere in promising to relinquish power should they be defeated in an election after obtaining it, it is increasingly clear that they do not think it realistic (especially after Chile) to expect their opponents to hand over power to them without a fight – a fight which communists would be as unlikely to win in Western Europe as in Latin America.

The conclusion seems to be, at least as far as the PCI is concerned, 'if you can't lick 'em, join 'em'. The Italian and (so far on a more limited scale) Spanish communists seem to be saying to the establishments of their respective countries, of the European Community and of the Western Alliance: 'All right. We understand that you are not willing to trust us as adversaries. But please accept us as partners. We are anxious to make our contribution to solving the economic crisis and strengthening democracy.' As an earnest of their good faith, the Italian communists go out of their way to consult and cooperate with Christian democrats and other 'bourgeois' parties in local government, even in areas where there is a clear left-wing majority. This behaviour is not necessarily reassuring. Rather than a free choice for the electorate between Left and Right, it seems to foreshadow a process whereby both Left and Right will be spared the risk of electoral defeat (because they will confront the electorate in alliance) and a system in which any real opposition whether from Left or Right will be frowned on as irresponsible and extremist. To a considerable extent, that seems already to be the PCI's attitude. (Its treatment of the Radical Party is particularly instructive in this respect.)

Mitterrand in France, Moro and Andreotti in Italy, Suárez and King Juan Carlos in Spain: all these are men who have encouraged Eurocommunism, seeking to limit the damage which communism might do to their respective countries by involving the communist leaders in a web of democratic commitments and patriotic responsibilities from which they would have difficulty in escaping. (Asked, on a visit to Madrid, whether he believed in the French communists' sincerity, Mitterrand replied: 'I don't know. My job is to give them no alternative but to act *as if* they were sincere.') The démarche can be compared to détente on the international level, as practised by Kissinger, though interestingly its practitioners seem to have had rather more encouragement from the Carter administration than they did from Kissinger himself. But, as Godfrey Hodgson's chapter shows, there is no slackening in Washington's vigilance to see that the risks taken with Eurocommunism are not too great. And the same is true in Bonn. If Eurocommunism is too successful, the destabilizing effects on the Western Alliance and the European Community will be considerable.

At first Eurocommunism could be seen simply as an extension of the Soviet Union's own détente strategy: in an era of peaceful coexistence, the task of the Western communist parties was no longer to carry on a kind of guerrilla warfare behind the 'enemy' lines, but to establish good relations with the non-communist political forces in their respective countries. Certainly détente was a necessary condition for Eurocommunism's development, and the Eurocommunist parties have consistently proclaimed their support for it. Indeed, when possible they have actively contributed to it. (Giovanni Russo has mentioned the PCI's role in the origins of the *Ostpolitik*.) They have perceived, moreover, that their chances of political success in their own countries are much better in the absence of major international crises such as would be provoked by any major shift in the existing strategic balance in Europe. They have thus been led to support the diplomatic and military *status quo* in each country, largely, no doubt, as a way of reassuring both superpowers. Thus the PCF accepts France's continued membership of the Atlantic Alliance, but opposes any reintegration of French forces into the military organization of NATO: and the PCE is willing to accept the retention of American bases in Spain (arguing that these are balanced by the presence of Soviet forces in Eastern Europe) while opposing Spanish membership of NATO. On this last point, the interests of the PCE and the PCI are closely interlocked, since Moscow has suggested that Spanish membership of NATO would have to be balanced by Yugoslavia joining the Warsaw Pact. The PCI's prospects in Italy would be adversely affected by the presence of Soviet troops on the Yugoslav-Italian border, and a check to the advance of Eurocommunism in Italy would almost certainly be reflected in Spain.

But the trouble with this strategy is that the success of Euro-communism would, in itself, be regarded by the superpowers as a major change in the *status quo* in Western Europe, carrying with it the possibility of a corresponding change in Eastern Europe as well. Henry Kissinger and his advisers viewed both these changes as dangerous. At a conference of American ambassadors in Europe in December 1975, Kissinger warned: 'The progress of left-wing politics [in Southern Europe] threatens to undermine the security relations and defence policies on which the [Atlantic] alliance was built'; while Helmut Sonnenfeldt expounded his famous 'doctrine' about the need for a more 'organic' relationship between Moscow and its East European satellites. The Carter administration's position seems somewhat more ambivalent. They give the impression that they would regard a degree of destabilization in Eastern Europe as encouraging, but are clearly not anxious to pay a high price for it in terms of actual power conceded to Eurocommunists in Western Europe.

A similar ambivalence affects the Soviet attitude, as noted by Brown and Schöpflin:

A Eurocommunist party in power practising what it currently preaches would be an even greater potential attraction as a model for East Europeans, and a correspondingly greater threat to the dominant position of the Soviet Union in Eastern Europe, than any communist party in opposition can possibly be . . . [yet at the same time the Soviet leaders] may reasonably hope that a Western communist party in power would be driven into dependence on them, precisely because of the domestic and foreign hostility which such a party would encounter in the West.

If Eurocommunism is seen as an ideological 'third force', causing inconvenience and embarrassment to Moscow and Washington in almost equal measure, the optimum diplomatic conditions for its further development might seem to be provided by the emergence of Western Europe as a third power-bloc, the notion of which has an appeal to certain strands of public opinion in the countries where Eurocommunism is strong. Again it is Santiago

Carrillo who has gone furthest along this line, but again it is what the PCI is doing in a quieter way that might in the long run be more significant. For the PCI is almost the only major party in any European country today that is seriously devoting itself to the further political and economic integration which is an indispensable condition for the transformation of the EEC into an independent politico-military power-bloc. But such a bloc is certainly not the proclaimed objective of the PCI, which – on the contrary – habitually adopts a most conciliatory tone towards both the superpowers.

The same is certainly not true of the PCF, but its attacks on the superpowers are launched not in the name of Europe but in that of France. The PCF remains deeply hostile to the idea of a supranational European Community, which it believes would be dominated to a very large extent by Federal Germany. That is indeed a plausible view, given the Federal Republic's economic weight, and this is arguably the most serious drawback to the idea of European independence as a slogan for Eurocommunists. For the main political forces in West Germany remain implacably hostile to communism in any form. It is, in fact, the German social democrats who have had the most effective counter-strategy against the rise of communism in Southern Europe, which consists essentially of promoting 'Eurosocialism'. The Portuguese Socialist Party was actually founded in Bonn, and both it and the Spanish Socialist Workers' Party – and more recently the Italian Socialist Party – have received a great deal of German advice as well as moral and, in some cases, financial support. Bonn has encouraged both French and Italian socialists to demarcate themselves more clearly from the communists (even though not concealing its preference for the *status quo* represented by Giscard d'Estaing), and in Italy has made its massive loans to the near-bankrupt state conditional on the communists' being kept out of government.

For West German leaders, as for many of the more conservative politicians in other West European countries, Eurocommunism is a particularly dangerous phenomenon because it coincides with (indeed, may be partly the consequence of) an apparent wavering, after the Vietnam defeat, of American resolve to stand up to communism overseas. There is a natural fear that Soviet power might be allowed to push into a European vacuum, as it is now pushing into an African one. To see Eurocommunists as an advance guard of Soviet power, after all the pledges they have given to NATO and all the insults they have incurred from Moscow, may seem grossly unjust, but it is, of course, possible that they would play such a role objectively, even without wishing to. The question is, whether they can best be prevented from doing so by rejection into the 'ghetto', or by cooption into the defence of the democratic system.

It is the economic crisis that is, perhaps, gradually tipping the scales in favour of cooption. The crisis cannot be solved democratically without the voluntary cooperation of the organized working class. The communists are, for historical reasons, the main organizers of the working class in Latin Europe. Their cooperation is therefore needed in the implementation of economic policy, and that in turn implies their participation in the making of policy, and hence in political power, within the existing democratic system. Eurocommunism is an ideology corresponding to that social and political process.

Paolo Filo della Torre
Edward Mortimer
Jonathan Story

Summer 1978

Appendix One

Joint Declaration of the Italian and Spanish Communist Parties, 12 July 1975

With the fall of the fascist dictatorships in Portugal and Greece, and the irreversible crisis through which the Franco régime is passing in Spain, Europe sees opening before her the concrete possibility of a continent without any fascist régime, while Spain can, at last, glimpse the prospect of a régime of democracy and freedom. In the new conditions created by the positive progress of international détante, it is increasingly urgent and necessary for the labour and democratic forces to point out, both at the level of each country and at that of Western Europe as a whole new ways of bringing about closer cooperation among all democratic forces for a policy of democratic and socialist renewal of society, and for a positive outcome of the crisis now affecting European capitalist countries.

This crisis shows the incapacity of capitalism to meet the general demands of society's development and the problems it confronts today, as well as its incapacity to achieve in all fields the profound structural reforms which alone can guarantee the development of nations. This crisis is constantly deepening the gulf between, on the one hand, a policy imposed by the monopolist groups and the big multinational companies, and, on the other hand, the need to give positive answers to the demands for freedom, participation and economic, social and cultural progress, of the great popular masses. It is necessary and possible to find a positive way out of this grave situation, through a development of understanding and of the closest cooperation among the forces with which the labour and democratic movement is identified throughout the continent: something which is also indispensable if the attempts of certain capitalist groups to impose an openly reactionary and authoritarian solution to the crisis are to be scotched.

Conscious of this responsibility, and determined to spare no effort in achieving this convergence and understanding, the Spanish and Italian communists solemnly declare that their conception of the march towards socialism in peace and freedom expresses not a tactical attitude but a strategic conviction: a strategic conviction born of reflection on all the experiences of the labour movement and on the specific historical conditions of each country in the West European context. It is the common task of communists and democratic forces in general to provide a real satisfaction of those social needs and human values, namely freedom, justice and civilization, which capitalism is sacrificing and crushing more and more; and through their action to find a solution to the problems posed for the great popular masses and for society as a whole.

Today the prospect of a socialist society springs from reality itself, and is rooted in the conviction that in our countries socialism can only be strengthened by the development and full operation of democracy. This conviction is based on the affirmation of the value of individual and collective freedoms, on their guarantee – which means that there must be no official state ideology – and on their democratic articulation. Likewise it affirms the value of the plurality of parties in free dialectical activity, the value of trade-union independence, of religious freedoms, of freedom of expression, of culture, of the arts and sciences. In the economic field, the socialist solution is called on to ensure a great productive development by means of a policy of democratic planning which will galvanize the different forms of enterprise and management, both public and private.

Starting from these conditions, which form the very kernel of their political and theoretical line, the Italian and Spanish communists are working to ensure that the reconquest and affirmation of democracy in Spain, and its development in Italy, make possible the broadest convergence of all the political forces which sense the need to provide a positive answer to the great and serious problems posed by the present crisis. Only this convergence, realized in the complete respect and complete independence of each one of the forces concerned, will make it possible to point the way to a prospect of progress and freedom, the way to promote the interests of the working class, peasant masses, intellectual and middle classes, and thus to create the national unity of democratic and progressive forces, isolating the socially conservative and reactionary ones. From now on we need new political perspectives, a new method of government, rooted in the broadest possible participation of the popular masses and of young people as well as of their organizations.

As the Brussels Conference of European Communist Parties indicated in January 1974, it is urgent and necessary to promote – both on the level of each country and on that of Western Europe – the widest possible exchange of opinions on these problems, and to complete a thoroughly responsible investigation of points of convergence and agreement with all the political forces – socialist, social democrat, Christian democrat, Catholic, democratic and progressive – which are willing to take action to ensure that Western Europe's great democratic potential finds a field of understanding in a policy of renewal and progress.

Yesterday's obstacles and traps are today being successively eliminated by the development of international détente. This is a fact which will shortly be expressed by the Conference on European Security and Cooperation, an achievement in which a key role has been played by the convergence of the foreign policy of peace pursued by the Soviet Union and by all the other socialist countries with the new realistic tendencies which are coming to the fore in Western capitals. All these new possibilities must be channelled to give the countries of Western Europe, and the latter as a whole, the capacity to make their own original contributions to the creation of an international society based on respect for the right of each people to choose its own way freely, on the elimination of imbalances, on justice, progress, development and peace. For the realization of all these great objectives, the formation of a new Western European policy based on relations of cooperation and friendship, on a footing of equality with all countries of the world – and first and foremost the United States and the Soviet Union – and on new relations with the developing countries, constitutes, without doubt, an irreplaceable contribution.

Both in Western Europe and in the Mediterranean zone, the Spanish and Italian communists propose to intensify their efforts and initiatives in this direction. The reconquest of democracy in Spain and democratic development in Italy – both linked to the new processes that characterize the life of so many European countries – can give Western Europe a new momentum for the solution of the problems it has to confront in a perspective of freedom, democracy, progress and peace.

The Italian and Spanish communist parties, which work out their internal and international policies in complete autonomy and independence, are fully aware of their grave national and European responsibilities. From these common viewpoints they will in future develop their fraternal relations sealed by a broad and solid friendship.

Appendix Two

Joint Declaration of the French and Italian Communist Parties,
15 November 1975

The situation in France and Italy is characterized by the worsening of a crisis affecting all aspects of economic, social, political, moral and cultural life.

In its economic aspects, this crisis – which is an integral part of the crisis gripping the capitalist system as a whole and worldwide in its effects on all economic relations – has heavy consequences for the working people and popular masses, hard hit by unemployment and rising prices. At the same time, the peasantry, artisans and small and medium-sized businesses are struggling against serious difficulties.

The institutions of civil life are encountering increasingly severe problems. The political crisis is deepening, and social and moral relations are affected by phenomena of degeneration.

This crisis reveals the inability of the capitalist system to answer the need for development of the productive forces, including science and technology; the need to ensure the right to work, a rising standard of living, the development of culture and the affirmation of all human values. In the two countries, as, in different forms, in other countries of Western Europe, serious social deterioration is threatened overall.

The forces of big capital and imperialism are attempting to take advantage of this situation to undermine the economic, social and political gains of the working people. But through their struggle, the working class and popular masses can defeat these attempts, making new gains and opening the road to further social and democratic advance.

To this end, the PCI and the PCF, while fighting for the immediate interests of the working people, are working at the same time for a policy of far-reaching democratic reforms, capable of solving the grave economic, social and political problems of their countries.

For France and Italy, the present crisis has more clearly than ever revealed the need to develop democracy and advance it towards socialism.

The two parties conduct their action in concretely different conditions, and, for this reason, each follows a policy suited to the needs and characteristics of its own country. At the same time, since they both fight in developed capitalist countries, they observe that the essential problems facing them present common characteristics and require similar solutions.

The Italian and French communists hold that the march towards socialism and the building of a socialist society, which they propose as the prospect for their countries, must be achieved within the framework of a continuous democratization of economic, social and political life. Socialism will constitute a higher phase of democracy and freedom: democracy realized in the most complete manner.

In this spirit, all the freedoms – which are a product both of the great democratic-bourgeois revolutions and of the great popular struggles of this century, headed by the working class – will have to be guaranteed and developed. This holds true for freedom of thought and expression, for freedom of the press, of assembly, association and demonstration, for free movement of persons inside and outside their country, for the inviolability of private life, for religious freedom and total freedom of expression for currents of thought and every philosophical, cultural and artistic opinion. The French and Italian communists declare themselves for the plurality of political parties, for the right to existence and activity of opposition parties, for the free formation of majorities and minorities and the possibility of their alternating democratically, for the lay nature and democratic functioning of the state, for independence of the judiciary. In the same way, they declare themselves for the freedom of activity and autonomy of the trade unions. They attribute essential importance to the development of democracy in the workplace, allowing the workers to participate in the running of their firms, with real rights and extensive decision-making powers. Democratic decentralization of the state must give an increasingly important role to regional and local governments, which must enjoy broad autonomy in the exercise of their powers.

A socialist transformation of society presupposes public control over the principal means of production and exchange, their progressive socialization and implementation of democratic economic planning at the national level. The sector of small and medium-sized peasant farms, artisan industry and small and medium-sized industrial and commercial enterprises can and must fulfil a specific, positive role in the building of socialism.

The transformation can only be the result of great, powerful struggles and broad mass movements, uniting the majority of the people around the working class. It requires the existence, guarantee and development of democratic institutions fully representative of popular sovereignty and the free exercise of direct, proportional universal suffrage. It is in this framework that the two parties – which have always respected and will always respect the verdict of universal suffrage – conceive the rise of the working people to leadership of the state.

The Italian Communist Party and the French Communist Party attribute a value of principle to all these conditions of democratic life. Their position is not tactical, but derived from their analysis of the specific objective and historical conditions of their countries and from their reflection on international experience as a whole.

The two parties uphold in relations among all states – which must be characterized by increasingly close cooperation within the framework of a new international division of labour – the right of every people to decide in sovereignty their own political and social régime. They therefore stress the necessity of struggling against the presumption of US imperialism to interfere in the life of other peoples, and declare themselves against all foreign interference.

The two parties hold that to guarantee success in the fight against the principal enemy of the working class and popular masses – monopoly capitalism – it is essential to achieve a free understanding among different social and political forces, within which the united working class must succeed in establishing its capacity for leadership. These broad alliances are necessary both in the present phase and for the building of socialism.

The development of solid, lasting cooperation among communists and socialists constitutes the basis for this broad alliance. Furthermore, today broad strata of the Catholic world are becoming increasingly aware of the contradiction existing between the reality of imperialism and capitalism and their deepest aspirations to brotherhood among men, social justice, the affirmation of higher moral values and the fulfilment of every personality. This fact creates growing possibilities for a coming-together among communists, the whole of the working-class movement and the popular forces of Catholic inspiration. These forces can and must play an important role in the creation of a new society.

In this situation of crisis, with the big tasks it implies, the two parties are fully conscious of their growing responsibilities and their irreplaceable functions.

In conformity with the conclusions of the Conference of Communist Parties of capitalist Europe, held in Brussels in January 1974, the two parties reaffirm their will to work to promote common action among the communist and socialist parties and all the democratic and progressive forces of Europe against fascism and all attacks on freedom, in defence of the interests of the working class and popular masses and for far-reaching democratic transformation in the economic and social structures.

Faced with the stance, profoundly opposed to the interests of the people, that is being taken by the monopolies and those ruling groups whose policies are aggravating unemployment and social imbalances in Common Market Europe, the two parties attribute great importance to the development of united initiatives by the popular forces and the left forces – within the framework of the European Parliament as well – for democratization of the orientations and modes of operation of the European Economic Community and for the progressive building of a democratic, peaceful and independent Europe.

In the same spirit, in this crucial hour for Spain, the two parties condemn all attempts to perpetuate the Franco régime, in one form or another, certain that in this regard they are interpreting the conviction of all democrats. They reconfirm their militant solidarity with the working class and all the anti-fascists of Spain, who are fighting to save and free the political prisoners and establish a system of full political freedom.

They express, moreover, their concern for the difficulties encountered by the young democracy in Portugal and their hope that all the working-class and democratic forces will again succeed in finding unity in the struggle to bar the road to all reactionary threats and to guarantee the democratic and social progress of that country.

The Helsinki Conference of European States – to whose convening and success the Soviet Union made an outstanding contribution – marked an important step forward along the road of international détente and towards the creation of a system of collective security in Europe. Peaceful coexistence is the only alternative to a war of extermination; it is a condition for solving conflicts among states and developing the broadest international cooperation in all fields. Peaceful coexistence, which does not mean the social and political *status quo*, offers the most favourable terrain for struggle against imperialism and for democracy and socialism. While pursuing this struggle, the two parties develop their action in favour of new progress for peace, for gradual mutual arms reduction – with the final goal of total disarmament – and for a gradual overcoming and dissolution of the military blocs. They express their will to contribute to union among all forces interested in halting the arms race.

In reconfirming the principle of the autonomy of each party, of respect, non-interference and internationalism, the PCF and the PCI intend to pursue and strengthen their fraternal cooperation.

Notes on the Contributors

Archie Brown is a Fellow of St Antony's College and Lecturer in Soviet Institutions at Oxford University. He is the author of *Soviet Politics and Political Science*, co-editor (with Michael Kaser) of *The Soviet Union since the Fall of Khrushchev* and co-editor (with Jack Gray) of *Political Culture and Political Change in Communist States*.

Godfrey Hodgson is an associate editor of the *New Statesman* and the presenter of London Weekend Television's 'The London Programme'. He is co-author of *An American Melodrama* (with Bruce Page and Lew Chester) and author of *In Our Time*, a political history of the U S since the Second World War.

Stuart Holland is the Labour Member of Parliament for Lambeth Vauxhall. His books include *The Socialist Challenge*, *Beyond Capitalist Planning* and *The Regional Problem*.

Arrigo Levi is a former editor of *La Stampa* and author of *La Lunga Marcia verso il potere*.

Neil McInnes is Deputy Director-General of the Office of National Assessments, Canberra. He is the author of *The Western Marxists* and *The Communist Parties of Western Europe*.

Edward Mortimer is a foreign specialist and leader-writer on *The Times*. He is the author of *France and the Africans, 1944–1960*, and of the forthcoming *The Rise of the French Communist Party*.

Peter Nichols is Rome correspondent of *The Times*, and author of *Italia Italia*, *Politics of the Vatican* and *La Scelta Italiana*.

Giovanni Russo is specialist in communist affairs for *Corriere della Sera*.

George Schöpflin is joint Lecturer in the Political Institutions of Eastern Europe at the London School of Economics and the School of Slavonic and East European Studies. He has written widely on current developments in Eastern Europe and has visited the area frequently.

Diana Smith is a *Financial Times* correspondent, at present in Brazil.

Jonathan Story is Associate Professor of European Business Environment, INSEAD, specializing in current affairs in Western Europe, on which he has written widely.

Paolo Filo della Torre is London correspondent of *La Repubblica*.

Index

Index

More About Penguins and Pelicans

Europe Since 1870
An International History
James Joll

The years from 1870 to 1914 were a long crowded period of history: a time of confusion and contradiction, when the main themes were provided by great mass movements – liberalism, imperialism, fascism and communism. And ironically, this was the era of the conflicting concepts of both 'national self-determination' and European unity. Professor Joll places these factors in their historical context, tracing their origins and following their development. Within the political and ideological framework, he studies the artistic and intellectual influences of the time, exploring their transformational impact on European society.

The New France
A Society in Transition 1945–1977

John Ardagh

The author's many years as *The Times* correspondent in Paris, together with his intense but critical sympathy for things French, have enabled him to look at France from within and present a sparkling and intelligent picture of a rapidly changing nation. John Ardagh travelled all over France to prepare this book, talking to technocrats and schoolgirls, prefects and peasants, grocers and film directors. He avoids straight political analysis – and in doing so explains recent French politics more incisively and clearly than most conventional textbooks.

The Spanish Civil War

Hugh Thomas

What was it that roused left-wing sympathizers from all over the world to fight for a cause for which their governments would not give active support? In this completely revised edition of his famous history, Hugh Thomas presents an objective analysis of the conflict – where fascism and democracy, communism and Christianity, centralism and regionalism were all at stake – and which was as much an international civil war as a Spanish one.

The European Parliament
A Guide to Direct Elections

Robert Jackson and John Fitzmaurice

Two people directly involved in the European elections – one a Tory, the other a Socialist – examine the circumstances of the campaign, the way the European Community is governed, the power of the European Parliament, how it works, how the various parties line up and, most important, what constitutes party policy.

The European Parliament affects us all directly, and will do so more and more. This straightforward book explains the significance of direct elections and provides the pertinent information we need if we are to understand the way our lives are being run.

Comparative Government

S. E. Finer

The Professor of Government at Manchester University identifies five principal types of government and examines many different styles of politics and rule.

'A considerable *tour de force* . . . Its scope is not confined to "the great powers". It is written in vivid, personal English. Above all, it is the work of a great teacher who breathes into every page his own enthusiasm for the discipline' – Anthony King in *New Society*

International Politics
Conflict and Harmony

Joseph Frankel

Today peace is harder to maintain than it has ever been, and the situation is aggravated by the growth of power blocs and ideologies, so that countries like Russia and China tend to become isolated. In the search for peace, Dr Frankel urges the West to accord equal weight to more exotic if less traditional modes of government, and not to regard failure as grounds for disillusion.

'A judicious and comprehensive introduction to its subject' – *The Times Literary Supplement*

Political Identity

W. J. M. MacKenzie

Professor Mackenzie examines the concept of 'political identity' in four main phases: its linguistic basis; its relationship to the concept of personal identity derived from philosophy, psychology, sociology and anthropology; its political basis in connection with current world problems of nationality, class and colour; its role within the language of political science.

Written like a whodunnit – but without a villain – the book searches through interlinking word and theory 'histories' and back again to the tantalizing questions: 'At what stage do *I* say *we*?' and 'with whom do *I/we* identify?'.

Political Ideas

Edited by David Thomson

The theme of this book, which is the work of a team of specialists, falls into four consecutive but overlapping parts. The discussion on Machiavelli, Luther and Hobbes deals ultimately with the creation of political sovereignty; the essays on Locke, Paine, Montesquieu and Rousseau are more concerned with the relationship between government and governed; Burke, Hegel and Mazzini represent the concept of the Nation-State; and Mill reasserts the claims of individual personality against excessive governmental authority, whilst Marx evolves his theory of revolutionary communism.

And if, as David Thomson suggests in his conclusion, the emphasis in future politics is on Equality rather than Liberty, the debate highlighted in this book will be a continuing one.

Progress, Coexistence and Intellectual Freedom

Andrei D. Sakharov

In one of the most radical polemics to come out of Russia, Sakharov foresees a world in which East and West have come together against the messianic threat of China. Writing just before the invasion Czechoslovakia, he castigates all aspects of neo-Stalinism in Russian life – and compares Stalin directly with Hitler.

But Sakharov's argument for world cooperation is of broader application, and his recognition in the West augurs well for its increasing acceptability.

Anarchism

George Woodcock

In this history of libertarian ideas and movements, George Woodcock shows the true face of anarchism as a political philosophy – a system of social thought which aims at fundamental changes in the structure of society and particularly at the replacement of authoritarian states by free cooperation. As such it has a respectable pedigree.

Proudhon adopted the label with pride. But before him there was William Godwin and the German egotist Max Stirner; and after him followed Bakunin, Kropotkin and the great Tolstoy. The ideas of these six men are minutely studied here, along with the anarchist movements which sprang from them and a postscript on the development of anarchism after 1939 – particularly in the last decade.

Fascism

A Reader's Guide

Edited by Walter Laqueur

Recognizing that there are not one but several fascisms, the authors have produced one of the first completely interdisciplinary works to examine all aspects of the phenomenon. Among the contributors, all authorities in their fields, are historians, political scientists, sociologists, economists and a psychoanalyst. Their discussion is systematic and comprehensive; an original work of synthesis and a new interpretation.

'This book represents a stocktaking which should determine any future debate about the nature of fascism . . . basic for our understanding of fascism' – George Mosse in *The Times Literary Supplement*

The Theory and Practice of Communism

R. N. Carew Hunt

'The best short account of Marxism and its Russian consequences written from a highly critical standpoint that has come my way' – Edward Crankshaw in the *Observer*

This concise and critical study of Marxism and its interpretations in practice has quickly become a classic. The author clearly shows how modern Marxism is a sythesis in which the basic creed of Marx and Engels has been tailored by Lenin and Stalin to fit the twentieth century. In analysing the relationship and the contrasts between Marx's predictions and the policies of the communist governments today, he provides an excellent outline of the institutions and events which have helped to shape the map of our world.

The Problem of Party Government

Richard Rose

Professor Rose provides a detailed anatomy of how **parties are
organized, recruited, financed, staffed, mobilized for elections, and led,**
or misled, to victory or defeat. He includes the findings of modern
research into the sociology of political parties, at national and local
level, in and out of government. The book also discusses the ways in
which party platforms are constructed – that subtle blend of the main
chance and ideology which makes them objects both of ridicule and
partisanship.

'It is a delight to read a serious study on the subject' – Terry Pitt in
the *Guardian*.

Voters, Parties, and Leaders
The Social Fabric of British Politics

Jean Blondel

In this original book Professor Blondel examines the background,
outlook and interests of voters, party members, politicians, civil
servants and party leaders, and endeavours to trace some of the subtle
threads that tie certain individuals to certain organizations. In an
anatomy of the political world he asks: 'What is the "Establishment"
we talk of? Does it exist? And if so, does it rule?'

This latest edition takes note of the voting trends of the seventies
and detects signs of disillusionment with both the major parties.

Thinking Politically

Jean Blondel

Politics deals in human behaviour, the struggles and arguments of
passionate and wilful individuals. It attracts adventurers and poets,
pragmatists and dreamers. And the political scientist must embrace all
these in his analysis.

Professor Blondel shows that if we are to think sensibly about politics
we must study theory (Aristotle etc.), institutions (parliaments etc.) and
everyday political behaviour. Only if we combine all aspects of political
life will our thinking about politics have any relevance for the future.